HATREDS

HATREDS

RACIALIZED AND SEXUALIZED

CONFLICTS IN THE 21ST CENTURY

ZILLAH EISENSTEIN

ROUTLEDGE
NEW YORK   LONDON

Published in 1996 by

Routledge
29 West 35th Street
New York, NY 10001

Published in Great Britain by

Routledge
11 New Fetter Lane
London EC4P 4EE

Library of Congress Cataloging-in-Publication Data

Eisenstein, Zillah R.
    Hatreds: racialized and sexualized conflicts in the twenty first
century / Zillah Eisenstein
        p. cm.
    Includes index.
    ISBN 0-415-91220-2 (CL). — ISBN 0-415-91221-0 (pbk.)
    1. Racism. 2. Sexism. 3. Patriarchy. 4. Post-communism. 5. Feminism.
I. Title.
HT1521.E44 1996
305.8—dc20   96-3657
                                                                CIP

for my daughter Sarah's generation of girls across the globe

CONTENTS

Acknowledgments   9

Introduction   13

PART I   DomiNATION/SubordiNATION

1   Writing Hatred on the Body   21

2   Writing Bodies on the Nation   43

3   Writing Multiculturalism for the Globe   63

4   Writing the Globe on the Nation   85

PART II   Beyond Nations

5   Feminism of the North and West for Export   109

6   Feminisms of the Global South and East   137

Notes   171

Index   217

ACKNOWLEDGMENTS

There are many people I wish to thank for their help in writing this book. John Borneman, Asma Barlas, Sandra Greene, Mary Jacobus, Mary Katzenstein, Chandra Mohanty, Susan Buck-Morss, Renata Salecl, Tom Shevory, and Anna Marie Smith all read and commented on several chapters. Their critiques have made this a much better book.

I also very much want to express my enormous gratitude to Miriam Brody, Patricia Zimmerman, and Rosalind Petchesky for reading and commenting on the entire manuscript. Their unique standpoints each demanded further clarity of me. Miriam even revisited parts of the manuscript a second time. I feel very lucky to have such talented and committed friends. Our sharing of ideas often leaves me not knowing where my ideas stop and theirs begin, or vice versa.

Anne Sapanaro and Kim Conrad were invaluable research assistants. Donna Freedline helped me with the difficult international communications and correspondence so necessary to my project. Jim Meyer of the Ithaca College Bookstore kept me supplied with all the newest writings I needed, and he checked more than a few footnote queries. Sarah Dean assisted me with her keen secretarial and computer skills. Mary Jacobus and Linda Zerilli helped me sort through the psychoanalytic literature.

If Sally McConnell-Ginet had not asked me, in the wake of the '89 revolutions, to explore racism for the Cornell conference

"Women in the New Germany and Its Neighbors," I am not sure this book would have developed as it has.

My work owes an extraordinary debt to Ann Snitow and Sonia Jaffe Robbins of the Network of East-West Women. Because of their initiative I was able to meet with women from eastern and central europe at conferences they arranged. The women I met at the Nationalism and Feminism conference held in washington, d.c., in October 1993 have been crucial to the writing of this book. I could not have completed my study without the incredible generosity of Zarana Papic and Lepa Mladjenovic of ex-yugoslavia.

I also wish to thank the New Jersey Project, Cornell Women's Studies, and the Whitman Series in Political Theory at Rutgers University for inviting me to lecture from sections of the book while it was in process.

My thanks to my seminar classes at Ithaca College, spring and fall '94, on the "New Nationalisms" and "Post–Cold War Isms," which supplied a vital dialogue for many of the ideas discussed here. Students in my '95 Feminist Theories class provided fertile ground for exploration and exchange.

Given my heavy teaching load, it would have been very difficult to complete this book without Ithaca College's institutional support by way of the reassigned-time program, and faculty research and travel grants.

And then there are those who sustain me, and allow me to write, even when they are not part of the writing process. So "thank you" to my mother, Fannie Price Eisenstein, for supporting me in every avenue of my life; and "thank you" to Richard Stumbar, who nurtures my imaginings; and to Ellen Wade, who is always there, through anything and everything. And I want to express my deep love and devotion to my sisters, Giah and Julia, who always asked about HATREDS even when their bodies hardly allowed them to think beyond their pain.

I also want to acknowledge and thank my incredible editorial team at Routledge. Cecelia Cancellaro's support and enthusiasm for the book made the entire project easy; Claudia Gorelick oversaw initial production with an extraordinary clarity; and Christine Cipriani and Norma McLemore went over the manuscript with a critical and talented eye. My heartfelt appreciation to each of them.

Last, I want to acknowledge my daughter Sarah's part in my writing of this book. She directed me to nazi germany when I had no initial intention to look there. Her own independent passion to know about the children living during world war II—especially those who lived in hiding from the nazis, but also those who were forced to die in the concentration camps—pulled me there. She would often look at the books in my study and say that I was not reading the really important stories. So at night we would read together Judith Kerr's *When Hitler Stole Pink Rabbit*, Jane Yolen's *The Devil's Arithmetic*, and Howard Greenfeld's *The Hidden Children*, to name just a few. The horror *and* the spirit of these books is, I hope, found in my writing, and I thank Sarah for this.

INTRODUCTION

My ten-year-old daughter and I recently read Nelly Toll's story of her terror-filled years in hiding from the nazis in poland.[1] At the time of her hiding, Nelly, a jewish girl, was not much older than my daughter. My daughter said Nelly reminded her of another girl she had read about, a runaway slave named Harriet Jacobs, who had hidden under the floorboards of an attic while her master hunted for her daily.[2] Black slave girl and jewish girl both barely escaped death by hiding. For years this was all they could do. Sarah saw beyond their differences and connected their pain and suffering in order to better understand them.

The racializing of difference—be it of "the" jew or black or girl/woman—requires that we look through and in between the horrors of hatred. The slave trade, black slavery, and racial lynchings do not bespeak the same hatred as do the expulsion of jews from spain in 1492 or the concentration camps of nazi germany or bosnia. Yet the slaves who died on the slave ships share a later history of hate with the jews and gypsies (*roma*) of the holocaust. The histories of the girls/women of these years further interweave the atrocities through rape and sexual torture. The particular histories must be recognized, explored, and compared because these accounts are part of a similar, though not identical, "otherness."

So I begin by asking you to see many kinds of hatred, written on similar kinds of bodies.

I start with the body and never quite leave it behind. I don't follow a traditional straightforward narrative, so let me give you a road map for this book's geography.

Black african slave bodies were shackled, and beaten, and castrated, and raped, and starved. In nazi germany, jews' bodies were tattooed with numbers, their heads shaved, and their limbs tortured and destroyed. In rwanda, noses were sliced and bodies macheted. In argentina and chile, rebels are decapitated and castrated, and breasts are cut off.

Borders have become problematic for international capital while political boundaries remain central elements of an identity politics rooted in "otherness." Bodies locate the borders for hate while nations are reconfigured. It is this highly racially/sexually charged political and psychological geography that I explore. It defines the transnational and multicultural borders for the twenty-first century.

On hatred... The wars in bosnia and rwanda force me to confront the agency of racialized/sexualized hatreds. The horrific spectacle of needless and endless death splashed on TV screens and newspapers, the crushed skulls of little children, the starving men and women in prison camps, and the unspeakable rape and torture of young girls alongside their mothers have made me query the inexplicable realm of murderous hate. I have been dragged here unwillingly.

My discussion of psychic hate takes me to the space of the repressed, the space of injury, hurt, and fear, *and* the space of desire, imagination, and fantasy. It is an irreducible space that resides in individuals, triggered by context and history. I do not make much sense of this mind's-eye place as I revisit it again and again. Maybe I think I can undo the hate by challenging its bordered constructions.

On gender and transnational feminisms... Diversely situated feminisms across the globe hold out a possibility for transgressing deadly hatreds. So I look to make women visible within the discourses of the twenty-first century. I want to do so through multiracial and transnational viewings of the new-old nationalisms and global capital. My argument rests on the complicated interweavings between racialized boundaries as sexual, and sexualized borders as racial.[3] (This discussion is indebted to the feminist politics and theory of the last two decades, which was initiated by women of color and which critiqued white/western feminism.) My hope is for the development of multiracial, transnational feminisms across the globe: for women to refuse nations and stand instead as communities of sisters. Their refusal to be "mother" of the nation, and its imaginary unifier, would begin the process of moving beyond the hatreds of the body.

On nationalisms... Postcommunist nationalisms in eastern and central europe and their masculinist borders are carved from racialized and sexualized hatreds. They are "new-old" formations that demand exclusionary boundary lines. I entertain the necessity of anti-colonialist feminism's embrace of nations as an intermediary step. But I continue to believe that no nationalism can fully include a multiracial/woman-specified democracy.

On "new-old"... President Bush promised a "new world" post–cold-war order, which has turned out to be completely disorderly. The "new world" order is "new-old" anyway: Hitler promised it as his post–world war II utopian victory.[4]

In this new-old morass, it is hard for people to know what to believe in. Global telecommunications let us look just about anywhere and see just about anything. But we don't really see anything and everything because telecommunications are not all that democratic. Global capital defines the viewing and the seeing.

Nevertheless, after we see more than we may want to in rwanda, or somalia, or bosnia, it is harder to think of "ourselves" in the ways we used to, whatever they were. The twenty-first century demands a clarification of the "we" in these viewings.

We view and see in racialized/sexualized ways. Despite corporatist multiculturalism, whiteness remains a key signifier, along with maleness, of first-world western/northern privilege. This privilege is re-coded for global capital, in "new-old" ways.

In these post–cold war, post-'89 times, the twenty-first century has already begun. There is no simple enemy, like the soviet union. Enemies have pluralized. They are now everywhere. Inside and outside.

I am not comfortable with the designation post because it is a bit too neat for these messy times. The *post* is also *pre*, as the new is also old. The *post* as *pre*fix comes before: it is "at the beginning and precedes."[5] So when I use the prefix *post* it does not declare a clear demarcation separating the past from the present. Much is contiguous between communism and postcommunism; the seeds for *perestroika* grew under communist rule, and much of communism remains as new markets develop. Much of the cold war also remains with us even in our defense industry. And our hatred of communism is retained, only the soviets are no longer the enemy: instead, our own poor are.

Most significantly, the race/gender structures of nations, which stand outside the target area of cold-war politics—communism/anticommunism—are retained as well.

So these are not simply *post*modern times. I use postmodernism to help describe global developments more than I use it as a theoretical stance to sort out the future.

Global capitalism rearranges economic borders. As the borders shift, so do the relations of transnational domination. The neat divide, although always problematic between first and third world, becomes even more problematic when some geographical areas contain aspects of both external *and* internal colonization. North and south/east and west become categories that are less significant geographically than they are culturally and politically.

"The" west and north do not exist homogeneously, yet they operate with hegemonic privilege as a euro-american masculinist narrative. "The" west and east are fictional constructs made of myth and fantasy;[6] they are geographical imaginaries. As imaginaries they retain enormous force long past their historical efficacy.

So I use the terminology of "first-world north and west" and "third-world south and east" to connote both changing borders *and* the continuation and exacerbation of global inequality. I use a language in this book that both calls forth essentialist categorizations *and* challenges them, because the globe seems to be unchanging while it changes. Globalism itself has become the newest imaginary to unsettle the "othered" mentalities of "east," "the orient," and "islam."

In order to call attention to the "man"-made content of geographical places, like nations, I do not capitalize countries in my writing. The small-lettered country/nation asks you to see differently; to *not* see proper naming, and thus clear boundaries/borders.

I will argue throughout this book that when one questions borders one is questioning the boundary markers of race. The black/white divide oversimplifies various borders that cannot be adequately defined by this bipolarity. Nevertheless, it operates as a western fantasy/nightmare.

When race is pluralized to encompass a notion of physicality that is not limited to the western black/white divide, difference itself becomes multiple and complex. "The" arab world will be seen with its own minorities: berbers, palestinians, kurds, bedouins, and yemeni.[7] Harlem, the cultural capital of the black u.s., will be recognized as more than 40 percent spanish-speaking, and blackness will widen to embrace peoples from jamaica, trinidad, panama, and the dominican republic.[8] Islam will be recognized as a grand and ancient monotheistic tradition with as many degrees and kinds of worship as believers. Jews will be seen in a variety of colors: the darker colors of the sephardim, the blackness of the ethiopian, the european coloring of the ashkenazi.[9]

In unsettling times—amidst unemployment, underemployment, or the fear of both—there is anger, which only makes the times more unsettled. Images present themselves for daily public consumption to assuage the tension. Some of the images depict heroes; some depict enemies.

Scott O'Grady, the pilot rescued from bosnia, was made a national hero of a war that we refused to enter. He made people feel better about themselves, feel that sometimes our military can do something right.[10] Mickey Mantle also filled the hero void. After his liver transplant, he received thousands of telegrams and cards every day from people needing to believe in something.[11]

The images also refashion enemies. Neocons have served up the u.s. government as our newest post–cold war enemy: it spends too many of the taxpayers' dollars. This depiction makes room for the rhetoric of hate toward affirmative action and the welfare state.

Forget the fact that the social welfare state has been under attack for more than a decade. The images still work.

The imaginary becomes the real. This applies to nations, worlds, and the racial/sexual borders that construct them.

PART I

DomiNATION/SubordiNATION

WRITING HATRED ON THE BODY

"Otherness" is constructed on bodies. Racism uses the physicality of bodies to punish, to expunge and isolate certain bodies and construct them as outsiders. The named "other" is a foreigner, immigrant, or stranger. Jews' and blacks' and women's bodies of all colors are used to mark the hatred of this "otherness." Racial hatred is not neat and separate; it is multiple and continuous. And much hatred spills over into the sexual aspects of racial meanings.

Yellow stars. White hoods. Both are symbols of specific hatreds and a grand narrative of hate, though the former marks those who are hated, while the latter marks those who do the hating. Hatred is unique and historically contextualized, but it also repeats itself as though it were intractable, as though it lay in our psyches ready to be pulled forward, outward from the deepest layers of our unconscious.

On the eve of the twenty-first century, hatreds explode in such places as sarajevo, argentina, chechnya, rwanda, los angeles, and oklahoma city. The hatred embodies a complex set of fears about difference and otherness. It reveals what some people fear in themselves, their own "differences." Hatred forms around the unknown, the difference of "others." And we have learned the difference that we fear through racialized and sexualized markings. Because people grow othered by their racialized, sexualized, and engendered bodies, bodies are important to the writing of hatred on history.

Hatred is not only color-coded but inscribed on such body parts as noses, hair, vaginas, eyes. I argue that physicality—our physical bodies—is key to constructing and seeing hatreds. Bodies are always in part psychic constructions of meaning symbolized through coloring hatred on sexualized sites. This psychic realm is a space of knowable and unknowable mental layerings that unconsciously and consciously frame our seeing. It is an unfathomable realm of desire and repression; of injury, hurt and fear, and imagination and fantasy. This non-corporeal arena of desire and escape is where one knows but does not know, sees but does not see. The psyche, our mind's eye, which *already* frames our experiencing of everyday life friendships, schools, neighborhoods, churches, mosques, is also constructed by this history. Within this psychic space we name and interpret what we think we see. Here we negotiate and renegotiate fear, desire, and difference itself.

The psyche both lies still, waiting to be called forth, and is already in play. Several available narratives can explain this psychic realm. I circle around the Freudian/Lacanian oedipal drama of repression and primal desire without wholly purchasing it. I have come to believe that hatred emanates from interiorized conditions that are in part unconscious longings and denials. Otherness is implicated here; we fear the escape of the repressed desire and project it elsewhere, onto "others" who then must be punished.

The unsettled psyches of borderless worlds and interconnected selves are localized in the fear and threat of women, semites, homosexuals, and colored people. These fears are repressed, and recast as hatreds. This hatred, in turn, orders and organizes the world. The repressed self requires the lies, the fantasized symbolizations. The fantasy framework is required by desires of the other as well as identification with the other.[1]

Jean-Paul Sartre calls this repression the "idea of the jew." It is the anti-semite who makes the jew.[2] But stereotypes are not merely false images. Rather, they are "ambivalent text[s] of projection and introjection...displacement, overdetermination, guilt, [and] aggressivity."[3] Racialized hatreds play back and forth between the mind's eye and its fears, and the peopled realities of daily life.

The chaos of the psychic realm has some people fearing in others what they most fear in themselves. These fears can elicit the different mindsets of colonialism, nationalism, orientalism, and imperialism.[4] The politics to be understood here extend from the real to layers of the unconscious. If serbs rape muslim women *as if* they are ethnic-cleansing, then the imaginary must be destroyed in order for life to be livable. Politics must allow people to embrace their own "radical strangeness" in an attempt to deny hatred.[5]

I do not view hatred as natural, or timeless, or homogenized, and yet it is something more than contextually specific. As a politics of "otherness," hatred calls forth the imaginings of unconscious fantasies. But the fantasies are changeable.

So I proceed cautiously here. There is no one kind of hate. No one kind of body. No one kind of psyche. Yet hatreds are reformulated continuously, and I keep wondering why. This leads me to focus more on those who hate than on those who are hated, or on those who hate those who hate them. I also say little about those who fight against hatred—those who fought, for example, against slavery, for civil rights, against nazism, against misogyny. I say little about them because they are not who I fear.

A problem with writing about hatred is that it makes the world seem completely hate-filled. Or, as Michael Taussig asks: "If life is constructed, how come it appears so immutable?"[6] Because we cannot make full sense of hate, because much of hate is unspeakable, or indescribable, it can seem untouchable.[7] By speaking hatred, I hope to touch it, and to begin to move through and past the trauma it creates.

BODY BORDERS AND PSYCHIC HATREDS

Hate is fueled by fictive symbols, by pictures in the mind. Serbian nationalists, the right wing in russia, the anti-abortionists of operation rescue in the u.s., skinheads in germany, the ku klux klan, and religious fundamentalists around the globe are violently committed to controlling the borders in which we live. As the world becomes more economically unequal and transnational, this border-consciousness seems to be more and more evident. Racialized ethnic nationalisms are in part a response to transnational capital in eastern and central europe. Ex-communists reposition themselves for the new world order by using old hatreds and wounds.

In other parts of the world—rwanda, iran, algeria—violent wars erupt or continue. Women are raped as part of a systematic campaign of ethnic cleansing in the balkans. Muslims are massacred by a crazed militant jewish settler while praying in hebron. Khalid Abdul Muhammad of the nation of islam, in speaking of jews, "prays 'that God will kill my enemy and take him off the face of the planet Earth.'"[8] Snipers in sarajevo shoot at children. Maja Djokic, on her way home from a volleyball game in sarajevo, is hit by shrapnel and dies. Her father says, "There are perhaps 10,000 dead in Sarajevo, of whom 1,700 were children. So we cannot think that Maja's death was anything special. But of course, she was our Maja, so we think it is special."[9]

A truck bomb blows up a jewish community center in buenos aires.[10] A car bomb explodes near the israeli embassy in london, wounding thirteen.[11] More than sixty thousand have died in the war in chechnya.[12] Paramilitary right-wing groups and their fascist underworld are exposed by the bombing of the federal building in oklahoma city. Christopher Hitchens says that these "aryan fundamentalists" who present themselves as patriots and anti-government individualalists are a thoroughly racist movement.[13] Hate does not seem specific to any one corner of the world.[14]

The hatred is global, *and* it is specifically racialized along religious, ethnic, and gender lines. In apprehending it, we must take into account particular geographies, histories, and cultures, as well as psychic mappings and layerings that may still make a grand narrative of otherness.

The psyche is mapped with a tension between the unlimited, unbordered desires of our bodies *and* the truncated multiple needs of our consciousness. Denial and repression underlie fear and loathing. This fear makes the unconscious, for psychoanalytic feminist Jacqueline Rose, utterly political at its core, so that right-wing ideologies thrive on and push against the "furthest limits of psychic fantasy."[15] Psychic sexual desire becomes the ground of political manipulation.

Desire is not easily controlled or erased. Fear of the unbridled self requires the construction of an "other" who/which must be shut out. Repression is recast as fear and hatred. For Mikkel Borch-

Jacobsen, "unconscious desire is undoubtedly not (re)presented to consciousness." Consciousness is exceeded continuously. The realm of desire, and with it the forbidden, is always waiting to express itself. Repression negotiates the inadmissable.[16] There is a constant struggle to contain desire.

Ronald Takaki depicts a process of separation from the instinctual (sexual) self as integral to the racializing of identity. This cultural construction of race forms any individual's psychic construction. People of color are then identified with the body, not the mind. And to be in control of the instinctual body is to establish whiteness over the black, indian, mexican, asian.[17] Fear dominates in the realm of unconscious desire because racial and sexual fantasies are limitless in these arenas. As Rose argues, "Freedom may not be sexy, but fear of it is wholly determined by sex."[18]

Wilhelm Reich argued that fascism directs itself to the unconscious; that sexuality is repressed and located here; and that repressed desire is not open to conscious knowing.[19] Fear becomes a major resource of fascism.[20] If desire is structured sexually, and we come to our sexuality through racialized fantasies, then, as Frantz Fanon argues, the racist must create his/her inferior. As such, "the myth of the bad nigger is part of the collective unconscious."[21] Racism itself, for Paul Gilroy, becomes a part of the process of denying and repressing the historical and unconscious experience.[22]

Fear and hate bespeak anxiety about the borders of an individual's desires. Experiencing differences, or even just seeing them, challenges and uproots certainty about the self. Jonathan Rutherford views this realm of personal anxiety as a threat to the dissolution of the self which demands new boundaries. The right wing always plays with the anxiety about difference and the unknown,[23] using racialized fantasies of orderly patriarchal families to set the borders and boundaries of desire.

Psychic meanings, as the mind's eye, represent and (mis)interpret for us. We see, or do not see, accordingly. Those germans who claimed to have known nothing of the gas chambers during world war II did not let themselves know, or were not able to know, or could not fathom that they knew. I wonder what we will not let ourselves see today in sarajevo or rwanda. We see through an elaborate system of screens. And this seeing has only become more complicated with CNN coverage and the global communications network, which broadcast immediate and continual pictures of violence and hate. So we *think* we know; and yet we know only what is screened for us and what we allow ourselves to see.

Race (the often-times colored body), sex (the sexed/biological body), gender (the cultural/biological body), and sexuality (the various sexual/cultural desires of the body) inflect on each other. The lack of boundaries unsettles desire itself. We see body color(s) from bodies that are already marked by the phallus, or by the lack of it. We know the male muslim or jew by his circumcised penis, which bespeaks a partial lack of the true phallus, which in turns suggests the female. We know the black man by his oversized penis, which suggests the excesses of black sexuality and a protectionism of white womanhood.[24] Or, as Judith Butler says, the black male body in the public psyche is always performing as a threat no matter what it is doing.[25]

Fanon wrote of the black man as a penis symbol, and of black men being lynched as a sign of sexual revenge. "We know how much of sexuality there is in all cruelties, tortures, beatings," he said. So the jew is killed or sterilized but the negro castrated.[26] Hitler spoke of the u.s. as a "niggerized jewish country," of jews and other minorities as guilty of the "syphilitization of our people," and of homosexuality as a "symptom of racial degeneracy."[27] Reich notes that the swastika, as a sign of racial superiority, was originally a sexual symbol.[28]

The writing of new-old borders through the racist, anti-semitic, misogynist history of the globe defines multiple nationalist struggles today. Michael Ignatieff writes that "the repressed has returned, and its name is nationalism." It is a nationalism defined by male resentment and a loathing of peace and domesticity.[29] Today's nationalisms represent a collective and individual paranoia resulting from unbridled fears and envy.[30] Serb nationalism is full of hate, and is completely bent on destroying the multicultural society of ex-yugoslavia with its fluid identities of muslim, croat, and serb. Zlata Filipovic, a thirteen-year-old bosnian girl now living in france, says that the war is "between idiots, not between Serbs and Croats and Muslims...

They're crazy."[31] One could also say that Hitler too was crazy. And Stalin also.

But *crazy* is not quite helpful here, because illusion is a profound part of "othered" politics. Politics is very much about a symbolization that allows for, creates, and even sometimes demands that people live *as if* they believe in the representations, the distortions, even when they do not.[32] It makes no sense to speak of aryan or serbian racial purity when blood is mixed all the time. And yet we speak *as if* such racial lines exist, and then they do.

Serbs have married croats who have married muslims, and they have had children. Nada Salom, a journalist, is serb on her mother's side, slovenian on her father's, jewish in last name, and sarajevan through and through.[33] And yet we speak *as if* there is such a thing as a serb. When Lani Guinier was nominated for a position in the civil-rights division of the Clinton administration she was treated *as if* she were (only) black even though she has a white jewish mother. So is she a "light-skinned black or a dark-skinned jew"?[34] When Farrakhan pits black against jew, or when jews become fixated on black anti-semitism, they deny their shared otherness in order to draw boundary markers that let them feel safer. They imagine themselves in control.

SHARED "OTHERNESS" AND FANTASY

Because we often fear that which we do not know, that which is strange to us, we take this fear and use it to smash difference, to try to annihilate it. This fear creates new ambivalent borders: we do not know which ones we want to cross or what we want to keep out.[35] In this reading, life is part fiction, part fantasy, in Slavoj Zizek's words, and the fantasy reflects the repression of unbridled desire.[36] The fantasy makes life bearable because it enforces borders and limits. It makes the unimaginable manageable through an enforced closure. White vs. black; man vs. woman; west vs. the orient; hetero vs. homo; christian vs. muslim; aryan vs. jew—the fictive divisions are clear-cut and apparently soothing for many.

For Slavoj Zizek, fantasy is a screen for the desire of the other; it is a screen masking a void, concealing inconsistency. It is a mask on whose presence we insist. One may well know the falsity of the mask but still not renounce it.[37] The imaginary works because we are deeply invested in it for the way it mystifies the "real," which itself is part fantasy. The imaginary makes life bearable.[38]

Bruno Bettelheim charges Otto Frank, Anne Frank's father, with not allowing himself to *really* believe that the concentration camps existed. Because he did not believe, or could not, he hid his family and tried to go on with life as well as one could while in hiding. Bettelheim believes that if Otto Frank had let himself *see* and *know* what was happening to jews—"to believe in Auschwitz"—he would have either left amsterdam early on, or devised some plan of resistance for the inevitable moment of discovery. Bettelheim also charges the rest of us with fantasy: we embrace Anne Frank's story because it lets us think that life went on for the Franks despite the horror. Her story allows us "to retreat into a private space."[39]

For Zizek, an unconscious fantasy structures social reality itself. So even though we may not believe something is true, we still act as though it is: "even if we do not take things seriously...*we are still doing them*."[40] Even though the president does not really represent all the people, we act *as if* he did. Even though all jews are not alike, homogenizing stereotypes operate *as if* they were. Even though anyone can be infected with the HIV virus, many act *as if* they could not.

Knowing and seeing take on new, fantasy-like meaning. Fantasies are partially true and partially untrue; and they are utterly real as fantasy. Many german women of the third reich say "they saw nothing, knew nothing." Some say they knew of the camps but did not know of the crematoria. One woman who survived auschwitz said she did not know of the gas chambers. A german prison guard at allendorf says "there was so much people didn't know at all...but thinking about it in hindsight one really had a pretty thick 'board in front of one's face.' There was so much one simply did not see." Yet one more woman states she knew "they were taken away to a camp. One could not imagine more."[41]

These women feared that if they did not obey the nazi edicts they would be killed. Some chose not to get involved, chose to be passive "little people"; others speak of needing extraordinary courage and not having it; others speak of fearing the "more" of what might happen if they disobeyed.[42]

Hannah Arendt writes of the "banality of evil" as encompassing jews themselves. If jews had not cooperated with the nazis, she says, the total number of victims would have been much less. Yet she also wants us to "see" those who resisted: "Under conditions of terror most people will comply but *some people will not*." And it will always matter because "one man will always be left alive to tell the story."[43]

Many german women were well aware of the dissonance of nazi propaganda. There was a big difference between "the other jews" and the ones you knew. "If all Jews were like you, we would have nothing to hate, or persecute."[44] But the construct of *jew* is retained and maintained intact: "The others are pigs, this one is first rate." Even Hitler is said to have acknowledged knowing 340 "first rate jews."[45]

The fear is not just of desire but of one's lacking, one's incompleteness. Jacques Lacan sees the lack in terms of the phallus.[46] The fear of our own lacking is displaced onto another. The fear of becoming feminine, of being penetrated, is displaced onto the woman. Men fear that they are like women. Rape allows them the fantasy that they are men.

BORDERING MULTIPLE IDENTITIES

Borders define and differentiate an inside from an outside. They are constituted through a construct of difference that is singular and exclusionary. American slavery defined racist borderlines between white and black. Civil-rights legislation rearranged the boundaries. Marriage defines the heterosexual borders between man and woman, and gays are outside them. The boundaries constructed through one's race, sex, gender, and sexuality cut apart and dissect the multiplicity of any one individual's identity. Any one identity embraces multiple borders: black women, muslim girls, gay men. Maria Lugones speaks of her multiple identity: "I realize that separation into clean, tidy things and beings is not possible for me because it would be the death of myself as multiplicitous and a death of community with my own." Whereas you can separate an egg yolk from the white of the egg, people exist in in-between spaces.[47]

Gays and lesbians represent uncomfortable identities for the heterosexual world. Gays and lesbians, particularly in their fantasized constructions, represent multiple, fluid, connected imaginings.[48] The homosexual is said to not "know the boundary of his own body—where his body ends and space begins."[49] Transvestites and transsexuals destroy the boundaries of gendered bodies. AIDS, although initially presented in the west as a gay disease, today knows no borders, crosses borders, breaks down old borders, creates new borders. It is a transnational disease that unsettles neat and tidy, singular identities.

But instead of radically pluralizing identities, singular difference is naturalized by the hetero/homo polarity. This normalizing of "difference" maintains a fantasmatic inside and outside for the increasingly complex global system. An inside space requires outsiders.[50] The division between homosexual (unnatural) and heterosexual (natural) is then written on the body through a system of signs: color, musculature, sex, gender, and so on. We are presented with a "body politic";[51] difference and otherness are inscribed on the body as fantasy.

The difference of *hetero*sexual is applauded while the sameness of *homo* is deplored. *Hetero* is naturalized by genitalia. Yet femaleness represents otherness as it is postioned against the white phallus. Homosexuality with its possible invisible (bodily) status is, ironically, marked by the phallus as danger itself.[52]

Difference—outside the construct of heterosexual—is treated as strangeness. And strangers are easy to distance and blame. The "other," as "woman" or "black" or "muslim," is translated and re-translated in relation to the changing world. So the world of transnational corporations attempts to adapt to a multicultural globe *as if* the borders of rich and poor did not still hold. And the u.s. speaks of protecting its borders, and limiting immigration, and maintains "difference" as strangeness, while insisting on a global vision.

Julia Kristeva argues that it has become normal to assume that there always will be foreigners among us. We navigate between national imperatives and universalist fantasies when we imagine that we all are one. Inherent in nationalism is the concept of foreignness, and it is this part of the self that we fear. Kristeva believes we are all foreigners to ourselves, because the foreigner lives within us. The foreigner "is the hidden face of our identity"; the otherness and strangeness within us. It is this same foreignness within that allows us to live with others. "If I am a foreigner, there are no foreigners."[53] Or we all are.

Jeanine Amber, a black jewish woman who could not find refuge either inside the nation of islam and its hatred or outside with the other hatreds, chooses to circle the group's circumference, preferring to try to get inside rather than be inside struggling to get out.[54] Yet for others, what Freud termed the "narcissism of minor difference" looms large. In this scenario one imagines and sees difference where it hardly exists. It is precisely the minor differences in people who are otherwise alike that form the basis of feelings of strangeness and hostility between them,"[55] says Freud. People exaggerate what separates them from others as part of their search for identity.[56]

BODY MASKS AND FANTASIES

Bordered identities are also constructed out of blood/racial lines. Women are needed to reproduce these lines. War is made with this blood; masculinist nationalisms use these bloodlines while they write territorial conquest on the bodies of women through forced prostitution and war rape. Klaus Theweleit explains that "fascist rituals went directly inside men, taking their material from the male unconscious." Men themselves were split into a female interior and a male exterior in the process.[57] For Kristeva, the imaginary and symbolic cultural order bespeaks the truth of desire even if it lacks reality.[58]

Bodies as representations of the phallic symbolic order define one's physicality as a system of signs in which the psyche is layered inside the meanings. Given that bodies are already layered in and through their psychic meanings, there is constant slippage between these meanings. Therefore, the physicality of the body is never completely discernible or retrievable from any one historical reality.[59]

The fear of the vagina, as expressed in the mythic notion of *vagina dentata*, which imagines the vagina eating the penis with its razor-sharp teeth if they are not excised, imagines the "warrior marks" that Alice Walker and Pratibha Parmar write of. Female genital mutilation—the physical and psychic maiming of 100 million girls and women in africa, asia, and the middle east—is demanded by male fears and desires, but also continually executed by women. Figuratively this demand is spread all over the bodies of women *even* in the west: breast implants, removal of ribs and fat, starvation, changed noses.[60] The body is a symbolized site because it is such a "basic political resource."[61]

The symbolizing of the physical traces back to racialized and sexual psychic borders; the signs on/of the body seem naturalized in this process. Bodies and their sexualized/racialized meanings are hidden psychically and also have what Judith Butler terms "surface appearance."[62] The signs of racialized gender written on the body also have psychic resonance. Or, as Mary Douglas argues, bodies represent and symbolize sexual dangers.[63]

The vagina can symbolize possible castration. Menstrual blood, for Kristeva, can represent the danger issuing from within identity or an unnamable otherness. The chador and the veil supposedly cover fears of the body, while pornography exposes the fear as desire. Radical feminists have long argued that the fear of women reflects a fear of procreative possibility, of the generative power of women. Pollution rituals and sexual prohibitions are intended to insure men's power over women.[64] Fearing women is a form of hating them and their differences—while also desiring them.

PHYSICALITY AND BODY CONSTRUCTION

Physicality—body color, shape, size; facial structure, noses, eyes, hair; sexual body parts, penis, breasts, vaginas, clitoris—is symbolized as *the* body. The body is not a constant, but remains a constant site of political struggle. The female body operates as spectacle; its physicality is given meaning by marking its difference(s). Sandra Lee Bartky describes the female body as a "body on which an inferior status has been inscribed."[65] The meaning of a female body never exists outside context even though the body is never just contextual. As I have written elsewhere, "However contextualized, [the body] is also real. There is no innate body, but there are bodies."[66] There is no body, as fact, without interpretation, and yet the body according to Leslie Adelson "is more than a discursive sign."[67]

Identities are constructed on bodies, for bodies, by political discourse. Although a "history without bodies is unimaginable" for Adelson, it is a history made of "images of bodies imagined to be real." The body is then many things simultaneously: "It is a thing and a sign, an inside and an outside, a boundary constantly crossing itself."[68] Bodies absorb meaning and elicit meaning. Politics processes the definitions.

But the body also has meaning before we see it.[69] Fanon bespeaks this dilemma when he states: "My blackness was there, dark and unarguable." He is thus, he says, "overdetermined from without."[70] Lisa Jones writes that hair is already given meaning as the key racial signifier after skin.[71] In rwanda thousands were hacked to death according to the shapes of their noses. Tutsis tend to be taller with narrow features and high cheekbones; hutus tend to be shorter and have flatter, broader noses.[72]

The physicality of the body becomes a horribly powerful resource for those who wish to conquer, violate, humiliate, and shame.[73] The body's power—its intimacy, its creativity against systems of power, its physical dignity and integrity—is also its vulnerability.[74] We can feel our body as we can feel nothing else. Its pain, its illness, its thirst, its hunger demand strength in our attempt to meet their needs, and make us despairingly vulnerable in the process. The vulnerability inside our strength is why rape is so brutalizing. In the oppressor's hope of smashing the body's spirit people are starved, mutilated, tortured, shaved, and made deathly cold and sick. Our bodies have an enormous claim on us. They force us to know and feel what we otherwise would never allow ourselves to imagine.

Mikhail Bakhtin argues that the body represents openness and incompleteness; it transgresses limits. The open mouth, genital organs, breasts, phallus, and nose leave the body unfinished, in process. Official culture seeks to close it down; to bind it.[75] For Kristeva the body is a territory of orifices, surfaces, and hollows where the differentiation between the possible and impossible is exerted.[76] Michel Foucault argues that politics is played out on the body.[77] Dorinda Outram speaks of the body as "a producer of knowledge for its owner"; as a vehicle and transmitter of political intentions. As such the body is not merely acted upon. It is both utterly personal, private, and intimate, and inescapably public.[78]

Elizabeth Grosz thinks of the body as "a writing surface on which messages can be inscribed." Graffiti-like body-writing engraves men as phallic, women as castrated. But the body always has the possibility of being self-marked, self-represented. And its representation shifts through time. Whereas the primitive body was read as "all surface," the modern body is read in terms of what it hides.[79]

Elaine Scarry writes of the pain of the body as "an invisible geography." Pain shatters and resists language. "The body in pain" makes and unmakes the world. Physical pain is both a "spectacle of power" and "read as power."[80] The extreme vulnerability of the body in pain becomes a resource for the regimes in power.[81]

Eating, sleeping, and defecating remind one of the body's needs. And the body is humiliated, numbed, and traumatized by the denial of these needs. Bodily violation terrorizes, and "trauma repeatedly interrupts." One's concept of safety is destroyed as the self's "connections are shattered"; and one is left with "utter abandonment."[82] In this process of annihilation, the person ceases to exist. And the horror becomes impossible to translate.[83]

The body is a visual site, which makes it crucial for marking difference, and it is a felt site: one feels one's body. This utter intimacy makes the body unique as a location for politics. One hears the body cry out for its safety when one hears of torture, slavery, and death camps. Slavery bespeaks the "slow throttling and murder of nine millions of men [and women]" shackled, whipped, and beaten on the basis of the color of their bodies.[84] In the nazi death camps people craved warmth, food, water, medicine, and the list goes on and on. In the bosnian concentration camps the horrors sound too similar: filth, hunger, starvation, rape, death.[85] One begins to suspect that the destruction and annihilation of bodies are attempts to smash difference itself.

The body could, instead of marking "otherness," be a democratic site for politics. The body's utter variety and uniqueness is shared. After all, "the human body is common to us all."[86] It is ironic that the body, the one thing all human beings have in common, becomes a site for demarcating difference, hate, and pain. We each start with our bodies; no one can escape its reality. Yet we do not

experience our physicality as an open potential of multiple meanings. Instead, we live in our bodies as they represent the fears of difference and strangeness. Color, vaginas, noses mark us as others.

RACIALIZING THE SEXUALIZED BODY

Purity of blood almost never exists, so neither does purity
of race. Yet we live as if both were real qualities. The construction of
the "other" or "others" depends on this notion of purity, of separate-
ness. Yet racial purity is a construction of the mind's eye: a fantasy, a
fiction. According to David Theo Goldberg, race has a "veneer of
fixedness," yet is "almost, but not quite, empty in its own connota-
tive capacity."[87] Race in this sense is never just biological. But the
idea of race is always in part fixated on the body; hence the notion of
"the" jew, or indian, or chicano. Race is, then, at once both fixed and
utterly unstable. Its meaning is always contextualized, yet the meaning of race precedes its context. Colors, noses, and hair are defined
before they are seen, yet one sees them only through the context of
their world.

So I disagree with Etienne Balibar when he states that "racism
has nothing to do with the existence of objective biological 'races'" if
he means to completely contextualize racialized bodies.[88] Shirlee
Taylor Haizlip pushes this point to its limits. She began the search for
her mother's family assuming she would find black people passing
for white. What she found instead was "black people who had
become white. After all, if you look white, act white, live white, vaca-
tion white, go to school white, marry white, and die white, are you
not 'white'?"[89]

Racism may exist without race,[90] as when muslims were sus-
pected of bombing the federal building in oklahoma city even after
pictures of two white men were splashed across our TV screens as
the suspects. However, racism was already in play and completely
foregrounded the incident. Some people saw muslims as the terror-
ists, as if they were the actual bombers. Racism is constructed
through fictions, which is not to say that race is a fiction. The concept of difference is so contaminated that we need to be cautious
about how we choose to deconstruct it.

Nazism was built on the fiction of purity: the daughter born of a jewish father and an aryan mother was a jew in Hitler's germany even if the father had lost his life in world war I fighting for the fatherland. The jew is always in part a social construction: there are 1/2 jews, 1/4 jews, "decent" jews, "prominent" jews, "foreign" jews.[91]

Slobodan Milosevic depends on racialized fantasy in his construction of serb nationalism, while ex-yugoslavians look about for identities to justify the carnage. A bosnian muslim says, "banjaluka is our jerusalem." A bosnian serb says, "Like the jews...we will prevail in the end."[92] Complicating the racialized fantasies is the fact that it is often quite difficult to physically distinguish between serb and croat.

The nation of islam assumes racial purity while Lisa Jones writes how her (white) mother raised her to think politically about being a black woman. "African-american" might include people of african, native american, latin, and/or european descent.[93] There are no purist, singular visions here. French tennis star Yannick Noah, the son of a mixed marriage says, "In Africa I am white, and in France I am black."[94]

Color is an already "naturalized" sign for race. But color itself is never simply one thing. Haizlip says color is shadings of red to brown, and tan to pink. We call "ourselves honey, caramel, ivory, peaches-and-cream, mahogany, coal blue, red, bronze, amber, chocolate coffee."[95] According to Sander Gilman, color itself represents a quality of "otherness." So racialized meanings are represented through color and as though they mean color: black vs. white; ayran vs. non-white; oriental vs. non-oriental. The jew, the muslim, the roma, the algerian, all are/become "black." Dark skin as far back as ancient greece is a sign of illness.[96] W. E. B. Du Bois' color line—from light to dark skin—continues to demarcate the world system.[97] The foreigner, the stranger, the "other" is colored. And color, as symbol, connects the jew to the muslim to the african, to the generalized "other."

So there are multiple racial dimensions to the systemic system of racism. Balibar argues that there is "not merely a single invariant racism but a number of racisms." There are open series of situations and historical formations that define any particular racism. In this sense today's racism has little if anything to do with actual "objective biological 'races'." The biological theme has a "fictive essence." It is, and always has been a "pseudo-biological accounting."[98]

Today the theme of racism is less biological heredity and more the insurmountability of cultural differences. Historical cultures outline the "other"; the language of incompatibility displaces the superior/inferior divide.[99] Boundary lines are therefore being constantly redrawn and must remain flexible. Yet, "the cake of custom," as W. E. B. Du Bois calls it, remains very much in place.[100] This survival is easily seen in the revival of the hereditary bell-curve view of racial intelligence.[101]

So racism is both old and new, static and changing; tied to darkness of skin color and pluralized to encompass ethnic/cultural meanings that are not simply based on an inferior/superior divide. One can neither understand contemporary racism as simply a black/white divide nor as a system that has left the divide behind. This black/white divide is particularly true for western societies with a history of black slavery. Blackness sets the context for the meanings of otherness rooted in color.

If racism exists with and without race, anti-semitism exists with and without jews. Fictional constructions stand in for "real" blacks, jews, muslims. We hate on the basis of fictional beliefs about the "other," which is why truth does not matter much. So what if our neighbor is different from the stereotype of the boisterous jew, or terrorist muslim, or swarthy black? The rule, a fiction, still holds.

The west has characterized much of the bloodshed in bosnia as a morass of irresolvable ethnic hatred, and bosnia has become "the other."[102] This depiction ignores the intense ethnic/racial conflicts existing within the u.s., france, england, etc. I do not clearly demarcate race and ethnicity because they are so similarly constructed as fantasy at this particular time in history. Both are constructed from exclusionary conceptions of difference. Race and ethnicity interweave much the same way nature is mixed with culture, sex with gender, and the physical with the psychic. As such, race and ethnicity are constructed out of classifications based on ascriptions to the body, when the body is already imbricated in cultural/politicized meanings.

Racial conflict can be ethnically pluralized, and ethnic conflict can be polarized by racial fictions. The conflicts between koreans and blacks and jews and asians in los angeles or new york city reflect the tensions of a highly racialized society along cultural and colored lines. Race and ethnicity blur. This also is true of serbs and croats and muslims in bosnia.

RACIALIZING THE PHALLUS

Color is also symbolized by the phallus and the fear of sexual desire, given the intimate history of racializing sexuality and sexualizing racism. Thus racism and the phallus are intimately connected. Edward Said argues that there is always an undercurrent of sexual exaggeration when constructing racial others.[103] Winthrop Jordan describes how the black male is associated sexually with the bestiality of animals. His penis is large and unruly.[104] He also describes the sexualization of the racialized african female by seventeenth- and eighteenth-century european males. Calvin Hernton writes that black male sexuality is demonized as a "walking phallus."[105] Sander Gilman shows how the male jew is seen as effeminate with his circumcised (castrated) penis.[106] Faisal Fatehali Devji, discussing the circumcised muslim male, says: "Racism is when life hangs upon a foreskin."[107] The sexualized meanings of racial fears reflect the phallocratic construction of racism. Or as Bankimchandra Chattopadhyay states, "As the Europeans always allege, the 'Hindoos' are 'effeminate.'"[108]

Gilman explores the hypersexuality of the jew(ish male) and his circumcised penis as a marker of sexual threat. Circumcision and castration form a fantasy about the entire body.[109] The woman's clitoris was understood in viennese psychoanalytic circles at the turn of the century as a truncated penis. Interestingly, the clitoris was referred to, according to Gilman, as the "Jew" (Jud). Female masturbation was referred to as "playing with the Jew."[110]

Both the jewish male and female (jew and non-jew alike) with their defective sexual organs, are set apart from the phallic order. The body writing of the phallus is more visible than the writing of the clitoris, which is not seen. The invisibility underwrites the lacking.

Male jews share a particular otherness with male muslims and women and foreigners in general. Black men share the phallic space differently from the male jew or muslim; they are an unruly threat.

They occupy the space as bestial "other." They too are the stranger, the foreigner.

Bosnia's muslims are said to be the new jews of europe,[111] while the blacks of somalia and haiti and south africa are pushed off the front pages of newspapers by the destruction of sarajevo. Nevertheless, the black/white transnational divide continues to construct the variations of ethnic "otherness." This divide is why vietnamese and african guest workers in germany are called "niggers," and why roma are hated for their dark skins.[112] According to Gilman, jews were metaphorically described as the negroes of europe in the 1920s writings of Milena Jesenka. In the late nineteenth century the views that jews had black skin or were "swarthy" and that their circumcised penises carried sexual diseases were general consensus in ethnological literature. Gilman concludes that "The Jews' disease is written on the skin." Their foreignness was a sign of racial otherness.[113] Color comes into play in Frau Anna Fest's denial that most germans think jews are cheats. She says, "The worst is the 'white Jew'; the 'white Jew' is a Christian."[114]

While color has marked the jew, this marking does not mean that the racial history of blacks and jews has been one and the same. Rather, this marking is very different from that which has characterized the racial history of blacks. Yet the hatreds of blacks, jews, and muslims are deeply tied to signs and fictions that are color-coded according to sexualized meanings. Signs of race and color are easily transposed to signs of sex and gender.

Race is encoded in and through the uncontrollable arena of sex. Racial fears bespeak the openness of sexual desire. Black male slaves were viewed as potential rapists of white women, while white masters raped their black female slaves. Jewish men were depicted as vile and effeminate while nazi officers starved and raped jewish women. Serb and croatian nationalists speak of racial purity and ethnic cleansing and systematically rape muslim women. Serbs describe Tito as not-a-man; they say, "He was a woman," which represents the serbs' sense of having been emasculated by history.[115]

To speak of the war in bosnia as one of simply ethnic/religious hatred masks the fantasy structures of racialized sexuality and the significance of women within nationalist struggles. When a serb general demands that a woman be raped "first before the eyes of those whom she bore, then before the eyes of those who bore her, then before the eyes of her husband who fathered children with her,"[116] we see woman defined as the fulcrum through which the "other" gets continually reproduced. Traumatize and destroy her children, her parents, her husband, the nation, by conquering her.

BORDER WRITINGS ON WOMEN

In nazi germany, green triangles noted criminals; black triangles noted anti-socials; red triangles noted politicals; yellow stars noted jews; pink triangles noted homosexuals. There was no colored triangle or star for women, no marking as such. Jewish women wore the yellow star; their identity was marked by yellow. Their identity as women was not specified. They were just jews. It is usually not mentioned that at least half of those persecuted on racial grounds in nazi germany were women.[117]

Aryan women were identified as women, as mothers of the race. Their job was described as kinder, kuche, and kirche (children, kitchen, and church). They were expected to be dutiful wives and mothers and "receptacles of the seed of the race."[118] Policies directed at these women focused on creating a "racial consciousness." Procreation was the responsibility of aryan women; abortion and sterilization were required for non-aryan women.[119]

Women throughout time and place have been used to reproduce "the" race: as breeders, as mothers, and sometimes as wives. Aryan women were defined as reproducers of the race in nazism through their racial status as "pure." As "mother of the nation" she defined the racial borders against non-aryan women and men.

Women, as female, are naturalized as "mothers" and as such can never be named as complete outsiders, like "the" jew, or black, or muslim. Their bodies are used to normalize "the" race, or family, or nation. They mark the inside, by reproducing it and naturalizing it, and in doing so are made invisible as border markers. They remain visibly invisible though present; systematically and perpetually semi-oticized. This symbolization is unsettled by the visibility of non-docile women. The unruly behavior of women, symbolized as a (feminist) sisterhood, makes women visible in unsettling ways for the nation.

Women are symbolized and represented according to Sandra Lee Bartky as "docile bodies" that are used as "ornamental surfaces."[120] As symbol, the woman is not-man, not-citizen, not-phallus. She is not-outside and not-inside; she is the invisible border. She represents our deepest fears and longings of sexual desire, obligation and duty, uncontrolled passion, and reproductive capacities.

Women, *as a fantasmatic*, construct the very meaning of stranger because they are different *from* men, strangers to them. They, as a homogenized fantasy, are the absolute other while never being named specifically as such. They represent the unnamed, the absence, in order to name the "other" others. Woman is in the nation but not of it; she is present but not seen; she is named, but not for what she is. Woman as translator of the bloodline constructs the nation, but through the naturalness of blood has no specified significance. The nationalizing of identity makes the woman visible while ascribing invisibility to her.

Women of color are the double foreigner, the double stranger. Their absence is twice effected, their presence twice negated. They are held up to the fantasmatic and found doubly wanting.

Women bear the new bodies for the nation state, and/or their rape represents conquered territories. Although the nation is psychically positioned against women, it is also reproduced through them. Women exist within as a male fantasy: silenced, conquered, soft. Women, though not-men, are included as "mother" of the nation. The insider/outsider status of women is necessary because the mother can comfort while she keeps borders intact. Women, as mothers and daughters, are distanced, silenced, without making them the outside.

The veil worn by muslim women elicits the psychic borders differentiating east from west, innocence from sex, availability from denial. The veil symbolizes the purity of denial, and also a rape fantasy.[121] In western fantasy, the veil hides, separates, marks a border and a forbidden space. It also sometimes comforts the muslim man as a "time-mirror"; it reassures him of "his" traditions.[122]

For muslim women the veil can liberate or confine. In sarajevo during world war II muslim women shrouded their jewish neighbors in their veils to protect them from the nazis. Today, the western media depicts muslim culture through its veiled women as backward and anti-modern. Such pictures during the gulf war and the war in bosnia reproduce "otherness" as part of the meaning of war itself. And western women are supposed to feel free and liberated compared to the "orient."

Women are symbolized in homogenized form; differences among them are denied in order to make them the "sign" of the authentic nation. Women become the absolute fiction and the transnational desire/fear. This hatred, written on the body, is then written on the nation.

To return to my daughter, and her trying to imagine the horrors of slavery and the concentration camps: I don't want my daughter to have a daughter who grows up reading the diary of a girl who had to spend her life in hiding, behind secret windows or floorboards, trying to escape hate.

WRITING BODIES ON THE NATION

I ask you to see the nation as an invention, completely mythic and unnatural. National identities and geographies shift and change. The idea of nation is a fantasmatic imagining that misrepresents the diversity that exists within the borders it names.

To the extent that I theorize the masculinist aspects of nationalism I risk overgeneralization, almost a kind of essentialist viewing of nation. Although no one viewing grasps the varieties of nationalism, I think I agree with Aijaz Ahmad that "an essence is *given* to it, in particular situations."[1] So I may unintentionally homogenize the gender exclusivity of nation, in order to eventually divest nationalism of its masculinist borders.

The nation constructs gender, sexuality, and their racial meanings through moments of nation building, such as the gulf war, "when the nation becomes a family";[2] or the video beating of Rodney King, when the nation becomes white;[3] or when President Clinton equates securing u.s. borders from haitian refugees with national security.

The fantasized bodies of an homogenized "womanhood"—maybe a maternalized barbie doll—are used to mark "the" western nation. Nation building is already, then, encoded with a series of racialized/sexualized/engendered silences. The symbolized woman, as mother of us all, psychically attaches the nation to family and nature, with their racialized meanings.

Colored bodies are scrutinized in relation to this fantasmatic femaleness as though femaleness were a monolithic construction. This process makes euro-american women painfully visible to women of color, given the racial power they wield.[4] Yet these same euro-american women are made invisible as part of the fantasmatic gender hierarchy of the nation.

Post–cold war politics creates new challenges for masking the racial/sexual/gender exclusivity of nation building. On the one hand are the nationalisms of eastern and central europe, which manipulate racial/ethnic identities as nations struggle to establish a place in the new global marketplace. On the other hand is the nation building of the u.s., which requires the redefinition of politics and public life in light of a global economy. The u.s. no longer can think of itself as an economic nation; rather, it is a site within the transnational economy. In this process, the racialized/sexualized symbolization of the nation and its fantasy structure become recoded.

Salman Rushdie in *The Satanic Verses* says that because we have to live in the world, we have to "make believe."[5] It is tricky to know who is making believe, and what they are imagining when they do so. Is it that the end of the bipolar superpower world has instigated a crisis of masculine identity for some, just at the time when the need to strut should have been quieted? Are wars and violence today due to a new post–cold war "manliness" that leaves the world with a pure aggression that has no particular name?[6] Is this what Jacqueline Rose means when she asks if "war mimics and participates" in the ambivalence toward one's own difference? For her, "the familiar destructiveness of war represents not as is commonly supposed, finality, but uncertainty, a hovering on the edge of what, like death, can never be totally known."[7] Meanwhile, I wonder how we might "make believe" without war.

I assume that we will first have to move beyond the need to distance people not like ourselves, and beyond the need for nationalism, to be able to move beyond hatreds.

POST-'89 POLITICS AND EASTERN EUROPEAN NATIONALISMS

In the spring of '89, western journalists and politicians celebrated the revolutions in eastern and central europe as a victory for democracy. Little was made of the fact that they were, at best, male-dominated democracies or, at worst, examples of recycled ex-communist paternalist opportunism. By the early '90s the western discourse shifted; the new democracies were defeated by ethnic nationalist rivalries. Democracy supposedly replaced communism, then nationalism displaced democracy.

These new-old nationalisms define the twenty-first century. They have developed during *as well as* in response to the transnational economy, which has established a global telecommunications system that shrinks time and space. The rise of these new-old nationalisms is a reaction against former egalitarian communist rhetoric and the promise of new consumer markets. They are also continuations of old racialized hatreds such as anti-semitism. Thus they mix old and new: they utilize racialized/gendered hatreds but with a new license—restructuring imposed by the global economy. My discussion, then, is not about nationalism in general, even if one could theorize it.

Instead, I focus on the hateful nationalisms of the twenty-first century that have developed in post–cold war eastern europe. And I look for the dialogic relations between these nationalisms, and the western discourses of multiculturalism, transnationalism, and globalism.

My discussion is complicated because nationalism has become a central facet of the "west's" language for looking at "other" post-communist societies. The u.s. criticizes these countries for succumbing to ethnic hatreds. Clinton looks *at* bosnia and complains that it is a hopeless morass. By default the west looks good, even though we have our own kind of nation building and our own racial/ethnic/gender hatreds. Instead of looking elsewhere and seeing itself, the u.s. looks elsewhere to caution marginalized groups within the u.s. not to demand too much for themselves. Affirmative action for blacks is called balkanized separatism, and is challenged for destabilizing the common ground of the nation as a whole.

But the common ground is shaky. The los angeles rebellion following the verdict in the Rodney King trial revealed enormous rage within blacks toward racism within the u.s. Nazi graffiti on subway walls in new york city is a ready reminder of the anti-semitism that flourishes within our borders. The bombing of abortion clinics and the killing of their doctors constitute terrorist activity against women "within" the west. The paramilitary militia movement hates the federal government because it supposedly has given away the country to blacks, jews, hispanics, *and* women.

All this mixes up the way we see hate, and difference, and nations, and democracy. Old borders no longer hold: enemies exist inside and outside nations. Post–cold war conflicts are not easily cast within the bipolar framework of communist/anti-communist. Instead, (western) democracy is positioned against various other enemies: islamic fundamentalism, ethnic nationalism, foreign terrorism. As enemies are constructed, so are nations. And if all the enemies are not located outside, it becomes more difficult to project unity. Then fantasy becomes more prominent.

THE IN(EX)CLUSIVITY OF THE NATION

Nations provide an identity beyond the self, a sense of belongingness and connectedness. Individuals, their connection to others, and their sociality, are crucial to the construction of the idea of "nation." Any notion of "we" is in part an "imaginary community."[8] Nationality provides an identity that exists outside the self[9] at the same time that it constructs a notion of self that is exclusionary of other identities. The notion of likeness *can* be dangerous if it is used to exclude, and silence, and punish. Nazism, south african apartheid, serb nationalism—each provide an identity for some while declaring a non-identity for others.

The nation implies borders and boundaries that bespeak both openings and closings.[10] A nation requires an inside and an outside; natives and foreigners, immigrants, refugees, and the people coming from the outside. A nation is defined by its unity; differences and particularities within it challenge its universality. Shared commonness is privileged against diversity, which is problematized as disorderly. Why? Because diversity means difference, and difference means conflict, and conflict is disorderly.

Nationalism articulates a "communal loyalty" that is positioned against loyalties that are seen as subversive to the recognized shared identity.[11] So one person's sense of nation can easily not be someone else's. The idea that all (white) men (not women or people of color) are created equal supposedly binds the nation. It clearly binds some people more than others.

In the u.s. one usually speaks of patriotism rather than nationalism; of a melting pot or mixed society rather than a racial or religious state; of (liberal) pluralism rather than ethnic nationalism; of federalism rather than centralization. U.S. stands for "united" states; unity with its distinct parts. Yet the "unity" reflects a war of conquest against mexico and native americans; the black slave trade and the vicious practice of slavery; its own civil war. The nation utters different narratives for its different inhabitants. Not everyone is a citizen with full access to rights. And yet the discourse of liberal democracy promises the "dream" of the collectivity to everyone.

One's sense of nation shifts according to one's position within it or outside it. When living outside one's "own" country in a first-world country one becomes asian, or third world. Third-world identity "gives a proper name to a generalized margin."[12] Otherwise, from within their homeland these identities are specified as bengali, korean, japanese, chinese, etc.

In the two and a half decades of Reagan-Bush-Clinton privatization, in which individuals became expected to take care of themselves and government took less responsibility for the public welfare, nationalism became a curious attempt at publicizing individualism.[13] Self-interest replaced a focus on public responsibility, and nationalism became an attempt to fill the void. But the western post–cold war nation is left emptied of its publicness. The self-centered discourse of the privatized state denies the realm of public responsibility or public welfare. As governments are expected to do less for the individual, the very notion of politics, with its publicness, is undermined.

It is not clear for the twenty-first century what will become of nations without publicly minded (however partial) governments. Although a fiction, the modern nation depended on the differentiation between economic (self-interest) and political (public-interest) arenas. As global capital challenges the role of nation-states in this process, the construction of a nation devoid of economic borders becomes the new imaginary. Nation building becomes newly artificial. Rituals, emblems, flags, and anthems must stand for the old as the nation shifts.[14] Consider the yellow-ribbon campaign of the gulf war, or the storybook fantasy remake of Nixon's presidency at his televised funeral.

RACIALIZING THE EXCLUSIVITY
OF THE NATION

Serb nationalists specify their racial blood as formative of "the" nation, much as Hitler defined germany by aryan blood. In these cases the specific racial category becomes the statement of the collectivity. Unity is defined by singularity and exclusivity. The nation has no universally inclusive meaning beyond this. Nationalism instead becomes a form of racism, although always set in particular context: croatian, german, american. Or as Hannah Arendt argued, race becomes a substitute for the nation.[15]

Nazis were consistent here: the "decent" jews were zionists because they thought in "national" terms.[16] Today the question of israel has become much more complicated: jewish nationalism looks different from how it looked in 1948, and there are new "victims" to be considered. Non-jews in palestine have their own experience of zionism.[17]

According to Paul Gilroy, race often coincides with national frontiers; the nation distinguishes itself from immigrants and foreigners.[18] One can assume that global capitalist markets will continue to rename nations and their racialized borders through a multiculturalist twenty-first-century vision. The relationship between race and nation develops together, but they are not, as David Goldberg argues, synonymous or fixed in meaning. Instead, "as *concepts* race and nation are largely empty receptacles...population groups...invented, interpreted, and imagined as communities or societies."[19]

Nationalism, as such, is often disguised. In u.s. post–cold war nationalist rhetoric, racism is not defended by a blood/color exclusivity. Instead it is constructed by a "color-blind" language of democracy. This discourse claims that white males suffer today from reverse discrimination and unfair treatment that favors white women and people of color. White men, who still dominate in public office and the economy, use civil rights legislation to challenge the demands made by people of color and white women, to secure the nation for themselves.

The significance of racism in the american psyche must not be lost on the reader. Michele Wallace argues the place of blacks "as central figures in the national imagination."[20] The psychic construction of "the" nation is white; built on and out of black slavery. The imaginary remains somewhat sedimented in the black/white divide with a "veneer of fixedness."[21] This residue threads through new as well as old circumstances. Racist arrangements change, but also do not.

Democracy, when used on behalf of nationalist rhetoric, allows racism to flourish. In many of the eastern european post-communist nations, freedom of speech has allowed hatred toward jews, roma, and other ethnic minorities to be spoken openly. When freedom of speech allows a freely spoken hatred, it is hard to distinguish masculinist democracy from ethnic nationalism.[22] This bespeaks the troubled relationship between freedom of speech and racial/sexual equality: one does not necessarily ensure the other.

The rhetoric of nationalism has also been used by marginalized groups like Queer Nation and the Black Panthers in the u.s. to legitimate a liberatory identity of the excluded.[23] When nation is used by "outsiders" to challenge the "inside" of the nation, these attempts are rejected by established authorities as divisive and separatist, and racist.[24]

Cold-war nationalisms positioned the nation for or against communism. The newer ethnic/racist nationalisms use the homogeneity of a racialized "difference" to draw borders where none were before. These post–cold war nationalisms construct nations out of geographical maps that are complicated by changed allegiances.[25] These identities emerge even when they are desperately fought against. As one sarajevan, Mikica Babic, angrily and sadly states: "'We never, until the war, thought of ourselves as Muslims. We were Yugoslavs. But when we began to be murdered, because we were Muslims, things changed. The definition of who we are today has been determined by our killers. In a way this means these Serbs have won, no matter what happens in the war.'"[26]

New geographical borders are formulated in and through these racialized imaginings. Multicultural expressions of difference either destabilize the nation, as in ex-yugoslavia, or become suspect as separatist and divisive to the nation, as in the u.s. But these new "nations" are not able to encompass the plural, shifting, and multiple identities they confront.

A nation cannot encompass its diverse identities from a homogenized standpoint. Nationalism, imagining unity, simultaneously creates and excludes difference. As Faisal Fatehali Devji states: in india, the muslim, as opposed to the hindu, appears as a sign of national failure because of the very politics of nationalism itself.[27] One would need to envision universality differently in order that the nation not be confining and dominating.[28]

Multiculturalism signifies multiplicity rather than singularity. It is increasingly said that the united states is no longer a nation but a multicultural regime.[29] This reflects a shift within the discourse of multiculturalism from a vision defined by marginalized groups to a recognized necessity of the new regime. Multiculturalism becomes the language of the monocultural society in hopes of deradicalizing its original potential to subvert the universality inherent in the meaning of nation.

Post–cold war nationalisms fictionalize ideal ethnic-linguistic homogeneity, while they are more readily recognized as plurinational and pluricultural states.[30] As George Soros states, "Ethnic states leave no room for people with different ethnic identities."[31] They establish this exclusivity along racialized/sexualized lines that collapse into themselves. As Renata Salecl describes serb nationalism: if you add an albanian (dirty, fornicating, violent, primitive) and a slovene (antipatriotic, unproductive merchant, profiteering), you get a jew.[32] This kind of nationalism is a devastating mix of racializing sexuality and engendering race.

Racism always differentiates in order to establish hierarchy.[33] And the hierarchy is also coded through a gendered formulation of family that authenticates the nation. Even the liberatory discourse of black nationalism, which openly decried u.s. racism, utilized an "authoritarian pastoral patriarchy," according to Paul Gilroy. He argues that "an Americo-centric, postnationalist essence of blackness has been constructed through the dubious appeal to family."

This appeal images a racial family that is organic and natural.[34] Angela Davis celebrates aspects of black nationalism but also recognizes its misogynist overtones within hip-hop culture.[35]

A nation always has "a" gender and "a" race although the gender is usually not spoken. Racism is clearly spoken in nazi germany, south african apartheid, and serb nationalism, while gender is encoded (naturalized) through patriarchal familialism. The symbolization of the nation as the "mother country" em*bodies* the nation as a "woman." The imagined female body represents the nation and silences patriarchy simultaneously.

So nations are pictorially represented by women, depicted as mothers (reproducers) of the nation. As such, nationalism, as a form of familialism, is neutralized, and women become the mothers of "the" race. Gender is racialized in the process: muslim women raped by serb nationalists provide ethnic cleansing, and a greater serbia.

Mother russia: the nation as homeland. The language of male privilege (sexism) speaks through the metaphors of love. It embraces the feminine as mother, nurturer, caregiver. It is a symbolic motherhood: women are the mothers of *all* children of the nation. In nationalism the fictive power of motherhood stands against the varied realities of women's experiences in society.[36]

Interestingly, though the nation is sometimes spoken of as the fatherland, it also imagines the brotherhood of fraternity. This is not the case for the mother country, which imagines the nation as a fraternity, *not* as a sisterhood. Nationalism reduces women to their motherhood. Nowhere in the iconography of nations is there space for women *as* sisters, *as* a sisterhood.[37]

The war memorial chosen as the symbol for the reunited germany intended to honor the war dead is a statue of a mother and son. The statue was criticized by many for "using the image of a suffering mother to promote national unity," writes *New York Times* reporter Stephen Kinzer. "Perpetrators and victims are gathered into her lap."[38] The unity expressed through mother's love and represented through patriarchal imagery is suppose to erase the hatred of nazism and its violations.

Nationalism calls to men and applauds the fraternal order while invoking women to call forth notions of motherly love. Hatred isn't spoken here. Love and duty are, so women are used as symbols of national identity.[39] Hate is instead spoken in terms of the racialized identities of men or women. Those who differ from us in color or ethnicity cannot be "our" mother. So one is free to express the fear, the anger, the blame.

Virginia Woolf in *The Three Guineas* wrote that as a woman one has no country.[40] Women do not belong to a nation. They instead construct the mythology of nationhood. Anannya Bhattachardee argues that nationness is inextricably linked to the fiction of womanhood. The myth of indian womanness is a signifier of the indian nation. Indian women represent tradition and custom as metaphor for chastity and sanctity. However, live women, rather than mythic ones, can always subvert this representation and the national boundaries constructed by it.[41]

NATIONALIST IMAGININGS AND WOMEN'S BODIES

Nations are a blend of fictive imaginings and pose the problem of an impossible unity.[42] Benedict Anderson writes of nationalism as an "imagined political community" that thinks of the nation with love. Nationalism allows a new way of thinking about fraternity, power, and time. The nation appears "interestless" and demands devotion as such.[43]

Anderson's community is made up of men and their devotion to a "deep, horizontal comradeship," a passionate brotherhood. As such, he thinks nationalism is an identity like kinship, or religion, rather than an ideology like liberalism or fascism.[44] He does not recognize that nationalism is an instance of phallocratic construction, with brotherhood rather than sisterhood at its core. Nor does he recognize racism as part of the historical articulation of the nation.[45]

Nations are made up of citizens, and the fiction here requires that anyone can be of the nation. W. E. B. Du Bois clarified early on that the nation echoes and enforces inequity for blacks.[46] Citizenship has long been shown, by excluded groups, to exclude them: people of color, white women, and the other "others." Minorities who are excluded by the nation as deviant are positioned against the silent standards of the nation as a whole.[47]

This "imagined community" is a fantasy world with women present, but silenced. The fraternity is masculine. Women are given no
citizen voice, although they often take it. Instead they create the
borders for the fraternal order. Geraldine Heng and Janadas Devan
describe this: "Women, and all signs of the feminine, are by definition
always and already anti-national."[48] Women guard the home and create domesticity, against which men construct their fictive manliness.[49]

We are presented with what Heng and Devan call "uterine
nationalism," which derives "out of the recesses of the womb."[50]
Women are the procreators and not the citizens.[51] The female/mater-
nalized body becomes the site for *viewing* the nation. It is an imaginary site that is wholly naturalized through the symbolization of the
female body. Or, as Anne McClintock states, "All nationalisms are
gendered."[52] It is the bordered differentiation of women's bodies
from men's bodies, rather than the bodies themselves, that construct
the fiction of nations.

Because the nation fantasizes women in a homogenized,
abstracted familial order, women become a metaphor for what they
represent, rather than what they are. First-world women of the west
represent modernity; women of the third-world south and east represent tradition. As symbolizations, they become static and unchanging, like the constructions of timeless motherhood. Their representation, as the nation, defines them fictively, and reproduces the fiction.

Women lose their own identity when used as markers for the
nation. Their status stands in for the progress of the nation, rather
than their own.[53] They become political signifiers because of their
"phantasmatic investment and phantasmatic promise," Judith Butler
writes. The symbol, rather than describe "real" women, "produces
the expectation of a unity, a full and final recognition that can never
be achieved."[54]

As mother of the nation, woman is invisibly visible as a symbolic fantasy; she is at once present and not seen. And the different layerings of invisibility are accorded along racial, economic, and sexual
lines. A black lesbian reflects this complex invisibility. She is *not* the
mother of the nation; she is not white, not a wife. In contrast, the
fantasmatic woman becomes the body of the nation. In the process
she is desexualized and "regulated" as the mother of us all. Her

maternal body fictionalizes motherhood and the nation simultaneously. She represents safety through the boundaries of her body. She
is embraced by the glorification of womanhood. She represents
morality itself.

No wonder real, actual women pose a problem for the nation;[55]
much of this fictive symbolization does not resemble life or common
sense.[56] Yet, two Barbie dolls are sold every second. In life-size
terms, Barbie's body would be 40-18-32; and although we all know
she is just a doll, she is also very real.[57] She represents the symbolic
use of women in what Natalini Natarajan, in another context, calls
the "erotics of nationalism": the "dream image of women" servicing
the "psychic needs of the male subject." Although Barbie is not symbolic of motherhood as a "spectacle" that "cements" and "unifies,"
she operates to legitimize the fantasy structure that underlies this
construction: the homogenized and congealed (hetero)sexuality that
sediments and contrasts with motherhood.[58]

Women, as cultural symbols[59] representing particular communities, become the site where tradition is "debated and reformulated,"[60] and where the nation is "regenerated."[61] The present situation
of algerian women reflects the importance of traditionalist patriarchy for religious islamic nationalists. Women are the symbol of
what the future algeria will become, so women who defy their traditional symbolic role—by not wearing the veil, or holding a job outside the home—are subject to grave danger.[62]

PSYCHIC NEEDS AND THE
RACIALIZED/GENDERED NATION

Nationalized identity blends real and unreal constructions
with a psychic resonance that is imaged in real and made-up ways,
with no consciousness that it is not "perfectly true."[63] Edward Said
elicits a similar understanding when he describes how one's mind
designates familiar spaces as "ours" and unfamiliar spaces beyond
"ours" as "theirs." The distinctions, often geographical, can be
entirely arbitrary.[64]

Said writes of myths/images that use all material for their own
end, to displace any other thought. Orientalism, as a myth/image,
explains the familiar—europe, the west, us—by contrasting it with

the strange—the orient, the east, them. The orient, like nation, is a creation that is essentially an idea; a "man-made" idea that has little connection to a real orient. Said argues that we endow things with meaning all the time and that this is an imaginative, figurative, interpretative process. It even has a quasi-fictional quality. "Imaginative geography and history help the mind to intensify its own sense of itself by dramatizing the distance and difference between what is close to it and what is far away," Said writes. An imagined geography draws dramatic boundaries.[65]

Nationhood is constructed in and through psychic identities that institutionalize "difference." People experience this identity—the psychic knowing of their sex, gender, and race—through their bodies. Women are the "boundary subjects" defining this process.[66] Gender, according to Nancy Chodorow, has an "individual, personal, emotional and fantasy meaning." It is an "intrapsychic experience" that resonates differently according to one's experience and one's unconscious fantasies.[67]

Because gender and nation are always being negotiated, femininity is not the same as femaleness; gays can be feminine, or effeminate. So can muslims and jews. Masculinity is not one and the same with maleness; masculine males are "men," whereas non-masculine males are not-"men." Learning one's gender is no easy or automatic process, which explains why moving into adolescence can feel, as it did for Marianne Hirsch, like "emigrating to a foreign culture"; girls must leave home and learn a new language.[68]

Imaginings, which are always part fantasy, are activated through different means. For Julia Kristeva, woman is never fully represented as she is because she is unrepresentable, a poetic version of femaleness as mother, suggesting incest, or the repressed maternal element. "Woman" reinstates maternal territory for Kristeva.[69] Then the nation becomes the imagined fantasmatic investment.[70] Women, being not-men, are included inside the nation as "mother." As mother, she can be distanced without being made an outcast.[71]

Salecl, a slovene feminist, views the traumatic gender fantasy structure that supports ethnic hatred as interlaced with nationalism. To unlearn nationalism is to unlearn the psychic physicality of racialized bodily borders.

South africa, the newest of the post–cold war attempts at democracy, faces the conundrum of a multiethnic democratic nationhood. According to Mark Gevisser, a south african journalist, non-racialism has been the guiding principle of the African National Congress (ANC). Zulu ethnic identity politics stands counter to this non-racial democratic vision. And "coloreds"—those of mixed race identity—are weary of a black identity considered more pure than their own racial mix. "To fight apartheid, the ANC chose to erase differences—to espouse a non-racialism that did not address ethnic identity." Zulus, coloreds, and whites each cling to a racial/ethnic/bloodline identity. It remains to be seen if a multicultural democracy and not a new racial (and male) apartheid can emerge out of this mix.[72] I think, with Craig Charney, it is a bit early to declare that south africa has "the makings of a wobbly but workable, wheeling-and-dealing, pluralist democracy." But we can hope.[73]

Rey Chow argues that "the west" owns the codes of fantasy. So imaginings will be westernized while also produced locally. The politics of seeing is simultaneously a politics of not seeing. Nationalized identity involves a "positional superiority"[74] of homogenized masculinity produced locally.

According to feminist and ex-yugoslav Zarana Papic, nationalism smashes democracy. For her, in belgrade there is only the national truth as stated by serb nationalists. Serbian nationalism is so deeply patriarchal, historically and culturally, it does not have to articulate or accentuate its control over women.

Papic makes clear that serb nationlism requires an aggressive violence that many men cannot sustain. In the beginning of the bosnian war twenty thousand to thirty thousand men left the country so as not to have to fight. She tells the story of one young man who was not so lucky. "In one unit somewhere near Sid some soldiers wanted to desert and go home, but others decided to stay. One unhappy young man of 18 first went to the line of deserters, then changed his mind and went back to the line of those who decided to stay. But he could not stay in that line also. He left both lines, stood for awhile and shot himself."[75]

Psychic hatreds are mobilized in the balkans. Anti-semitic and xenophobic violence is on the rise, and neo-nazis continue to gain strength.[76] Slobodan Milosevic, formerly a loyal communist-party hack, invented serb nationalism to reposition himself for the post-communist transnational economy. Although his real commitment is to his own power, he has been able to re-instigate psychic racialized/gendered hatreds for this purpose, all too easily.

More recently Milosevic has found that whipping up "pan-serbian fervor" does not serve him well. Instead he paints Radovan Karadzic, leader of the bosnian serbs, as the lunatic of serb aggression and presents himself as reasonable and open to negotiation. Predrag Simic, director of a foreign-policy center in belgrade, says that Milosevic was never a nationalist. "He was only a politician surfing on the nationalist wave. That explains how he was able to change course so easily."[77]

On the other hand, the people of sarajevo will not leave. As the well-known bosnian journalist Zlatko Dizdarevic says, "We simply refuse to die—as a city, as a people, as a future... if we only had a little more peace and electricity." And fantasies of all sorts die hard as well. Dizdarevic reports that a six-year-old in sarajevo has said, "Who knows, maybe Santa Claus will bring me a leg for the new year. I'd sort of like that, if he can. If he can't, maybe it'll happen another time."[78]

The use of violent nationalism and ethnic cleansing have created thousands of refugees. These refugees have become the new "others" in western europe. England and germany have tightened their borders against them. Once again, one hears that germany is for the germans. And while a revisionist reading of the holocaust is embraced by some, the gulf war has also made germany a world player for the first time since world war II.[79]

Against this ethnic disintegration and nationalist fervor is the privileging of the patriarchal family unit. Nationalism demands a pre-communist moral renewal: return women to the home.[80] Women are imagined as mothers and protectors of hearth and family. The psychic connectors between nationalism, racism, and women's lives are continually rejoined. Ethnic nationalisms tell only part of the story. They speak the anger of racism and cover over the intimate relationship that defines the constructs of race, sex, and gender.

MASCULINIST NATIONALISM AND WAR RAPE

Because nations are symbolized by women, ethnic cleansing directs its fears and desires onto the bodies of women. On the one hand, women are idolized and revered; on the other hand, they are brutalized, tortured, raped, and often killed. The war rape of ethnic cleansing in bosnia is set on destroying and annihilating the "mother"; if she can no longer comfort, or create safety, she can no longer defend the nation. Shame her, and her family, and her nation, and they are defeated.

Lydia H. Liu sees rape as an appropriation of the female body by the nation to eroticize women's victimization.[81] War rape uses the devastation of women and their families to represent the plight of the nation. The ties of homeland and nation are played out in nationalistic fixations about the mother.[82] And these unconscious fantasies are let loose in times of crisis.[83]

Women become the objects of hatred when men play out their psychic fantasies of desire and fear. Women are targets because of who they are, and how war expresses a militarist masculinity. Rape constructs men's domi*nation*, and women's subordi*nation*.

Ethnic nationalisms are racialized through sexual violation and strip the "imaginary community" of its love. Raping women in war defiles the nation of which she is a part, while marking nationness. When this war rape is described as ethnic hatred, women are given no specificity.

Women's bodies, then, are used, literally and figuratively, in shaping national identities.[84] Masculinist nationalism is why rape has been consistently used to exert a kind of "male apartheid"[85] in bosnia. Serbian nationalism violates women bodily. It nationalizes identity along bloodlines. It defines legitimacy in terms of birth. It uses old patriarchal familial traditions to elicit the naturalness of the nation as such.

Serbian nationalist ethnic cleansing requires the complete annihilation of women's identity. Serb men plant their serb seed in muslim women, and supposedly serb children will be born. The fictive purity of this ethnic identity demands the entire negation of the woman's identity. She becomes a hollowed vessel for serbia. Even in nazi germany, women played a part in the jew's racial identity. If born to a jewish mother and christian father, one was considered half-jew; if one's grandmother was a jew, one was a quarter-jew. Not so, in serb fantasy.

Ethnic cleansing focuses the violence on bloodlines even though it is played out on and through gender.[86] To name only the ethnic hatred is to make gender hatred invisible. It names the gender violence as something different from hatred. It normalizes the violence against women by not naming it. This invisibility of violence toward women sustains it, as in domestic violence, in violence toward women refugees, etc.[87] Or as Catharine MacKinnon states: "What is done to women is either too specific to women to be seen as human or too generic to human beings to be seen as specific to women."[88]

Many bosnian and croatian women's and refugee groups have protested the depiction of mass rape as simply a "weapon of war." They argue that the "genocidal particularity of rape" is very *ethnically* specific to muslim and croatian women in bosnia-herzegovina and croatia. They argue that if this particular aspect of rape is not understood, the specifically genocidal use of rape by serbian soldiers goes unrecognized.[89] For them, this is a different kind of rape. It is nationalist in its origin and a "war crime."[90] Although initially the U.N. Balkan War Crimes Commission did not conclude that a "systematic rape policy by the serbs had been proved,"[91] Judge Richard Goldstone has now included rape as a war crime.

Genocide is the attempt to destroy a people's identity. War rape is sexualized violence that seeks to terrorize, destroy, and humiliate a people through its women. Rape is being used as a tool of ethnic cleansing, but as Rhonda Copelon advises, one does not want to exaggerate the difference between genocidal rape and "normal" rape for fear of obscuring the atrocity of common rape.[92]

But genocidal rape has its own horrors. It takes place in isolated rape camps, with strict orders from above to either force the woman's exile or her death. Rape is repeatedly performed as torture; it is used to forcibly impregnate; it is even used to exterminate. Women in the camps are raped repetitively, some as many as thirty times a day for as long as three consecutive months. They are kept hungry, they are beaten and gang-raped, their breasts are cut off, and stomachs split open.[93]

The war rape of women is aimed at the destruction of their physical and personal integrity. Inger Agger explains how women's body borders and boundaries are violated to create sexual trauma.[94] War rape politically uses sexual trauma as shame. One's body is exposed, abused, and violated; there is no private self left.[95] Rape itself is like war: "a violent invasion into the interior of one's body."[96]

Sexual humiliation and degradation is an integral part of the rape camps. The terror is brutal and deliberate. The "rapes stifle any wish to return" to the "cleansed area" if one survives.[97] And the rape and humiliation are not limited to women. In some of the concentration camps men have also been raped, castrated, and forced into brutal homosexual acts.[98]

Less has been reported about the sexual abuse and torture of men because it destabilizes the very notion of gender that is central to nation building. The homoerotic and its relation to masculinist fears and desires is kept silenced, while the war rapes of women are sensationalized.[99]

Rape transcends historical eras and national borders.[100] Frantz Fanon discusses the rape of an algerian woman by french soldiers: she was raped to dishonor her husband, she was told to tell her husband what was done to her.[101] Mass rape has been a part of most wars; in serbia it is said to be a war strategy. In rwanda's ethnic massacres in '94, thousands of women and girls were reportedly raped. The scope of the rapes "defies imagination—every girl and woman not killed—was raped." The rape was "systematic, arbitrary, planned and used as a weapon of ethnic cleansing to destroy community ties."[102] A nineteen-year-old air force cadet, Elizabeth Saum, in training at a u.s. academy, was required to take a survival course that included a mock rape scenario. Still suffering from the humiliation, she says: "I felt so hated and degraded."[103]

On a visit to belgrade in May 1995, I met with the anti-war activists, "women in black,"[104] who stand every Wednesday in the center square to voice their opposition to serb nationalism. I also met with women from the "autonomous women's center against sexual violence." These women assist victims of war rape. Many of the raped women—croat, muslim, and serb—try to find abortions and/or a place to stay in belgrade until the dreaded birth.

The feminists I met in belgrade say that the sensationalized reporting of war rapes has been used now to create nationalist fervor on all sides rather than to help the traumatized women.

The tragedy is deep and profound. Many of these rape victims are unable to say anything at all about what happened to them. Some were or are only fourteen years old. Some recognized their rapists as their neighbors. Some of the women are serb, raped by muslims and/or croats. Some of the women are muslim. Some of the women are serb/muslim by marriage; others croat/serbs; others muslim/croat. None of the women I met was a nationalist of any sort.

Post–cold war politics has decentered the superpower struggles and dispersed warfare and hatred to multiple local sites. At stake are the meanings of racial/ethnic identity, multiculturalism, and nationalism for global capitalism. Women's bodies, as an imaginary construction, are central to these negotiations. Gender, however, falls off the international map when the politics of the twenty-first century is theorized.

Economic globalism and local nationalisms mix uneasily. New-old nationalisms exist within a cultural and economic network that is global. Transnational economies require multiracial workers. Whereas economic transnationalization articulates an imaginary of "new world unity," ethnic nationalisms splinter the world into separate identities.[105] Woman, as the embodiment of the nation, begins to unravel as an imaginary construction along with economic borders themselves.

The challenge remains to dislodge the fiction of universality through exclusion and reframe transnational economies into richly diverse cultures. Nations will move beyond psychic fantasies of racial purity and misogynist fraternities. Diversity will still exist, but it would simply be outrageous to think that rape and/or torture could ever bring closure to fear or desire. Differences would be so pluralized that they could only create an anarchy of pleasure. Then gender and its multiracial richness could be theorized as part of the liberatory politics of the twenty-first century.

WRITING MULTICULTURALISM

FOR THE GLOBE

Nation building constructs a contradictory identity. It is exclusionary, yet the people it would attempt to contain are complex and diverse. Individuals, as well as nations, are defined by race, gender, sexuality, religion, ethnicity, age, geographic location, ad infinitum. Today, as the discourse of "globalism" competes with the discourse of "nation" in first-world countries, a particular multiculturalist stance is adopted by the transnational marketplace. This corporatist multiculturalism attempts to rewrite difference and "otherness" for the twenty-first century in order to contain the disruptiveness of diversity.

So I now ask you to see the nation as it is being rewritten through and by a corporatist multiculturalism for global capitalist markets. At the same time, we need to remember that multiculturalism has many meanings today. For some, it describes the origins of the u.s. For others, it delineates new immigration flows for the twenty-first century. For still others, it suggests a richly plural and democratic society.

Multiculturalism, as a politics, can be used for very different purposes by those who seek to use diversity opportunistically for corporate interests, or by those who wish to destroy the euro-american hegemony of corporatist transnationalism. Both of these usages often employ multiculturalism as a code word for race, sometimes creating a racist backlash.[1]

There are also variations on the above themes. Multicultural-ism, then, has become a little bit like democracy: everyone is for it, but it has no one meaning. Sometimes it evokes a serious commit-ment to an identity politics that challenges the dominant silencing of diversity. As such it operates as a counter narrative from the nation's margins against what Flora Anthias and Nira Yuval-Davis call the "totalizing boundaries" of the nation.[2] Other times it is used by mar-ginalized peoples as a therapeutic stance for raising minority self-esteem. Other times it is used to pejoratively position special inter-ests and "their" foreignness against the general good; many "nations" against the single nation.[3] Yet still other times it operates, according to Benjamin Schwarz, as part of an historical myth that the u.s. was formed by conciliation and compromise rather than con-quest and force. In keeping with the myth, "we are all pluralists now; everyone favors 'tolerance' and 'diversity.'"[4]

Global markets and multiculturalism—as fact and imaginary—have been developing alongside and in relationship to each other in first-world countries since the early 1970s. By the 1990s globalism seems to have come into dominance. Or, as Salman Rushdie says, multiculturalism has become "a sham" and cover for other interests, such as "racial harmony in Britain."[5]

When multiculturalism challenges false eurocentric univer-salisms, it operates as a militant discourse demanding the radical racial/ethnic pluralization of knowledge, experience, speech, and the way we "see."[6] In contrast to this radical critique, a deradicalized official discourse is used by many in government and corporate cir-cles to advance their own agendas.[7] Ignoring the distinction between multiculturalism as radically militant and as liberally pluralist (read assimilationist), neoconservatives caricature it as the balkanization and destruction of the nation as a whole.

These neocon fears reflect "the west's" nightmare of its own dispossession and displacement in the "new world order." This oppo-sitioning between multi- and monocultural positions privileges "imagined" universalism against particular identities, and sameness against difference.

In sum: multiculturalism can be commodified for transnational capitalist markets that manipulate, accommodate, and assimilate notions of difference. It can also be used by civil-rights activists to challenge white privilege and present a richly diverse notion of color itself. It can also be a messy blend of each. In these scenarios, new possibilities for cultural change are opened up, although never as broadly as intended by those articulating serious and radical revision-ing; *and* new methods and markets for exploitation are developed.

These first-world developments take place alongside the disin-tegration of the once effective multicultural experiment in bosnia-herzegovina. As Isak Samokovlija wrote in 1928: "We ate cakes on Passover, round flour cakes on Bayram, and pretzels on Easter."[8] In the documentary "We Are All Neighbors,"[9] croats and muslims tell of their friendships before the balkan war, and how the war put an end to friendship.

In jackson heights, n.y., a turkish moslem speaks of celebrating christmas with his neighbors while they celebrate his holidays with him. "Why shouldn't Hindus celebrate Christmas?" asks Mr. Kohli. "I am part of this society so I must participate in it."[10] But being a part means participating in a world where christianity is privileged, and converting is seen as a way of getting ahead. This *mono*cultural stance marginalizes *multi*cultures and religions at the same time that it recognizes their presence.

The u.s. is defined by a dominant white and christian culture with multicultural margins—african-american, latino, korean, pacific islander. The suspicions of muslim involvement in the 1995 bombing of the federal building in oklahoma city reflect the racial tensions between the dominant culture and its multicultural margins. The 1992 los angeles riots after the verdict in the Rodney King trial reflect these tensions as they exist within and among the marginal-ized groups themselves.[11]

The globalized world economy and transnational communica-tion systems of the post–cold war period utilize a marginalized mul-ticulturalism and yet reveal its inconsistencies and incompleteness. Global economies use inter*national* workers. Transcultural communi-cation systems beam a monocultural first-world fantasmatic across the globe. *Nation*alized racisms define a myriad of post-communist societies, while racialized identities tear at the core of first-world countries. Global capitalism creates new immigrants and refugees—homeless, displaced, dislocated people. The post–cold war world is simultaneously borderless for capital and rebordered by cultural/racial identities defined by "difference."

Within these global changes economic nations are undermined; cultural practices are internationalized; and multicultural societies are enhanced within parts of the world and smashed in others. This is the context of today's multiculturalism(s) as practice *and* political discourse.

The twenty-first century will be defined by monoculturalism, multiethnicity, and transnationalized capital. Threaded through these *networks* are the racialized and gendered constructions of "difference" that are contextualized through the specificities of particular cultural histories. The variations of cultural experience and individual identity formation are continually in flux and in contention within this global process.

Identity politics and the search for personal and collective ties underline the trans (through), multi (many), inter (between) construction of economies, cultures, and nations. What will a nation and personal identity become in all this? A revisioned and radically pluralist multiculturalism must rework the fantasmatic of differences enriching communities and communities enriching personal life to allow for new publics free from hate.

UNIVERSALISM AND THE PROBLEM OF MULTICULTURALISM

The "unity" of the north american republic was a fiction from the start: native americans and black slaves, chinese railroad workers, and white women were not part of the nation.[12] Diversity was not definitive of citizen rights; the similarity of white men constructed the universality.

A (liberal) democratic nation supposedly represents all its people, and in the *same* way. Sameness of treatment means fairness. But north american pluralism has never been egalitarian. Some groups have always counted more than others. European immigrants were expected to assimilate: to be the same, rather than different. Likeness is privileged against diversity; the nation, against its different parts. The common culture privileges what is universally shared. Cultural/racial/ethnic distinctness is subversive to the disguised exclusivity of liberal individualism.

North america was a racial/ethnic/religious mix at the start. Precolumbian north america was first inhabited by the tainos and other native tribes. The enslavement of native americans defines the start of u.s. history. Early colonists warred with the spanish, french, and mexicans to carve out the boundaries of the new nation. The black slave trade was deeply embedded in every aspect of this nation building. However, there is no romanticized immigrant narrative for the african-american.[13] Slaves came here not of their own free will, but under brutal circumstances.

Ronald Takaki says that native americans were used to draw the borders of the u.s. while blacks became its bosom.[14] In this process white men were privileged against all other groups. The laws and the language were not multicultural, or multiethnic, or multiracial. Women were excluded legally and constitutionally *as women* and as members of each of these collectivities. The intersection of race and gender in women's lives complexified this further:[15] women of color had to contend with both racial and sexual bias.

Today's corporatist attempts at pluralizing the nation are mere attempts to incorporate and capitalize on the global changes already in place. Seventy-five percent of miami residents and 41 percent of new york city residents speak languages other than english in their homes.[16] In arizona and california a majority of public-school students are not white anglo-saxon protestants, and 25 percent speak languages other than english at home. Over 150 languages are spoken, though not taught, in the schools.[17]

Migrants from latin america and asia continue to emigrate to first-world countries. The latino population in the u.s. now outnumbers blacks in four of the nation's ten largest cities.[18] Although blacks remain the largest minority, this will probably change soon.[19] The increasing number of non-white north americans visibly challenges the pretenses of universalist/white privilege.

By 2005 the u.s. will probably be 15.8 percent black, 10.1 percent asian, 27.8 percent latino, and 46.3 percent white. Whites may be less than a majority in california as early as 1997. These demographic shifts have little to do with who votes. In the 1992 presidential election, 82 percent of the voters were white.[20]

The u.s. ethnic/racial/cultural mix differs from east to west to south. Latinos, mestizas, and native americans are disproportionately found in the south and southwest; european immigrants still populate the northeast; blacks' largest concentration is in the south, but large numbers of blacks live in northern industrial cities. The greatest concentrations of koreans, vietnamese, thais, japanese, etc., are found on the west coast. Latinos are expected to make up 40 percent of california's population by the year 2000.[21]

Major population shifts were already clearly under way by the early 1970s in the u.s. as well as in other western, first-world countries. By this time in australia, multiculturalism, had become the "official" stance toward assimilation and the hegemony of anglo-celtic tradition. Cultural pluralism and ethnic identity displaced an economic class identity and emphasized the welfare of the whole society.[22] Multiculturalism was embraced as a holistic approach to "difference." And nothing was terribly new about this. Gayatri Spivak says she was brought up twenty years ago reading indian schoolbooks calling for and using the "tired slogan... unity in diversity."[23]

White dominant culture dislocates the migrant, who is homogenized as "ethnic."[24] As ethnic, one's migrant identity is defined by one's past, by one's point of origin, rather than by the present. The statisticity of the construction preserves one's "otherness" and limits the possibilities of a radically pluralized multicultural present.[25]

When used as a militant demand for uncompromising pluralism, multiculturalism speaks a language different from those of assimilation and integration. If culture is a system of discriminations as well as a system of exclusions,[26] multiculturalism multiplies culture to *embrace* a pluralism that is more inclusive than exclusive. Multiculturalism multiplies differences in the attempt to undermine discrimination. It is positioned against a notion of arbitrary cohesion and is, according to Sneja Gunew, suggestive of paternal confusion and maternal promiscuity.[27] It challenges the state's authority of inclusivity and universalized rights. Multiculturalism as militant discourse can uncover the paternalism of racism and the racialized aspects of patriarchal authority.

The early u.s. civil rights movement spoke the language of integration with its universalist epistemology: blacks should have the same legal rights and opportunities as whites. But opportunity was insufficient in our deeply racialized and sexualized society. Affirmative action was instituted as a corrective to make opportunity equal. Whereas the 1960s and '70s saw much new civil-rights legislation, the 1980s saw it denuded and destroyed. The Reagan/Bush administrations treated racial/gender affirmative action as unfair to white men. Civil rights were criticized as "special rights" and are sometimes still considered to be so; and "special" meant unfair to the "general" white male public.[28] As such, multiculturalism was rejected by neoconservatives as a new tyranny of divisiveness and political correctness.

In its militant form, multiculturalism has much in common with the Black Panthers and the black nationalist movement of the early 1960s. These groups challenged the integrationist mode of their time by focusing on racial liberation, rather than integration. "Black is beautiful" rejected the silent and silencing white standards of commonality. Equality and freedom for african-americans required a dismantling of white privilege and assimilation to this standard.

Multiculturalism, in its similarly militant form, also rejects equal-opportunity rhetoric, which assumes assimilationist and integrationist positions that leave white male monocultural standards in place. Black militants, women's liberationists, and gay activists, as part of an extended multicultural agenda, demand in varied ways that the standards of "like a white man" be rethought. Equality cannot mean simple sameness of treatment. There are/were inequalities that must be remedied and differences that must be celebrated.

An insurgent multiculturalism, unlike integration(ism), does not assume that the excluded group wants to become a part of the larger collectivity; to be treated *like*, the same as, the others. Whereas integration does not necessarily involve a criticism of the larger collectivity except for its exclusivity, multiculturalism queries the construction of the collectivity itself.

Commonality, defined as an abstracted universalism, cannot encompass diversity adequately. Arthur Schlesinger distinguishes earlier immigrants from present-day ones on this basis. "They *expected* to become Americans. Their goals were escape, deliverance, assimilation."[29] He argues that they did not want to preserve their old cultures but instead wished to become a part of american society. Or as Mary Antin wrote in 1911: "With our despised immigrant clothing we shed also our impossible Hebrew names."[30]

This sort of immigrant narrative might be met with skepticism. After all, there was little choice for most eastern european immigrants but to adapt. The "new" world they came to was a land of opportunity in comparison to what they left. But the opportunities of russian jews, italians, poles, etc., were predicated on their willingness to assimilate and their capacity to conform. Schlesinger elicits a folk memory of immigration rather than an account of the limited options and constraints these people faced.[31] And he says nothing of the blacks and native americans who, given their skin color, did not have the option of simple assimilation.

Mestiza feminist Gloria Anzaldua, recalling her childhood along the texas-mexico border, remembers trying to correct her teacher's pronunciation of her name and being told: "If you want to be American, speak American."[32] The pressures to be like everyone else were extreme. Through the promise of inclusion one is seduced to create a voluntary assimilation. Correct your speech and become one of us. Exclusions are re-coded as a moment of tolerant inclusion.[33]

Many of today's immigrants reflect the new displacements of labor as a result of global capital. Many south american immigrants, according to David Rieff, "don't come here to be ethnic forever, they come here to make money."[34] Many thai, latino, korean, etc., are not rooted in a militant identity politics, but rather identify with a pluralism that side-steps a critique of the dominant mainstream. Their children study english as a second language in the public schools while their children's classmates never entertain learning thai or spanish.

These thai, korean, chinese, and latino immigrants are similar to the european immigrants of the early and mid-twentieth century, although their difference is written more starkly on their bodies: by the colors of the third world, south and east. Their racialized bodies interweave with the discourses of multiculturalism—in their deradicalized corporatist and militant insurgent forms—to form a polyglot of identities.

INSURGENT MULTICULTURALISM:
REPLURALIZING DIFFERENCES

The contradictory uses of multiculturalism diminish its effectiveness as radical critique. Neoconservatives in the u.s. simultaneously adopt a corporate version of multiculturalism as official discourse and criticize its radical formulation as subversive to the community. They use it in hopes of what Gunew calls "camouflaging vested orthodoxies"; and keeping the "others" quiet "while the anglos go on running things."[35] And then they critique it as disruptive.

Multiethnicity, although descriptively accurate of most countries, is problematized as a viable political directive by neocons. They homogenize difference and then position it against a homogenized commonness. Individuals' identities, though plural, are viewed as though they were one and then contrasted against the multiple needs of the larger group. Gloria Anzaldua, self-defined as a mestiza, says she has no country, but countries, no race, but races. She is a blending, woven together through cultural and border crossings.[36] No difference is ever completely homogenous; differences exist within difference.[37]

Identities are plural both individually and collectively. No one individual has only one identity. No one group has only one identity. No one nation is constituted by only one identity. Yet oneness, as a fastasmatic, retains enormous power. Only when multiplicity at the core is recognized, however, can one displace the opposition between sameness and difference as exclusive of each other. Any two individuals will be similarly different and differently similar; no two individuals are completely different or completely the same.

A radically pluralist multiculturalism pluralizes the individual *as well as* the community. We not only have here what Jeffrey Weeks calls a "community of communities"[38] but a community of communities with endless individuality. This does not mean that differences are endless but rather that similarities are endlessly particular, while differences are continually similar.[39]

Identity identifies what you have in common with some people and what differentiates you from others.[40] These identities are not fixed, but are rather "flexible identifications."[41] Culture itself, along with its multiple identities, is continually in process. As Homi Bhabha says: there is no ordinary culture. But there is a constant struggle to privilege a universalist center that "authorizes or allows" diversity, in order to contain it.[42] After all, "the powerful are not accustomed to being relativized."[43]

"Official" multiculturalism manages difference by trying to keep the center intact. This represents difference as non-conflictual and assimilationist. "The" difference can be integrated into the whole. But if multicultural differences are plural and hybrid identifications, they demand a reconstruction of the nation.

Lisa Jones writes of these multiple identities. She describes one panamanian-american as deep brown, senegalese, and ethnically latino, but also black-hispanic. Someone else is described as a caribbean-american who lives on three continents, is gingerbread brown, originally from grenada, but identifies as african-american.[44] Jose Vasconcelos describes the role of white, red, black, and yellow peoples, along with spain, mexico, greece, and india, in the making of latin civilization.[45] The racial/cultural mixing is at the core, not the margins. And in order to rearrange the rainbow there will be displacement and discomfort for the privileged authors at the center.

The radical pluralizing of multiculturalism that challenges eurocentrism is different from the racialized ethnic hatreds in bosnia or chechnya. These hatreds are based on exclusionary identities that are synonomous with right-wing nationalisms. The insurgent multiculturalism I am writing of here imagines identities that are open, fluid, and multiple. As such they invite inclusion, not exclusion. This vision of multiculturalism celebrates differences—and the conflicts they provoke—in order to create a public space for shared individuality. Henry Louis Gates clarifies a similar vision: "So I'm divided. I want to be black, to know black, to luxuriate in whatever I might be calling blackness... but in order to come out the other side, to experience a humanity that is neither colorless nor reducible to color. Bach and James Brown. Sushi and fried catfish."[46]

Identity is itself an indictment of the self/community split because, as a politics, identity requires an identification that is simultaneously individual *and* collective. One's very identity presumes an identification with and as a part of a group. A woman who self-identifies as a feminist must be able to see herself as an individual

defined by a group status; without the connection there is no feminist consciousness. There is just a woman seeing an individual
female. Gay activists recognize a similar connection: their identity as
gay cannot be recognized without the group status naming the
identity.

Interestingly, identity politics subordinates the differences that
constitute any group, in order to be able to ensure or to be able to
build solidarity. It must believe in the similarity between individuals
in order to name "a" difference.[47] As a gay african-american, if one
identifies as gay, one may simultaneously construct and see the larger gay community, while subordinating one's african-american identification. This requires a partly fictional viewing that ignores the differences within the collectivity in order to see one of the
communities. From this standpoint one can more fully pluralize.

Only after one sees the collectivity can one individualize and
particularize it.[48] This poses the major conflict for a multicultural
perspective between plural identities and separatism, between militant diversity and nationalism. It also means that this viewing must
be scrutinized carefully. When marginalized groups seek an identity
connected to other excluded communities, they must do so carefully
and scrupulously. As Stuart Marshall argues brilliantly: likeness does
not mean sameness.

Marshall argues that gays should invoke the World War II genocide of jews carefully because their own treatment by nazis was
somewhat different: oppressive regulation of desire throughout the
entire population along with the confinement of known gays to concentration camps. The pink triangle identified known gay men.
(Lesbians were assigned the black triangle for anti-socials.) And
although the triangles meant horrific persecution, they did not represent the annihilation that the yellow star did.[49]

A multicultural viewing of the gay community itself becomes a
needed corrective for multiculturalists, as well as gays. Vinita
Srivastava, as "queer and asian friendly," "brown and out in n.y.," says
that on her way to a dyke bar she took off her turquoise rajasthani
mirrored vest and rolled it up, then carried the bundle with her the
rest of the night. She feels "caught between the past that formed her
and a future she has yet to create."[50] The past had posted clear

boundaries for her: she was either gay or pakistani. Now she moves across borders, hoping to make them more fluid.

Group identities demand the careful explanation of specified needs that are already defined in the spaces in between the universal and the particular.[51] Bhabha might call this a third space.[52] Julia Kristeva might call it a "union of singularities" that are "not homogeneous." They exist to counter the "leveling absorption" of a false universalism. And to create a human universality "which impugns supremacy without erasing distinctions."[53]

Racialized/ethnic states demand a leveling sameness of a oneness of kind. Singularity becomes the nation. Communist statist regimes—from the stance of a falsely inclusive universalized egalitarianism—enforced a leveling sameness that denied the notion of difference as individuality. Egalitarianism in this instance is destroyed by sameness.

Liberal and neoconservative states use the official discourse of universal individual rights to cover over the concept of difference altogether. Everyone is an individual; the group particularities of blackness, gayness, femaleness are politically irrelevant. Multiculturalism stands as both militant critique of false universalisms and as an authorized partial corrective.

HOMOGENIZING AND CORPORATIZING MULTICULTURALISM

Multiculturalism, when used as "catch-up" for changing demographics, lumps and codes differences as an overgeneralized "otherness."[54] Part and parcel of this racialized discourse about immigrants, illegal aliens, and foreigners is a demarcation of otherness in a falsely homogenized framework. Cultures are named and described in terms of homogeneities that do not exist.[55] This applies to the naming process itself. Whereas in el salvador one is not hispanic, but salvadoran, and in china one is not asian but chinese, in the u.s. there is an "overarching Hispanicity or Asianness"[56] that clouds the specialness of these distinct identities. It allows for a manufactured demarcation of difference, which reproduces the opposition between a dominant core and marginalized, fantasized racial "others."

Multiculturalism itself can suffer from similar fictions of homogenous publics. In these instances, Sneja Gunew says, "diverse cultures are returned as homogenized folkloric spectacle." Then multiculturalism becomes an act of recuperating nationalism and is depoliticized into a multimedia event.[57] When framed by the privileged monocultural discourse, multiculturalism is denied its open, fluid pluralism of identities.

The militancy of pluralism is easily lost because it can be so easily absorbed into the corporatist use of the racial and ethnic variety that already exists. But there is a big difference between gastronomic pluralism[58] and an insurgent pluralism that demands economic, racial, and gender equality and sexual freedom for individual cultural identities.

A deradicalized, corporatist multiculturalism uses difference to sell things. Ethnicity becomes a marketing strategy.[59] Multicultural advertising displays the "united colors of Benetton"[60] and Malcolm X regalia. Coca-Cola says, "We are the world." Walt Disney produces *Pocahontas*, which is advertised as "sensitive to minorities."[61] The *New York Times* markets a special advertising supplement called "the diversity challenge." Diversity is said to be "good for business." United Technologies advertises: "United by diversity... It's the differences among us that empower us as one." Nabisco states: diversity is in everything we do—in the products we make, the countries we serve, and the people we recruit.[62] Bellcore says, "diversity promotes ideas." Philip Morris says, "great ideas come in different packages." Scholastic's *Weekly Reader* tells us, "our staff is as diverse as the world we serve."[63]

Corporations advertise that they must become as varied as the customers they service. As one executive puts it, "Once companies realize that having Spanish-speaking employees can help them gain new customers in South America...diversity will receive the attention it deserves because it will be part of the company's overall business strategy."[64] IBM brags that diversity has been a way of life for the company since it began to expand internationally about eighty years ago.[65]

John Rutherford says that capitalism is in love with difference. It sells us things that supposedly recognize uniqueness and individuality.[66] So "brown plastic is poured into blonde Barbie's mold,"[67] and Disney World hosts tens of thousands of homosexuals for a gay-day carnival while in the rest of florida they can be arrested for sodomy.[68] The contrast between the center and its margins is reified in this corporatist multiculturalism. Difference remains "othered."

Chamcha, a main character in Rushdie's *Satanic Verses*, whose face is the wrong color for color TV, must shed his body for his voice and be invisible. When prime-time eurovision beckons, his face is covered with rubber, and he is given a red wig.[69] Corporate diversity does not dislodge the primacy of whiteness. It instead chooses to ignore the fact that difference is always charged with powerful meanings; differences are never power neutral.[70] It leaves unchallenged the euro-american centrism that reproduces hierarchical differentiations.

Because power differentials are neutralized within the discourse of corporatist multiculturalism, all discriminations can be treated as the same. So affirmative action, which highlights the discrepancy of racial power, is labeled a racism in reverse. Even though there is little if any similarity between using race in order to create equality (affirmative action) and using race to limit one's opportunity (black segregation), they are leveled to the same rhetoric. So the unintended consequences to white males are equated with the intentional discrimination of people of color[71]—despite the fact that the consequences appear quite limited.[72]

Multiculturalism, as part of mass-market culture, keeps the multiplicity at the margins. So the multiple identities within the nation are never fully pluralized as part of the nation. The differences of race, economic class, gender, sexual identity, ethnicity, religion, are homogenized within the discourse of multiculturalism, and multiculturalism itself gets homogenized as meaning "difference," or different from the center, with no real specificity, or recognition of the powerful differences that constitute the nation. Whereas multiculturalism developed in part as a reaction against the assimilationist view of difference, today strains of it have been integrated into the dominant culture in order to maintain the hegemony of universalism.

U.S. BACKLASH: US vs. THEM

Neoconservatives and right-wing republicans have successfully undermined the civil-rights legislation of the 1960s and renamed what remains of it the "new" racism. Insurgent multiculturalism has been painted with this same brush; it is called the "new tribalism" threatening "the" american way of life.[73] An organized backlash has already engulfed much of the u.s. electorate. Initiatives in california, texas, and florida sought to eradicate the multiple identities within u.s. borders. This initial politics of exclusion targeted "illegal aliens" as unworthy foreigners and attempted to exclude them from eligibility for social services.[74]

California's proposition 187—also known as "save our state" (s.o.s.)—would eliminate all public welfare, including non-emergency medical care, prenatal clinics, and public schools, for all undocumented immigrants.[75] This initiative, if applied nationwide, would affect 13 percent of all immigrants, who make up 1 percent of the u.s. population. Yet it smears all immigrants with the same charges even though immigrants (as a group) create more jobs than they fill and generate more revenues than they absorb in service.[76]

In response, legal immigrants, feeling stigmatized, are applying for citizenship in record numbers.[77] But citizenship will not protect them from the police state developing in the u.s. southwest, where no one of color travels freely.[78]

However, hysteria is never assuaged by facts. Newt Gingrich articulates a u.s. right-wing nationalism that rivals that of the balkans. Sadly, the privatized visions of selfishness and exclusivity know no party lines. In a *New York Times* article, Felix Rohatyn asks where his Democrats have gone; today's Democrats, he says, have become "kinder and gentler Republicans." Rohatyn, who came to this country at fourteen, in 1942, and could have just as easily ended up in auschwitz death camp, says he now feels like a political refugee again.[79]

Crime, unemployment, welfare abuse, and illegitimacy are labeled foreign, and imaged on immigrant bodies of color, or on african-americans.[80] The language of hate toward jews and blacks and latinos is increasingly used by reactionary factions in government right alongside corporatist multiculturalism. They critique "dependency" as the effect of an overgenerous and bloated welfare state. And dependency has been racialized and feminized, while welfare has been completely racialized and sexualized.[81]

As many as four million people in the u.s. live in walled communities. They think they are being overtaken by people who are not assimilating; in the southwest, according to Dale Maharidge, anglos think "everything's turning Mexican."[82] Given these attitudes, it is hard to fathom what Sheldon Hackney, chairman of the National Endowment for the Humanities, means when he says we must find a way to express a national identity rather than splintered interests.[83]

Racism splinters. As such, race itself becomes something to overcome, rather than embrace.[84] White racism seeks to erase race—which means colored—because whiteness remains intact in the process. Racial harmony then assumes sameness, as whiteness, or sameness to one standard. In japan, similarity, rather than whiteness, defines the image of racial homogeneity. The likeness is supposedly responsible for a more "civilized" lifestyle.[85] Recent difficulties in japan with cults and poison-gas subway explosions will assuredly lead to a review of this imaginary homogeneity.

Samuel Huntington and similar neocons worry that diversity will only further fragment the nation. He is troubled by what he sees as the subversion of individual rights, by group rights; and by the move from an ideal of a color-blind society to color consciousness.[86] He praises the politics of assimilation along with the mythic immigrant who wished only to become a part of society. It was a time when "those in charge had confidence in the universal application of their culture."[87] Today the universals have supposedly been displaced by chaos.

White males in particular respond by calling foul play. Reverse discrimination has become the major focus of this discourse; affirmative action is the culprit. Neocons call for color-blind politics. Multiculturalists respond by asking why color-blindness could not have been the politics of choice when they needed it years ago.[88]

The "imaginary" operating here is that affirmative action has taken away white men's jobs. However, this public imagination is quite different than the actual denial of opportunities for whites.[89] White men still dominate in professional and managerial jobs, holding more than 95 percent of them.[90] And when white men have lost their jobs, they have lost them to transnational corporate downsizing, not to people of color. The racialized culture of today makes it easy for whites to blame blacks for their problems, while whites accuse blacks of blaming everyone else for their problems.

When all else fails in the blame game, there is always "biology as destiny." Enter Charles Murray and Richard Herrnstein, who argue that blacks' IQ is fixed by nature and cannot be improved.[91] Much of the information cited in *The Bell Curve* is from writers of *Mankind Quarterly*, which is, according to Charles Lane, "a notorious journal of 'racial history' founded by men who believe in the genetic superiority of the white race."[92] Murray uses their data to argue that blacks are intellectually doomed by the "bell curve" to welfare dependency and poverty, and that the government can do little to change this.[93] This argument is then used to justify the privatization of the social welfare state. This neoracism openly rejects an affirmative-action state and recycles old hatreds to do it.[94]

The privatization of public services and the cutting of the federal government's budget is a centerpiece of right-wing reactionary politics. Gingrich's "Contract with America" is supposed to return the country to the way it used to be for men like him.[95] He'll take it back from blacks, jews, HIV carriers, immigrants, etc. Never mind that 99,000 people—half of all americans with AIDS—are either homeless or likely to become so. Our privatized state leaves them alone to wander the streets of n.y.c., miami, los angeles, and detroit.[96] "America" becomes a nation defined by those who are able to take care of themselves, like white men used to be able to take of their families.

It is harder for the imaginary to work today because the u.s. is populated by so many more people of color from all over the world. It is also harder to homogenize racial difference by the black/white divide. Nevertheless, blackness is made the bedrock signifier of race and racial hatred, and african-americans stand in for the multirace threat.

Blackness, repressed in the mind's eye, threads through the processes of creating "others," which is further pluralized by demographic changes. While u.s. whites partake in practices that they used to distance others by, boundaries of self/other are confounded. Difference appears everywhere when the food we eat comes from all over the world; when the transnational economy challenges our conception of nation; and when global communication webs make for easy transnational viewing. But the differences and desires are psychically distanced and translated as fear. Exclusion rather than inclusion repositions monoculturalism against its multiplicity.

As long as difference is positioned against sameness, and universalized symbols are left in place to cover over the interests of western white heterosexual male class privilege, then corporatist multiculturalism will remain a cover for marginalization. The marginalization silences radically insurgent pluralism, which demands a full rewriting of diverse and equal identities. However, as long as the dialogue remains here I cannot make the point I wish to: that until insurgent multiculturalists recognize the crucial place of sex and gender in building the racialized euro-american nation, their project remains undertheorized.

Interestingly, and problematically, the competing imaginaries of nation and multiculturalism do not specify sexuality and gender as particular identities. Sex/gender is effaced in *both* official and corporatist *and* radically insurgent discourse. The man/woman divide is kept invisible in its interwoven racial/gender complexity. But if, as I argue, nations are built in and on the racialized bodies of women, we must dismantle the fallacious naturalizing of the homogeneous nation by naming the place of sexuality and gender in the processes of racism.

Multiculturalism, when used by neocons as a signifier of "race," which is also a signifier for "homogenized otherness," makes women "in and of" the nation invisible. And when insurgent multiculturalists *also* demand a recognition of diversity based on race, but not sex and gender, they rewrite and reinscribe the privileged center. My point is that: where there is race, there is sexuality and gender. Where there is sexuality and gender there is always race. Together, they bind the nation and define its borders.

THEORIZING GENDER FOR A RE-PLURALIZED MULTICULTURALISM

Neither ethnic nationalism nor multiculturalism locates gender as constitutive of the power relations defining borders, margins, boundaries, or difference. Radically pluralist multiculturalists challenge the boundaries drawn around ethnic/racial identities and the surrounding culture while leaving intact the patriarchal and masculinist borders of the nation and its heterosexist culture. Although some radical multiculturalists have sought to broaden their agenda to include issues of gender and sexuality, most often these attempts are met with great hostility from inside as well as outside the multicultural camps. The rainbow curriculum for n.y.c. schools was rejected along with its chancellor for broadening its focus to issues of sexuality. Multiculturalists in the school my daughter attends in ithaca, n.y., have rejected attempts to redirect the racial emphasis of its multicultural curriculum to include gender and sexuality.

This construction of diversity, though recognizing race, is defined by a "liberal" pluralism. By leaving sexual and gender borders in place, multiculturalism becomes a form of assimilationism: black history told in its masculinist form reproduces inaccurate gender histories of black women and their particular place in nation building. Race is added, but with clear borders of containment in place; the old add-and-stir method. Additional stories are told but in the old ways, instead of telling new and old stories differently.

One needs to do more than broaden the multicultural focus. Women's identities as women must be interwoven through their racialized and sexualized experience. The viewing must be refocused and deepened. Otherwise the assimilation process has simply been pluralized and domesticated.[97]

The problem here is that radical multiculturalism, which is supposed to redress the monovision of multiple realities, leaves the monoviewing in place in relation to sex/gender diversity. By equating multicultures with their racial/ethnic meanings, multiculturalism misnames, because racial/ethnic identities are already gendered and sexualized. Gender is repressed, fictionalized as absent. By default gender is equated with whiteness, and whiteness is homogenized as middle class, while women of color are homogenized *into* their "other" identities as black, latino, korean, etc.

Multiculturalism, even in its insurgent form, becomes a cloak for covering over women's particular and specific identities, which cross economic-class and racial/ethnic lines. It covers over the multiple interwoven experiences of women of color and the class differences between white women themselves. These plural realities contrast sharply with "uterine nationalism" and are a major resource by which to challenge the *imaginary* of the monoculture. Multiculturalists who limit themselves to race miss all this.

Women's place within the racialized and gendered politics of difference is central to the way that racial/ethnic/gendered/sexual difference is constructed in the first place. If patriarchal structures and cultures are naturalized by leaving them in place, then multiculturalism cannot be fully effective in dislodging the universalized notion of the nation. The nation, as unified, is signified through the homogenized symbolism of a racialized and vaporized "motherhood."

Pluralize women to their differences from each other as well as their multiple individual identities, and you begin the process of radically diversifying the nation. Once the nation is pluralized at its racialized/sexualized/gendered core, multiculturalism is no longer positioned as simply a reminder of ethnic and racial difference. To leave the homogenized viewing of women in place is to construct multiculturalism as always the "other."[98]

The transnational economy requires a corporatist view of diversity in racially pluralized first-world countries of the north and west *and* third-world countries of the south and east. This global capitalism challenges economic national borders that reconfigure the role of nation-states and their governments. In the process of this reconfiguration familial and masculinist *imaginaries* become all the more important in providing stability and psychic order.

As women in third-world countries are exploited as the cheapest labor anywhere, and women from the third world living in the first world reflect new and different boundary lines, women's identities are re-raced and re-gendered. The processes of the global market use race to contain gender, and with it, the separation between the global center and its margins.

Multiculturalism, if it is to stand against the onslaught of the global market, must theorize women's specificity and use this to denaturalize the construction of "otherness" that allows the psychic parameters of racialized gender hatred to go forward into the twenty-first century, untheorized and unnamed.

WRITING THE GLOBE

ON THE NATION

Let me start this part of the nation's story differently. Instead of nation, think trans*national*. "Trans" asks us to think through and beyond the nation. This global image depicts a one-world economy that "we" all share. It masks the globe's multiracial, multicultural, multilingual diversity. And it cloaks the gender hierarchies that traverse and construct the global economy. So the twenty-first century will be multi—many, and trans—unified, while the (economic) nation is displaced by the corporatist-multicultural globalized imaginary.

The global economy symbolizes a wholeness of a world without divisions, difference, conflict. Some have called it a borderless world.[1] But this reduces and simplifies borders to an economic reading. Instead, religious, familial, heterosexist, and racial borders are called forth to renegotiate global spaces. Globalism, like nation, erases sex/gender hierarchies, while utilizing corporatist multicultural viewings of racial diversity.

I explore the pre-fixes of the "post"–cold war period in order to examine global capital's uniqueness. Without communism it is much easier to promote the vision of globalism as the only alternative; "capitalist universality" has triumphed to the point where it becomes invisible.[2] The mythic "oneness" of the globe ignores the first third-world divide and the devastating inequalities of rich and poor.

Transnational corporations speak of globalism rather than global capitalism; and the necessities of downsizing and being competitive, rather than the excessive wealth of a few and the unemployment of millions.

*Trans*nationalism stands in for capital. Corporatist *multi*culturalism uses and absorbs cultural/ethnic/racial diversity in order to naturalize and depoliticize multiracialism's potentially disordering aspects.[3] Or, as Terry Eagleton clearly states: "Difference, hybridity, heterogeneity, restless mobility, are native to the capitalist mode of production, and thus by no means inherently radical phenomena."[4]

The problem with the prefixes of "post"-times is that they misrepresent the newness of the twenty-first century. After all, Marx and Lenin argued early on that capitalism was an international system. Imperialism was their name for it. And they thought it created an international proletariat. Now, it is the capitalists, and "new democrats" like Bill Clinton, who argue the global necessities of the system, in order to defend it. The new is both different and similar.

The new globalism and its *multi*cultural agenda are "new-old" developments with transnational origins. Corporate structures are identified by their economic trans-status (across and through and beyond) rather than their 1970s multinational status. Multinational presumes at least two distinct entities, as *inter*national requires distinct nations. Trans cuts through and creates mobile borders. *Trans*national imagines beyond known boundaries and allegiances.

The anti-statist communist stance of eastern europe and western anti-government neoconservatism leave global capitalists with a fairly free hand. First-world national governments have less clout in this global framework. Governments are less and less accountable, so first-world countries become increasingly privatized. Post-modernism's skepticism of grand narratives, and transcultural, transhistorical realities, leaves it ill prepared to deal with these global trends.

Global capital operates in disguise with no clear culprit, especially in first-world countries. This disguise remains racialized and gendered: racism is still used to cover over the extreme poverty in africa, south america, asia, etc. Race stands as a silent explanation of the third-world status of rwanda, or haiti, or somalia. Kwame Anthony Appiah argues that if we take the poverty of africa as a given and do not ask why africa is poor, we can be excused of responsibility.[5]

Racism is used as a marker to naturalize new aspects of the global marketplace. Black disorder, pictured by somalians dragging u.s. soldiers through mogadishu as imaged on TV screens around the world, stands in for a rainbow of colors: shades of black, yellow, and brown. The rejection of haitian asylum seekers maintains the continuing relevance of color for the global economy.[6] In the global economy, plural colors, symbolized through a homogenized blackness, are positioned against a pluralized and fictionalized whiteness.

The opportunism of capitalism reconstitutes gender hierarchies while re-racing first- and third-world divides. Patriarchal familial and national allegiances are unsettled by global corporate searches for women's cheap labor in third-world-south countries. And new consumer markets in third-world-east countries redeploy sexuality to undermine former communist statist notions of woman's equality. Women, in these eastern european countries, are then summarily displaced by these same markets and sent back to the home. These women view the new consumerism, but with no money to spend. Women in first-world countries are used to symbolize the market's consumerist possibilities for women in third-world countries.

Global capital sends Avon to brazil, fancy lingerie to argentina, prostitution and porn to eastern europe. There is little new here, but there are new ways of doing it. Transnational corporations defy economic borders while utilizing and adapting old formations and constructions of race and gender. The question is whether capital itself will erode the racialized/gendered borders that it depends on.

Let me start unpacking this.

POST–COLD WAR GLOBALIZING OF MULTICULTURALISM

Many u.s.-based corporations were slow to recognize the limits of the nationalist fictions they used. Japanese companies such as Sony and Honda adapted their corporate visions more readily.[7] While thinking globally they developed radios and cars for local markets. They diversified in order to create and capture new market possibilities.

According to Richard Barnet and John Cavanagh, Ford wanted a car that could be sold anywhere in the world. That meant adapting to the local labor force and local suppliers. "Ford of Asia" was born. Product "purity" is as much a fantasy as racial "purity" is.[8] Instead of purity, the abilities of a diverse workforce are tapped for tomorrow's marketplace.[9]

U.S. corporations have been situated throughout the globe for a very long time now. So global production is not totally new here. What is new are the global channels of communication that shrink distance and speed up time.[10] The globe itself has changed so that being identified as stateless, i.e., global, is a new corporate goal. Barnet and Cavanagh argue that it is in the interest of corporations to lose their national identity, especially if they are u.s.-identified.[11] Multi/transnational-identified corporations pluralize their available markets for investment, production, and consumption.

Multiple markets provide global capital with wider arenas. Multinational/multicultural cars, hair products, video equipment, etc., sell better. These products identify local markets within a global framework. Global/local, universal/particular, similar/different guide the marketing and investment sites. The fast-food industry brings local tastes to the globe as a whole, and pizza and tacos have become global items.[12]

Finding a politically useful language for these changing times is difficult. Thinking globally and acting locally is further complicated because these spaces are not clear-cut. The global is lived locally, and the local is lived globally. As such, first-/third-world divides do not hold simply; nor do north/south, east/west divides. Yet these divides still resonate and continue to carve out punishing differences.

The former fictional clarity of national boundaries also destabilizes lines drawn between center/periphery and imperialist/dependent countries. However, the rich/poor divide remains, even if some rich people live in poor nations, and many more poor people live in rich nations. The first-/third-world divide may misrepresent the global multinational alliances that exist across this division, but revisioned racial conflicts are retained through and in this divide.[13] So is worldwide poverty among women.

The "post" in post–cold war also does not represent a clean

break with the past, though much has changed. The capitalist/communist opposition no longer is defined by the "threat" of the soviet union.[14] This threat has been replaced by the fear of islamic "terrorism," and the random violence of the globe. There are multiple enemies today: the concern with national security has been replaced by the concern with personal insecurity.[15]

So enemies are pluralized, and the global market is singular with no alternatives. This gives the u.s. more clear license than ever before to ignore its own poor, not to mention the rest of the world's poor.[16] And transnational corporations are now freer to move around the globe, regardless of geographical territory.

The end of the communist bloc, which once offered support to third-world countries to develop their own resources, such as oil, leaves these countries on their own as never before.[17] Hardest hit in lost soviet aid is cuba. In contrast, parts of vietnam's economy are booming. At the celebration of ho chi minh city in 1995, the buildings were draped in banners with hammers and sickles and Ho Chi Minh, but also with red, white, and blue logo flags, signifying Pepsi-Cola as an official sponsor of the event.[18]

Aspects of the cold war persist through these changes even in the post-'89 anti-communist rhetoric of eastern europe. Nations exist psychically alongside their economic demise; western/anglo hegemony exists alongside multiracialism; women are used to write national borders even while they displace them; the population of the u.s. continues to diversify racially and ethnically while anglo-americans challenge affirmative action law.

Today's nationalisms in eastern europe are a mix of intercultural and transnational developments.[19] They represent tensions that exist between nations and multiculturalism, between the understanding of universality and specificity. They cross the boundaries of individualism and collectivity. They exist within the intersections where old borders crumble.

The political priorities of nationness, which require an exclusive stance, run counter to the needs of mobile capital as well as the plural racial identities of west and east, north and south. After all, millions of europeans have black african ancestry; and black africans have lived throughout the western part of the globe.[20] But because national borders are constructed from sexual boundaries, moments that are perceived as political threats are transferred to the realm of sexuality.[21] And, as I have earlier argued, sexuality is already encoded racially. So, transnationalism—as it challenges geographical borders—undermines nationalism at the same time it instigates anachronistic versions of it.

In this post–cold war, post–gulf war, post-soviet world, the world splits apart in "new-old" ways. First and second worlds no longer exist as they once did. Instead the global north includes manila, nairobi, and mexico city. And the global south stretches through los angeles and chicago.[22] Taiwan, hong kong, and singapore represent the newest industrial parts of the third world.

For Aijaz Ahmad, we live in one world, not three, and colonialism and imperialism exist in each divide. He writes of the supranationalism of advanced capital that hierarchically structures the world as a whole. There is a transnational sweep of capital with nation-state locales.[23] This is the process of advanced global capitalism; no clear-cut "pre" or "post" anything, but new levels of excess. And the process initiates the psychic arenas of repressed fears and desires, which challenge the new global parameters of the nation. In sum: divides within the globe are real, and yet the globe is whole.

GLOBAL CAPITALISM AND TRANSNATIONALISM

Global capitalism's cross-border banking exists within *and* beyond nations. Therefore, nations are not completely at odds with transnational corporations; parts of a nation will benefit from seeing itself globally.[24] But the state, as the protector of the nation, gets caught in the threat of capital flight. As a result it has less power today, and protects less of the nation.

Robert Reich, Bill Clinton's economic architect, tries to clarify this new relationship. According to him, corporations used to be "national multinationals," still devoted to their host/home country, whereas today they are "pure multinationals," with no commitment to their home country.[25] With no loyalty but to themselves, they are scot-free to move around the globe. This is their new threat and their new power.

Reich warns that everything as we have known it is changing. That the u.s. exists within "global webs with no particular connection to any single nation." That we are laborers in a global market and that "nationalism is a hazardous sentiment."[26] That the globalism redirects financing, markets, and corporate executives themselves toward transnational markets. The allegiances to nation are outmoded.

Reich asks us to see corporations as complex networks of problem solvers and strategic brokers stretching around the globe. The webs of contractors, subcontractors, franchisees, and temporary alliances structure this economy. Products simply become the international composites of this process. Computers and modems thread the web; and "intellectual and financial capital can come from anywhere, and be added instantly."[27]

Because global capital can flow anywhere or everywhere, it makes its own rules. And as capital appears homeless, and authorless, it becomes blameless with sectors of the first world becoming more like the third world. Extreme poverty, though still concentrated in southeast asia, africa, and south america, is also dispersed to sites within the u.s. and western europe. The ruthlessness of the market spares few.

Transnational corporations, as stateless nations, escape accountability. They exist as vast bank accounts and global production sites.[28] There are no bosses to be angry at. Business is itself seen as a victim of the global competition. As one worker states: "My boss is trying hard, but there is nothing he can do, either."[29] Instead the global economy uses itself as its own cover: competition rules. Get competitive or pay the consequences.[30] Emily Martin describes how this economic/cultural moment defines fitness, in terms of flexibility and adaptability. The corporate body must be lean, agile, and downsized.[31] If you are going to get angry, get angry at yourself, or the "foreigner" within you.

Capital remains an unnamed enemy. The randomness of the victims even affects white professional-managerial men. It makes all the competitiveness seem inevitable and glosses over the intentional greed.

Instead, the enemy named in countries such as the u.s. and

great britain is the government itself. Big government must be stopped—while the transnationals are left to take over the globe. And big government, according to neocons, is best stopped by downsizing the public sector's responsibility for the poor. This anti-government stance takes on a specifically racist and sexist agenda. The u.s. right-wing militia movement takes this anti-government agenda a step further and turns it inside out, calling the u.s. government a nazi cancer and an updated gestapo in disguise.[32] In eastern europe, the anti-government stance is defined by an anti-communist statism.

Assisting global corporations and their global financial infrastructure is the global communications network. The "technical infrastructure" and megatechnology allow new levels of commodity movement and efficiency. This age of "mega-corporations" and "mega-technology" has created an "unprecedented corporate power grab."[33] The excesses are staggering.

The United Nations estimates some seven hundred million people are currently underemployed or unemployed in the third world.[34] At the other extreme David Rockefeller got the Mitsubishi Corporation to buy an 80 percent ($1.37 billion) share in Rockefeller Center, a bilateral arrangement that allowed the Rockefeller family to pocket $2 billion in profits and introduce the japanese company to bankruptcy. Robert Scheer asks: "Would you buy a new world order from a Yankee who swindled you on a Manhattan real estate deal?"[35]

More than one-fifth of cuba's total workforce will be laid off because of the post-communist global marketplace. They have had to "cut down on state subsidies to attract foreign investment." The cuban people have been told to get used to unemployment as the government restructures the workforce in order to be competitive in the world economy.[36]

In this world market there are new losers, even in the first world. The downward leveling is not limited to low-skill, low-tech jobs.[37] The new level of economic dispersion—developing everything elsewhere and in multiple sites—makes the world, according to one Wal-Mart executive, "one great big marketplace."[38] In this world, designer labels, trademarks, and brand names construct loyalties and create the new patriotism.[39]

The hegemony of the global market seems complete given the absence of the soviet bloc. Self-interest has new uncontested license. The u.s. has now become the most economically stratified industrial nation, with new levels of economic inequality on the rise.[40] Instead of millionaires we now brag about mega-billionaires. William Gates of Microsoft, now one of the wealthiest men in the world, has accumulated $12.9 billion thanks to changes in u.s. tax law.[41] While the super-wealthy continue to accumulate, even the professional wealthy are downsized.

G. J. Meyers, once a corporate mogul and now a victim of downsizing, writes: "I know an amazing number of capable, experienced, college-educated, unemployed people." He says that it seems like "we are evolving into a nation of native-born refugees." He describes the "unprecedented executive unemployment" and his own despair at endless job interviews and no hope of a job.[42]

THE MULTI-BORDERED, MULTICULTURAL U.S.

Instead of seeing multiraciality and globalism as part of an historical process that is plural at its core, a fictive vision of homogeneity frames the idea of more and more immigrants arriving at the "nation." Hence, the vision: globe vs. nation. The immigrant is "different" and "other." The immigrant symbolizes the globalization of the nation by representing the very borders they cross.

There is something wrong with positioning the globe, as holistic and inclusive, against the nation, as singular, when nations like the u.s. are global in origin. Mexicans were enclosed by north american expansionism. Blacks were forcibly transported as slaves. Chinese and japanese were the cheap laborers who built the railroads.[43] Native americans preceded the colonists.

Ishmael Reed argues that the world has been arriving at north american shores for at least ten thousand years from europe, africa, and asia. This process has only recently intensified with increasing numbers of mexicans, filipinos, chinese, taiwanese, japanese, indians, and dominicans emigrating through the 1980s. "The world is here," Reed writes.[44] The north american fiction of racial homogeneity unravels as more and more people trace themselves to africa, asia, the hispanic world, the pacific islands, and arabia.[45] Native american and african-american heritages of hispanicity further web identity.[46] Latinos from mexico, cuba, salvador, nicaragua, haiti, and brazil express plural ethnic/cultural identities. The global parameters of racial hybridity—with all its colors—shifts identities away from "the" nation.

But these identities are also marked by the "globe vs. nation" dichotomy. This division dislocates and displaces: people become homeless refugees and migrants.[47] By 1995, twenty-three million refugees had fled across borders, and twenty-six million were displaced in their own countries, according to the United Nations Commission for Refugees.[48]

More often than not, immigrants are imaged as illegal.[49] And they represent northern first-world fears of being overrun by third-world southern countries. The vision is of colored people of asia and africa seeking jobs in first-world countries. Even though immigration is tightly controlled in europe and north america, the fear is transposed to the supposedly illegal immigrant from south america, asia, and africa.[50]

California exhibits this troubled politics of dislocation and hostility. At present there is a great discrepancy between those who work and those who vote. This "foreign plurality" is politically disenfranchised but pays taxes. This process of taxation without representation is creating the "dedemocratization of California society." According to Jorge Castañeda, a form of "electoral apartheid" draws boundary lines between foreigners and citizens so that california's international citizenry is disenfranchised domestically.[51] Mexican-americans live in between the domestic/foreign border. This sense of present-day displacement stands in contrast to the chicano slogan during world war II, "Americans All."[52] In this earlier period, many chicanos saw their interests as aligned with those of the nation as a whole.

As the gateway to south america and asia, california symbolizes the fluidity of geographical borders, and the statisticity of racialized boundaries. As Gloria Anzaldua writes, the mestiza consciousness of indian/mexican culture from an anglo point of view requires juggling cultures, plural personalities, and contradictory consciousness.[53]

California represents the flux and change of the transnational economy where boundaries—racial, national, and economic—are reconfigured. The market economies of the pacific rim define new interdependencies where california has the third-largest market, japan the first,[54] and where los angeles is the capital of the third world.[55]

The economic relations between the u.s. and mexico—as orchestrated in the North American Free Trade Agreement (NAFTA)—reflect the regional aspects of globalism, rather than national realignments. Transnationalized economic patterns have shrunk the distance and challenged the political boundaries of the two nations. The political border between california and mexico both separates and connects; it creates differences where similarities also exist. Economic and demographic changes pull the two spaces together.[56] These changes have been a process of silent integration and economic interdependence.[57] NAFTA merely legalized and OK'd the process.

But Elaine Bernard argues that NAFTA is not about free trade, but rather is a protection of transnational capital. It provides new corporate protections and tariff reductions and amounts to a deregulation of international commerce. NAFTA frees business from government regulation and allows for "unrestricted movement of money, capital, goods and services."[58] It is a blueprint of neocon privatization: government has no business being in the global business. Instead, governments must get out of the way of the free flow of capital; hence, the privatization of the state.

This free flow of capital is a death sentence for the indigenous people of mexico who say they cannot compete with canada and california.[59] The Zapatista uprising in chiapas was a statement against the global restructuring of NAFTA by those dispossessed by it.[60]

Regional agreements such as NAFTA become the localized site for negotiating global trade. The Asia-Pacific Free Trade Agreement established "free trade" by dropping tariffs for the eighteen countries involved.[61] The General Agreement on Tariffs and Trade (GATT)—is a one hundred twenty-three-nation agreement affording corporate protection worth $744 billion in tariff reductions. Agreements like NAFTA harmonize standards downward, for capital enhancements.[62] Tariffs are dropped along with protections for workers and consumers alike. Profits go up while the quality of life is in a downward spiral for a majority of the world's people.

THE "WEST" AND THE GULF WAR

Anti-immigration, anti-haitian, anti-islamic politics reproduce racisms in and for the globe. The gulf war assisted in the post–cold war rearticulation of new-old racial hatreds by putting western cultural hegemony in full view. The western view of the war dominated the airwaves. Global information networks were singularly dependent on CNN as the source for news.[63] The images—smart bombs, pentagon-cleared reporting, and a sanitized war with little u.s. blood—triumphed. The informational monopoly concealed the devastation and ecological disaster the war caused for kuwait and iraq.[64] The "west" won; the "rest" lost.

The gulf war was to mark the new world order; the west would police the disorder.[65] Then came the messy situations in somalia, haiti, rwanda, and bosnia. And los angeles, the world trade center, and oklahoma city. The increased disorder triggers fantasmatic fears. And islamic fundamentalism has become a ready stand-in for the anxiety. Iraqis, bosnian muslims, and palestinians all get lumped together with Saddam Hussein and terrorism and his "holy war."[66] Islamic fundamentalism becomes an incongruous homogenized "other."

When "the" west is situated against "the" rest in overly homogenized categories, racialized others are easily garnered. And as complex and hybrid as the globe is, these coagulated homogeneities remain in play. Noted neocon Samuel Huntington invokes these constructions when he argues that "western ideas" such as individualism, liberalism, constitutionalism, human rights, democracy, etc., have little meaning for islamic, confucian, hindu, japanese, and buddhist cultures.[67] The Hapsburgs of the north and west and the Ottomans of the east and south are still at war here.

"The" west is constructed as distinct and apart: it is defined by rationalism and constitutionalism. "The" rest is defined as particularist and factional. If the "west" is homogeneously rationalist, then heterogeneity fragments. My point is that although some islamic fundamentalism—as well as some christianity—is in conflict with rationalism and constitutionalism, much of it is not.

The key global conflicts for Huntington are cultural. He demands that we see beyond cultural difference but thinks it is not possible. "Faith and family, blood and belief, are what people identify with and what they will fight and die for."[68] He homogenizes/naturalizes religion and culture, and erases politics with it.

Instead of theorizing cultural heterogeneity as part of civilization, Huntington problematizes it. The west has never been simply "the" west. Its development has been circuitous and warriorlike. Post–cold war, post–gulf war, transnational corporations operate similarly, but with new telecommunication possibilities. New levels of hybridity are in the making, and there is no simple or easy fit here.

Local sites outside the west sometimes adapt, and sometimes protest. So western Gerber baby food does not sell well to those used to making their own, as in poland, while some young bosnians dream of coming to the u.s. for a Coke and a Big Mac.

POLICING IMMIGRATION ON THE GLOBE

Immigration law polices u.s. borders. It defines who can come in and who cannot, who can enter and exit, who can be admitted or expelled. This exclusivity defines the boundaries of the nation and immigration at the same time. This right to include/exclude underlies the territorial jurisdiction of the nation.[69]

Immigration law is defined by economic concerns and familial priorities. Entry is often dependent on marriage and concerns for family unity. The reunification of married couples initiated the War Brides Act of 1945. Family is defined in its narrow heterosexist version.

Today, exclusions cannot be made on the basis of race, sex, nationality, or place of birth unless one is insane, a psychopathic person, "sexually deviant," a chronic alcoholic, a drug addict, or is infected with a contagious disease.[70] One gets the idea. Yet, the interpretation of these regulations fluctuates in terms of labor needs and familial commitments.

The Chinese Exclusion Act of 1882 stands in stark contrast to present-day law. Anti-chinese feeling, especially in california, fueled this legislation. Tolerance for chinese laborers declined after the completion of the Central Pacific railroad. The drought and depression of the early 1870s had also heightened anti-chinese feelings.[71]

However, the racial exclusivity of immigration law is not limited to this one departure. The National Origins Quota System of the 1920s was both anti-asian and anti-eastern and southern european. The Mexican Repatriation Campaign of the 1950s was also responsible for expelling large numbers of mexicans from the u.s.

The history of u.s. immigration tells a contradictory story of entrance and exclusion, promise, and restriction. After world war I there was a movement to americanize immigrants. Assimilation was the goal; citizenship training and english courses were expected of new immigrants. Cultural pluralism was rejected as an ideal. By 1921, quotas according to national origins were in place. Japanese immigration was prohibited at this time.

The quota system stood until 1965. During this decade of civil-rights legislation, immigration law followed suit. Mexicans and chinese were once again allowed entry as laborers. Shortly before these changes were made, President John F. Kennedy applauded the u.s. for being a melting pot. The pot symbolized a blending of many stripes into a single nationality, but with a recognition of particular ethnic identities.[72]

When Kennedy wrote of the melting pot he acknowledged that the negro had not been adequately included. According to him, they were the only minority that had not been integrated into the full stream of american life.[73]

Decades later, the melting pot has failed many more, and poverty among african-americans has increased. The brutal extremes of rich and poor visited on parts of the third-world-south and -east throughout the 1980s has created a newly migrant work force desperate for work. But to the extent the first-world-north and -west is no longer a strong and growing industrial economy, many of these would-be workers do not find what they are hoping for.

Immigration has always been, in part, about people looking for work. This is true across the globe. And today more people are looking for work than ever. Australia hosted migrants from britain, southern and eastern europe, and italy shortly after world war II. In the next stages of immigration, people seeking work from the middle east, especially lebanon and turkey, emigrated. More recently, south americans and southeast asians have sought work there.[74]

Migration flows fluctuate with the global economy. The excesses of poverty remap third-world countries. People come to the u.s. looking for jobs while more and more people in the u.s. are looking as well. Many of the jobs once located within the u.s. borders are easier to find elsewhere today—in the newly industrializing third world of south korea or taiwan, for example.

Meanwhile, corporatist multiculturalism covers over the imperialist relations of transnational capital. And neocons use the radically pluralist potential of multiracialism as a whipping post for attacking insurgent political movements. They defend the nation through the fear of white citizens who are without work, and want the few available jobs at home. But this does not sit easy with the changed economy. Rotoflow's two hundred-person work force in southern california includes thirty nationalities.[75]

Transnational corporatist multiculturalism transgresses the old boundaries of identity. And the configurations and reconfigurations create complicated new allegiances. Many chicanos in california support proposition 187, which would cut expenditures for undocumented workers. Why? Because they are tired of being lumped together and scapegoated with illegal aliens. The construction of "otherness" is rebordered once again, by transnational capital.

TRANSNATIONAL CORPORATISM AND EASTERN EUROPE

Global capitalism has dominated eastern and central europe since the revolutions of 1989. The disintegration of the communist world allowed for a mobility of capital that could ignore cold war boundaries. Corporations could operate not merely without borders, but without responsibility.[76] As a result, eastern europe has been repositioned globally as a new third world.

The mobility of capital has been enhanced by the anti-communist rhetoric of eastern europe and the neocon free-market model. The transition from communism to "free-market democracies" has left the most vulnerable people in eastern and central european countries—albania, czech republic, slovakia, poland, russia, romania—poorer and less healthy. People's living conditions have seriously deteriorated: alcoholism, infectious diseases, and malnutrition have increased.[77] With the privatization of the market in hungary, most people's standard of living has plunged. In poland, 38 percent of the people live below the poverty line, with more than 15 percent unemployed in 1994.[78]

Global capital has meant declining health and welfare for the people in eastern and central europe. Because money for public health has been sharply reduced, russia is plagued by infectious diseases; cases of cholera, dysentery, and diptheria have increased radically in the past year.[79] The health-care system is in ruins with cancer, heart disease, and tuberculosis all on the rise.[80] Meanwhile, moscow is filled with people from azerbaijan, pakistan, and armenia. Infant mortality is up in bulgaria, moldova, romania, and the ukraine.[81]

Global capital presents a conundrum: it is dispersed through the world but is completely self-centered. With governments shrinking and transnational corporations growing, the relationship between public and private space collides. We can see this most clearly in arenas such as public health, where the public cannot be wished away. As one russian health official says, "These infections often come from beyond one's borders, but once they are here it is a problem for all of us."[82]

Besides the problematic fallout for public life from privatized markets, the markets often do not work. General Electric bought the state-owned Tungsram in hungary (maker of lighting products) but has not been able to get it to turn a profit.[83] In russia, the market has been most successful for the criminal element. Seen from the eyes of a western businessman: "Russia is not an 'underdeveloped' or 'developing' country. It's a misdeveloped country."[84] Nevertheless, many young, newly middle-class russians luxuriate in their new-found freedoms.[85]

The privatization of capital and the transnational corporate structure of the privatization preclude public accountability. As a result, the process is highly undemocratic.[86] The transformations of state apparati by global capital requires downsizing; and the post–cold war pentagon becomes a little leaner and meaner.[87] But no matter how much the u.s. government shrinks, it still seems to operate as an imaginary enemy, displacing global capital.[88]

As governments get redefined for the global economy, so do militaries. So the u.s. sends troops across the globe, similar to capital itself. And the post–cold war global economy speaks the hegemony of free-market ideology.

TELECOMMUNICATIONS AND TRANSNATIONAL CULTURE

The enormous changes in telecommunications and data transmission knits a web of financial transactions between frankfurt, tokyo, and new york that exists beyond the control of any one government.[89] The intra/international demands of global capital decide investment, so local/national markets must be able to attract the attention of these investors.

The transnational aspects of corporate power are more obvious to people in the u.s. when japanese, korean, and german companies are based here. As key players in the global market change, the downward mobility of many in the u.s. becomes more visible, especially that of the white working and middle classes.

"The" u.s., however, remains dominant in the export of "western" culture: hollywood film, pop music, TV, fashion, etc. As Barnet and Cavanagh state: "The American Dream is the nation's number one export." The fantasy and promise of freedom (more than equality) is spread through u.s.-made films. Messages of individualist rebellion are spread through our cultural products.[90] The effect is not unidirectional or uniform but is transmitted through the onslaught of these products.[91]

CNN reaches seventy-eight million homes in more than one hundred twenty countries. MTV networks have over two hundred million viewers worldwide and are owned by Viacom, the second-largest transnational media company in the world.[92] This kind of daily media exposure begins to create new combinations of local/global reality because mass communications do not adhere to national boundaries.

A global cultural network begins to emerge. Time Warner Communications is the largest transnational media corporation in the world. Its globalization has allowed greater flexibility to adapt to market changes. The communication technologies allow for fast and necessary dispersion.[93] Walt Disney, though still american owned, makes most of its profits from overseas markets and amusement parks. With its acquisition of Capital Cities/ABC Inc., Disney now can further consolidate its dominance over the packaging of "image as product." Mickey and Minnie Mouse will oversee the conglomeration of information networking.[94]

Satellites, lasers, high-speed computation and travel, and instantaneous resource transfer all redefine time and space. The communications media "deterritorialize" cultures through the global circulation of images, sounds, and goods.[95] The electronic information delivery system of telephones and cable TV make voice, data, and image become one.[96] Consumer culture, exported by TV, pop music, and fashion, transmits the west all over the globe.[97] The Internet and the information highway defy nation, time, and space.

Arjun Appadurai says that there is a difference between the globalization of culture and the homogenization of culture.[98] The technological developments construct an international mass culture rather than a western hegemony. Or they create several mass cultures defined by local sites.

But there is something of a hegemonic influence here. Czechs are said to like Woody Allen; u.s. soap operas are popular among egyptians; israelis love Clint Eastwood; haitians went to see *Malcolm X* and *Indecent Proposal* in great numbers; japanese like the *Ed Sullivan* show; and poles watch *Dynasty*.[99] What these gross overstatements occlude more than they clarify is that these moments of culture are viewed, absorbed, and "repatriated" in a zillion different ways. As Appadurai convincingly argues, the global cultural economy has a series of building blocks of "imagined worlds" that are "historically situated imaginations of persons and groups spread around the globe."[100]

Computer technologies and information highways create their own boundary lines. As a consequence, the international media and entertainment industry have more influence than any "national political class."[101] Telecommunications centralizes the information and the products, while the effects can reflect a pluralization of meaning by those who receive them. This is more and more true as the networks become interactive and give more choice and control to the consumer.

With the end of bipolarity, cultural highways are more open. The effect on identities has been conflictual. Although hybridity can be nurtured in new ways today, so can exclusionary stances. And the fantasmatic "west" is still positioned against the fantasmatic "east," as islam, or the orient, or africa *alongside* the hybridity.

At this moment, global corporations are having an easier time adjusting than are nation-states. McDonald's adapts to the locale in which it will be housed. In japan, a Big Mac is made with soybean; in france it is served on a croissant. This global corporatism is continually adaptable and opportunist. But imagined communities shift more slowly. And "public" responsibility cannot be ignored forever.

TRANSNATIONAL RACIALIZED GENDER AND THE TWENTY-FIRST CENTURY

Even the united nations acknowledges that transnational corporations are the central organizers of the world economy and are fighting to establish themselves in each other's home markets. Each of them tries to build its own regionally integrated, independent network of overseas affiliates.[102] This requires building international networks within culturally specific locales. The troubling relationship between the universal and the particular, sameness and difference, transnational and national meet in this globalizing corporatism.

The global web is transstate and multination. Japanese corporate execs are controlling owners in CBS. Vast stretches of downtown los angeles are inhabited by internationally owned corporations. The "fortunate fifth"[103] who succeed in this global web can succeed without the rest. The well-being of any nation as a whole is no longer necessary for capital's success. Neither is the social welfare state.

Corporate america has never been dependent on the success of the nation as a whole for its profits, but today it has more opportunities to leave the rest of the nation behind. So the rest of the nation must become competitive with workers around the globe, or the u.s.—as distinct from corporate america—will become a part of the new third world. The key is not "which nation's investors own what part of them" but which work force is most valuable to the economic web.[104]

Eric Hobsbawm assumes that nationalism will die out along with national economies.[105] Zbigniew Brezinski wonders about the viability of the new "pluralistic free market democracies" while relegating ethnic nationalism to an "external complication."[106]

These analysts reduce the nation to its economic function. However, economic transnationalism stands in contrast to the political racial/ethnic/sexual nationalisms of eastern and central europe or the complex racisms defining haiti, rwanda, south africa, etc. As economies diversify and internationalize, they utilize and corporatize the racialized and gendered constructions of otherness while *also* naturalizing the more traditional roles of race and sex/gender in bordering identities.

Transnational corporations do not promote a racism that is co-equal with the nation. Instead, corporate multiculturalism pluralizes race for transnational capital, although there is no simple or complete absorption or adaptation here. So, nationalisms in the former yugoslavia and soviet union are partial reactions to outsider economies symbolized by McDonald's in zagreb, and Dairy Queen, Kentucky Fried Chicken, and Dunkin' Donuts in budapest.[107]

Hugh P. Price of the Urban League argues that the global realignment of work and wealth requires that blacks understand their commonality with other displaced workers.[108] Because the global marketplace is the culprit, he argues, blacks must understand their place within these new racial dynamics.

Immigrant identities are also constituted in and through these new racial dynamics. And the telecommunications transnational network allows some of them to retain local roots, routes, with their home country. So a more complex international identity can be sustained: they are both foreign and citizen, different and the same, multicultural and national. There is no simply constructed national identity here. They must see themselves in relation to the globe.

The globalization of capital and its mobility have diversified and dispersed corporate interests in multiracial and multicultural ways. Although power remains concentrated in first-world corporations, nations as well as their first-world status are in turmoil. This stirs up fantasies of nation building that resonate with a fantasmatic of gender hierarchy. The gender aspects of nation—the presentation of woman as never the sister, always the mother, and as the definer of border crossings—presses hard against the women of the third-world factories of the twenty-first century, the rape victims of bosnia and haiti, and feminists of the north and west, south and east.

As global capital spreads, women work harder, either in and from their homes, or in specified third-world markets. They become the third world of the third world, and the third world of the first world. They are the cheapest of the cheap workers. Reebok and Nike hire the women in indonesia for 16 cents an hour and the women in china for 10 to 14 cents an hour.[109] These women build nations from their families; and they build the global market from their families, farms and factories.[110] They supply the flexibility that global capital needs. Two-thirds of all part-time workers and 60 percent of all temporary workers are women.[111] These women also supply enormous sustenance in the families they rear, and private needs they meet within this domestic sphere. As privatized markets unemploy women and dismantle state subsidies and access in eastern europe, and superexploit women in southeast asian factories, the global market unsettles a key network of domestic support.

The global marketplace is premised on a transnational sexual division of labor. Global capital displaces the economic nation while relying on women in the family to nurture the globe. Women bear and rear children *and* they labor in the sexual ghettoes of the global market. In asia, africa, and the middle east, those women who work outside the home are mostly agricultural laborers. In hong kong, south korea, and singapore, growing numbers of women are employed in the factories. In first-world countries, women disproportionately provide the low-paid service-sector labor. This is also often true in south america.[112]

The fantasmatic anglo-western woman is marketed in and by the global economy, as symbolic of the market's freedom. This contrasts with the subordination of women in the global market. The contrast criss-crosses and unsettles the relations between family, nation, and globe. As public space is renegotiated, the masculinist dimensions of the globe are both exposed and promoted. This may just become a major stumbling block for global capital.

As global capital shrinks space and time it allows for the subversive possibility of women seeing beyond the local to the global. This move puts male privilege clearly in view, as never before.

PART II

BEYOND NATIONS

5

FEMINISM OF THE NORTH

AND WEST FOR EXPORT

I shift here to the use of western feminism by the global economy as a marketing device by first-world markets. Glitzy advertising and romanticized displays fantasize the freedom of the "west." Beautiful, healthy, fashionable women become images for the promise of democracy. This feminism of the west "for export" is used to construct the new-old gender borders of the global economy alongside and in dialogue with corporatist multiculturalism. This process utilizes multiracialism while establishing western cultural hegemony of the market. Women's bodies are the sites for these renegotiations.

This mass-marketing strategy has troublesome effects for women of color and poor women across color divides inside and outside the west. I'll show here how western feminism[1] is itself being privatized by the market and reduced to self-help strategies while women, especially poor women, are losing too much of their public assistance as government programs are downsized. This mass marketing of a de-politicized feminism is crucial to the downsizing and privatizing of the u.s. government. The market advertises the successes of feminism as justificatory of the rollbacks of an affirmative-action state. I'll also argue that the rearticulation of race/sex/gender borders for the twenty-first century is undermined by the global market even as the boundaries of the fantasmatic "east" and "west" are re-encoded in the "export" version of feminism.

Unlike other post–cold war, post–gulf war "isms"—nationalism, multiculturalism, and globalism—feminism calls attention to women. And western feminism is only one variety of feminism, and has itself multiple meanings. Women of the first-world west of differing economic classes view feminist concerns in a variety of ways. Further multiply these varieties with the differing views among women of color. Then criss-cross this diversity across color lines.

Within western feminisms there is debate and dialogue among radical, cultural, and liberal feminists. And these divisions exist within every racial/ethnic divide. Recombine this with a popularized media feminism that takes what it wants from each and forgets the rest, and you begin to fathom the difficulty of sorting out what any individual or media corporation means by "feminism."

This only begins to suggest the multiplicity within western feminisms. Yet feminism of the "west," as it is marketed, is a caricature of sex equality *and* victimhood; it becomes a fantasmatic nightmare, both locally and globally. Feminism operates discursively: a hatred of men, an insistence on equal rights, and a victim ideology that calls for protectionist policies which stand in for each other *and* are positioned against one another. To complicate things further, feminism "for export" creates its own allure.

This popularized/publicized[2] feminism is marketed domestically as well as offered as part of colonialist and global politics. Some of the variants hegemonize the "west"; others assist the porn industry in eastern europe; others are used to mass market products within our own borders. Some variants are used to demonize white women in communities of women of color; others are used to criticize women of color, saying they indicate racial disloyalty. Others are used to normalize feminism and strip it of its militant voice.

The market flattens out and transforms the complexity. Often it is these versions that women in the u.s. and third-world-south and -east countries reject as feminism. But before I turn to feminism in eastern and central europe and the muslim world, let me focus on marketized/popularized feminisms in the u.s.

My focus in this chapter is not on global feminism or feminisms across the globe, but rather on the dominance of western feminism

in the global market. This dominance does not occlude the development of other feminisms, in other countries, or subsume these feminisms to variations of western feminism. Margot Badran makes criti-
cally clear that egyptian feminism was not and is not limited to
dialogue with feminisms of the west. Instead, feminisms in other
countries develop within "their own political cultures and pasts and
might themselves have reconstructed western feminisms."[3]

Living in the west, and looking from the west where images for
export originate and are packaged, I explore, to better see, the writings on women's bodies in the global market.

"DISCIPLINING" FEMINISM FROM
INSIDE THE NATION

Much political talk today, about women, acts to neutralize
once-militant ideas. This happens more often as the borders
between public and private become further skewed and the lines
between politics and culture are muted. As the government gets
more privatized, our president visits talk shows. As the nation is
reconfigured for globalism, there is more need to co-opt political
militancy into the privatized stances of the market.

So Newt Gingrich embraces the Internet and seems quite modern. He appoints several Republican women to lead congressional
committees while also making clear that women do not belong in
combat if it involves hostile fire.[4] One is supposed to ignore the
inconsistency that combat means hostile fire. One is also to ignore
that Gingrich is *not* a feminist.

When Bill Clinton and Hillary Rodham Clinton moved into the
White House there was much noise about a new kind of democrat
and a new kind of presidential wife. Things would be different
because the world is changing: Bill would initiate a health-care plan
that would jump-start the economy and take us competitively into
the twenty-first century, and Hillary would oversee the process.

This seems like a very long time ago now, a time when there was
still some hope that Bill Clinton might hold the line against greed.

It was also before the multiply orchestrated Hillary transitions.
Her shifting borders and ambiguity are much like the contours of
gender today.[5] She is used to symbolize and write the contradictory

meanings of motherhood, wifehood, and nation as they collide with feminism. Given one read, she stands for the marketed/popularized version of feminism: she's white, and professional, and smart, and determined; she has a child but doesn't spend much time raising her; she appears aloof and focused on power; she cares about her maiden name.

But this is only one depiction. Hillary also changes her hairdos, wonders why she's not liked more by the public, and chooses not to identify herself with the women's movement. She carries a message to the nation in global times: as able as she is, she still is not president—she is *his* wife. It's her glass ceiling, and she'll live with it. But she tries to do it differently, more actively, as a professional type. She gets nailed at every turn. People keep asking, "Who elected her, anyway?" They forget to ask about all the men in charge we haven't chosen either.

Even though Hillary has never identified herself as a feminist activist, feminism has been attached to her: defame one and hurt the other. It is so much trickier than with Nancy Reagan or Barbara Bush. They stood clearly as wives, not as professionals. They deferred to their husbands in ways that made clear that their first duty was as wife and mother. They were first lady to the old kind of nation. The imaginary is what counts. To hear Patti Reagan's version of Nancy's style of motherhood, one is left to wonder exactly how the imaginary reproduces itself.

Barbara and Nancy did not ask the public to negotiate their selfhood, and Hillary does. Hillary wants to rewrite her role as citizen-wife for post–cold war times. As an active player/co-equal partner she needs new rules; just as global capital needs new rules. But gender changes are even more unsettling than global ones. So her media experts nervously write old stories on her: headbands, pageboy hairdos, pink angora sweaters.

Mass-media culture and politicized markets confuse feminism with successful women. This makes trying to decipher what all this means quite tricky. Not only are there a variety of feminisms, but the first lady, as successful professional woman, is supposedly one of "us," whoever the "us" is. The borders of feminism are left fluid and manipulable for the nation: popular culture vaporizes feminism while it privatizes it for the market and depoliticizes it for the state.

At stake here are the boundary lines of gender for the transnational globe. Gender borders are always being reconstructed, and Bill and Hillary are a national reminder of this process. Richard Nixon warned of this when he snarled that a strong woman makes a man look weak. The weakness in the national imagination reads as effeminate, or homosexual. No wonder all the upset surrounding Bill's draft dodging, and his early foray into the arena of gays in the military.

The assaults on feminism arise from multiple cultural spaces. Much like liberalism, feminism is attacked for being too radical in all its varieties: too committed to sexual equality, to its victimhood, to sexual freedom, to women's difference, to women's sameness. Forget that no one feminism is depicted fairly here. And forget that the earliest forms of western feminism were *radically* liberal in that they demanded women's inclusion into the bourgeois/liberal individualism of the day. The equal-rights doctrine followed suit.

The backlash today is deep and profound: it is against individualism as it operates *radically* for women. The market has to transform the militancy of this feminist individualism into consumerism. It attempts to do this by focusing on freedom, which the mass market absorbs, instead of equality, which the market rejects. Feminism gets redefined as an individualized consumer self-help market; and the politics surrounding the struggle for equality drops out the bottom.

MASS-MARKETED POP FEMINISM

Although few politicians call themselves feminist, fewer yet would publicly challenge mainstream equal-rights feminism. This absorption into the mainstream has neutralized liberal feminism, as though women were already equal and feminism were no longer needed.

Simultaneously, however, depictions of women's victimization and powerlessness blanket the media. Talk shows are filled with concerns originally articulated by radical feminists: date rape, pornography, incest, sexual abuse, etc. But the media disconnects the original critique of patriarchal privilege from the sexual battery.[6] Whereas radical feminists connected the personal to the political, media depictions of sexual violence appear individualized and privatized. There is no politics to the personal because the personal is made private. "Sexual politics" and the uncovering of power-defined private moments is mass marketed.

Patriarchal privilege is depoliticized through a stunning array of individual women's tragedies. Many of these moments are further appropriated by TV news. O. J. Simpson decries that his marriage was abusive for both himself and Nicole, and both become victim and victimizer. In this instance, the abuse is not merely neutralized, but concealed.

The consumer side of feminist discourse and its commercialization operate both to publicize feminist concerns and to disconnect these issues from their radical critique of male privilege. The popularization mainstreams their radically political content, although not completely. This process of depoliticization is similar to the corporatist use of multiculturalism, but in this instance the market focuses and isolates gender. Corporatist multiculturalism pluralizes ethnicity while privileging euro-american centrism. Feminism, in its mass-market guise, popularizes women's victimization while leaving the phallus intact.

Interestingly, the racialized aspects of sexuality recombine in the market's attempt at neutralization. Anita Hill[7] and O. J. Simpson became household names in large part because of the popularization and mass marketing of feminist concerns *and* the racialized content of their meaning. Both these cases, though quite different, are instances of the already popularized cultural discussions of sexual harassment and domestic violence, and their interplay with race. Anita Hill's testimony about her experience of sexual harassment mobilized women in extraordinary ways.[8]

The marketing of feminist concerns in the popular media crisscrosses the arenas of racial hate and sexual violence. It is why the Simpson trial was a media bonanza: domestic violence meets football star; interracial marriage meets racial hatred; racism meets sexism. Then mix up the players on both sides of the courtroom by race and sex, and one has a significant cultural event.

Take the media's attention to Hugh Grant's tryst with a prostitute. The excessive coverage positions the bad black hooker against the good, white girlfriend. They are treated quite differently by the media, although Richard Goldstein of the *Village Voice* points to their similarity. According to Goldstein, both of them "make their living by submitting to the dictates of male desire."[9] Meanwhile the tabloids recreate the racialized borders of good-rich girl/bad-poor girl. All the while, we are told this is a story about Hugh Grant.

Each media event is framed by a familiarized public/feminist discourse. Anti-porn, anti-prostitution feminism is the backdrop for the media's viewing of the Grant affair. Domestic violence and sexual harassment were already in dialogue before the Hill/Thomas hearings and the Simpson trial. These events would have never been publicized as much or as sensationally as they were if they did not intersect with these discourses. And the events further publicized the discourses they were dependent on. The contours intersect: feminist concerns are neutralized by endless media viewing of them, while the concerns are nurtured and reified by public exposure. There is no simple neat fit here.

The process of popularization blurs the lines between using women as icons for the market and encoding feminist claims. These conflictual processes operate to create the fantasmatic of success: of a Jacqueline Kennedy, a Hillary Clinton, an Oprah Winfrey, a Nancy Kerrigan, or a Madonna. The mass marketing absorbs, publicizes, normalizes and disciplines *all at the same time*. The marketing redefines the boundaries between privacy and publicness, inside and outside, mainstream politics and mass culture, feminist language and women's identities. Radical feminist politics drops out of the renegotiated boundaries, and woman's victim status becomes the new voyeurism.

Feminists are said to wallow in their victimhood while this very status is used to underwrite a huge industry. TV news, talk shows, newspapers, self-help books, videos, movies, tabloids, and MTV write their own texts with the words and images from feminist discourse. So even trials and politics have become a part of this mass-culture market. In this media-driven age, elections and courtrooms have none of the boundary markers they once had. Politics enters our bedrooms on TV and collapses the public/private divide, but not entirely.

One cannot completely neutralize/popularize feminism when the destruction of male patriarchal/racial privilege will never be fully popular. So pop feminism distorts feminism by depoliticizing it and burying its complexities, and in so diminished a state it has no power to vanquish the male privilege that women experience in their everyday lives.

So the language of sexual violence and battery is used to catch women's attention, rather than change their lives. This mass-marketed feminism is a bit like fat-free food. Fat-free food won't make you healthy, and pop/market feminism won't make you equal or stop domestic violence.

The trick of mass-marketed pop feminism is that it gets people's attention. Victimhood and sex sell. Liberal feminism's opportunity/equality focus isn't sexy enough for the market these days. And, sadly, its demands have either become neutralized or have (once again) become too radical for the neocons. Nevertheless, feminism of the west, as export, mixes the two. It advertises women in the u.s. as sexy—"free and equal"—to third-world-southern and -eastern countries. The media moguls just forget to mention domestic battery and the glass ceiling and poverty rates among women here.

Responses vary. Some women in eastern europe react suspiciously to the equal-rights stance of feminism, which sounds too reminiscent of statist communism. Some muslim fundamentalists, as well as women in muslim countries, reject the pop/market version of "man-hating" feminism as the worst of the excesses of western colonialism. These misreadings and misuses—with their transnational effect—construct anti-feminist stances both at home and abroad.

Pop/market feminism—which is in large part a deradicalized radical feminism in disguise—distorts the complex relationship and history between liberal and radical feminism. Whereas liberal feminism's commitment to legal/economic equality dominated mainstream feminism in the early 1970s, radical feminism existed on the fringes, demanding an end to the entire patriarchal structuring of society. This restructuring inaugurated a new politics of sex: masculinist sexual hierarchy and privilege was to be destroyed. Equality was not enough. Instead women needed freedom from masculinism to become what they might desire.

Today, although some aspects of liberal feminist equality discourse have been incorporated into everyday language, much remains unchanged. Making an idea mainstream is not equivalent to creating its reality. Saying women are to be treated equally is not the same as equal treatment. Expecting women on welfare to find jobs is not the same an enabling them to do so.

The limitations of political/legal talk are clearly in evidence if one is poor and needs an abortion. Even though one has the right to choose an abortion—as an idea—one may not be able to get an abortion—as the real.[10]

Some feminist successes act to conceal the continuation of patriarchal structures that radical feminists target for dismantling. I have long argued that feminism cannot be contained within the individualist model of opportunity. I believe that liberal feminism—with its individualism (liberal rights) and collectivism (recognition of women as a sexual class)—strains to radicalize beyond itself.[11] The inclusion of women is never simple addition; a fundamental rearrangement of some kind is always necessitated. And equality, even when it simply means sameness of treatment, is always destabilizing to racialized/patriarchal layerings.

Liberalism and liberal feminism have become way too radical for the new north american global state *at the same time* that they are marketed. Radical feminism has always been too radical. But the pop/mass/culture market has blended the two in brilliant fashion. The radical/structural critique of patriarchy has been reduced to a personal/individualized statement of victimhood. Therapy and recovery have become the solution. TV is very often its mode. The radical future of liberal feminism has been renegotiated to read as the privatized future of radical feminism.

An individualized and depoliticized feminism distorts women's lives. And in no time at all feminism is used to focus on men themselves, who we are told face these problems too. Sexual issues are disabused of their gendered and racial content, and white men become the renewed focus. Or as the film *Disclosure* makes clear: "if you want harassment to seem serious, do it to a man instead of a woman."[12]

So feminism is everywhere and nowhere. It operates in veiled references and orchestrated absences. It is disparaged at the same time that it is embraced. It becomes the perfect fictive symbol. Few ever quite know what it means, but it is the fantasy to fear.

FEMINIZING THE MAINSTREAM

Today, feminism is simultaneously text and subtext, named and unnamed. It has no simple narrative to chart. Instead there are multiple sound bites. It operates a lot like vaporized corporatist multiculturalism for transnational capital.

Enter Anita Hill, again. She's not a likely candidate for feminism of any stripe. She's a conservative republican black woman. But she tapped the fear/anger about sexual harassment of many women, and at first she evoked a tidal wave of "feminist" reaction. A group of black women formed a network called African American Women in Defense of Ourselves to have a forum for public debate on the hearings. Amid the concern, Carol Moseley Braun of Illinois was elected along with four other women to the senate. The next year, '92, was even said to be "the year of the woman." But still, one could say, little changed. Clarence Thomas sits on the high court and Bob Packwood, accused by many women of sexual harassment, remained in congress for too long.

Enter the military. Women have been trying to qualify for combat for years. Women fought in the gulf war in record numbers, and this demanded a rethinking of gender borders for post–cold war militarism.[13] So the rules have shifted some. Women can now fly combat planes and partake in combat as long as the combat is not likely to involve direct fire. I keep mulling over the distinction between combat and direct fire and cannot find one.[14] What this new rule changes is unclear, which is exactly the point.[15]

Enter the military again. This time the issue is gays in the military. Given the recent changes it is now OK to say that you are gay as long as you do not "act" gay; or you can "act" gay as long as you do not say that you are. Sometimes the status/conduct distinction does not hold, and then you cannot say that you are gay, unless you can prove you are not acting gay. This new unclear policy renews the old evasive, yet punitive policy: "don't ask, don't tell."[16]

Enter President Clinton. Right after the presidential election he

got angry with feminist groups for demanding too many appoint-
ments from his administration, and called them "bean counters."[17]
Then he consecutively nominated Zoe Baird and Kimba Wood for
attorney general. Both are successful professional women who were
pressured/forced to step aside because of their nanny problems.
Their nannies were undocumented immigrants. Illegal undocumented workers both stood in for and covered the problems of child care
for professional parents. Baird's and Wood's class privilege was easy
to use against them, positioned as it was against their practices of
motherhood; and feminism got encoded through rich white women
who hire undocumented workers on the cheap. This is all partially
true and partially not true. Through all of this Hillary, though clearly
a professional mom, said nothing.

It should not be lost on us that Clinton had to find an unmar-
ried woman with no children to fill the attorney general position.
She then told us, in code, that she is not a lesbian, that she really
likes men.

But there is no simple narrative or singular performance here.
Shortly after being elected, Clinton approved the Family Leave Act;
he changed constraints on the abortion pill RU486; he repealed the
gag rule limiting discussion of abortion in federally funded clinics; he
initiated, though later bungled, efforts to end the ban on gays in the
military.

The sexual/gender relations of family and nation and globe are
incoherently changing, *and* they remain strikingly unchanged. More
women enter government, *and* they still must find day care. There is
a family leave act, *and* women still can't afford to take leave without
pay. The gag rule was repealed, *and* federal clinics are being defund-
ed and closed. The chaos is *also* utterly orderly.

The nomination and then the quick withdrawal of Lani Guinier
for assistant attorney general for civil rights reveals the intense
political conflict over racial/sexual/gender borders for the nation.
Clinton's "waffling" is not simply a psychological disorder. Waffling is
in part a political stance amid flux, chaos, and change.

Guinier's nomination highlights the racial *and* gender challenges for defining today's public/political arena. She is a woman of
color who is supposed to enforce civil rights for a government whose

supreme court has already dismantled its affirmative-action law.[18]

Lani Guinier's nomination was dropped because Clinton said he did not share her vision of racial equality.[19] Supposedly, he did not know her views on proportional representation beforehand. If this is true, it underscores the tokenism of her appointment. Her ideas really did not matter. Her color and her sex did.

Clinton was so scared Guinier would be seen as a "quota queen" that he silenced public discussion before it could happen. Guinier wished only that a national conversation about race would be allowed.[20] Meanwhile she was characterized as a radical black woman who would unfairly enforce racial quotas. Her more complex identity, as a daughter of a white jew and black man, was pushed to the side. So were her complicated views about single-member racial districts.

Instead, Guinier was made to appear so reckless and radical that there was nothing more to be said; she exceeded the bounds of acceptable performance.[21] Dumping Guinier amounted to dumping the affirmative governmental civil-rights project. A narrowed, less interventionist government role in civil rights was put in its place. It is not completely irrelevant that this message is silently translated for us by a black woman: her body gives the double message that the rights of women *and* people of color are up for grabs.

When President Clinton fired Surgeon General Joycelyn Elders we were told that she had been continually stepping out of line, and this was the last straw. She was said to repeatedly speak out of turn so she had been under surveillance for some time before the final rebuke. Elders was depicted as untamable, and not a team player. Eventually she was fired for speaking about masturbation after being asked to address its appropriateness as part of an educational campaign to fight the spread of AIDS.

Elders had responded to the question about AIDS that full discussion and exploration of all sexual practices were required if the attempt to limit AIDS infection was to be successful. Right-wing groups, after hearing this response, said it was unacceptable. She then was told by Clinton that her remarks at the AIDS conference violated the administration's position on masturbation. One cannot help but wonder what this position might be: one can masturbate, as long as one does not speak of it?

The disciplining of Elders as another unruly black woman unleashes the multiple intersecting communities that are represented on and through her body: people of color and out-of-control sexuality, black feminists and their concerns with health care for the poor, AIDS, drugs, sex, and gays. Masturbation was the performance code word here.[22] She had crossed the boundaries of decency.

It's easy to forget in this cacophony of contradictory and elliptical messages that Clinton asked Maya Angelou to deliver the inaugural poem. Her voice was mesmerizing on that day. As a black woman she spoke of the multiplicity of peoples that constitute the nation. She was visually significant: her black skin and female body made the nation look a little different. But only a little different, because this same body contrasted with, and was a boundary marker for, *all* the white men surrounding her. Her bodily presence promised a different imaginary for the nation while *also* taking the promise back.

The color-coding of gender issues has been a theme for Clinton. During the summer of '92, shortly before the Republican presidential convention, Clinton denounced the racial hatred of rap singer Sister Souljah. He said that racial hatred by blacks toward whites would not be countenanced. Clinton's disciplining of racial talk was done paternalistically. He used his rebuke of Sister Souljah, who had shared the platform with Jesse Jackson, to distance himself from Jackson-style democratic politics. Clinton had a new racial style in mind.

Black women are key to the symbolized and coded messages about race and nation. Their radical and unruly fantasized status as black "bitches" and "welfare dependents" undermines the legitimacy of civil-rights talk, while displacing their womanhood. As displaced, they are used to undermine claims made by white women and people of color as the nation is re-raced and re-gendered for transnational capital.

The '94 congressional elections were a culmination of this racial/gender politics. White men and white women who spoke for the nation as such, won. The rest of us, actually most of us, stayed home. 1994 was an expression of a kind of new nationalism that has taken hold here: buy american and protect "the" nation and "the" family. This republican backlash, which also crosses party lines, defines the enemy as illegal immigrants, women and children on welfare, and an overly committed government that must be privatized. Feminism and civil rights are the enemies of this nation.

This backlash, in part, conflicts with corporatist *and* radically pluralist multiculturalism; and trans*nationa*list capital initiatives. The new boundaries of the economic nation highlight the boundary lines that circle around the family, race, and sexuality. This complicates the reactionary political offensive led by Bob Dole and Newt Gingrich: the global economy and multiracial globe create new challenges for their imaginary nation. And it is not only right-wing white men who are angry. New right-wing women's groups like the Independent Women's Forum seem bent on dismantling many of the programs initiated by feminist reforms of the last two decades.[23]

At present, *transnational*ism is vying against a protectionist u.s. *national*ism. Multiculturalism is vying against racial homogeneity. People of color and white women are vying against privatization of the state and the downsizing of their entitlements. The u.s. economy declines while an unthinking nationalism subverts twenty-first-century developments. And twenty-first-century developments subvert any conception of a social welfare state.

Jesse Helms, Strom Thurmond, and Bob Dole want to keep the twenty-first century from happening. Newt Gingrich wants the Internet, but otherwise his head is in the sand. Newt thinks women's readiness for combat duty is comprised by their "female biological problems" which would make them prone to infection if they had to stay in a ditch for 30 days. He *also* says that if combat duty requires "manning" computer controls, "a female may be dramatically better than a male who gets very, very, frustrated sitting in a chair all the time." He's willing to give women opportunity but leaves in place his biological myths: "males are biologically driven to go out and hunt giraffe" whereas women are more sedentary.[24] He naturalizes patriarchal assumptions while adopting opportunity rhetoric.

Newt's sloppy biologism is uncomfortably similar to Murray and Herrnstein's racial bell curve.[25] They use biology to undermine equality claims. And nature itself is called upon to undermine the demands of women and people of color. Women of color are the clearest losers here. They symbolize racial *and* sexual biological constraints. As such, women of color construct and define the limitations of what the nation *is not* and *cannot* be.

In spite of, and because of all the above, the "issue" of race will supply the narrative of the '96 presidential election. At the time of this writing, Clinton has decided to stand firm in his defense of affirmative-action hiring. He says that affirmative action "has been good for America."[26] We will have to wait and see if he holds to this global corporatist multiracial line or not.

"MASSIFYING" FEMINISM AND FEMINIZING MASS CULTURE

Movies, TV, and newspapers continually narrate the changes in women's lives. They visualize the changes for us as an unruly combination of conflictual images. They also are a constant reminder of what has not changed. The messages simultaneously naturalize women as part of the landscape and differentiate them as "other." Women have entered arenas that were once closed. They have also demanded fairness of treatment, thus bringing about constant critique if not actual effect.

Mass culture's narratives tell a series of stories without a story line. There are moments of intense exposure. Then silences. Memory becomes difficult. Between these media lapses "the" national imaginary is constructed.

Nancy Kerrigan and Tonya Harding were one such media moment. Kerrigan and Harding, representing "the" nation at the olympics, sent conflicted messages about womanhood and nation status. Tonya was ruined by the crippling effects of competitiveness as well as a dysfunctional family. Kerrigan, hard as she tried, was runner-up. In the end, Kerrigan was made to seem silly and petty waving alongside Mickey Mouse at Disneyland. Women are not able to represent "the" nation well, even when they are supposed to.

Another narrative came in Gennifer Flowers' and Paula Jones's claims that they had been involved in sexual liaisons with the president. It is open season on the public/private divide, and men are learning that there is less privacy for their duplicity today. The new state moralism publicizes the bedroom and privatizes everything else.

The Tailhook scandal, declaring the sexual harassment of women by uniformed officers for all to see, publicly interrogated the sexual behavior of the military. Few penalties of any consequence were handed out, however.

Madonna flaunts her sexuality as power. She, of course, can afford to pay for several bodyguards.

Abortion clinics are under siege, and doctors are murdered.

The film *The Piano* offers women muteness as a power stance.

Another film, *The River Wild*, presents a woman strong enough to tame the rapids but does not let us forget that the woman's son is in the raft with her, and that it is her husband who saves the day.

Little Women is not a huge box-office hit because men and boys choose not to see it. Its movie theaters are filled mostly with girls and women.

Interview with the Vampire homoerotizes the multiraciality of blood as women are sucked to death.

TV exposes and constructs sexual abuse, domestic battery, and rape as part of mass culture. They seem more a natural part of life than a concern of feminism. The violence seems inevitable whereas feminism demands a response. One can tune in to any talk show to hear people tell of their abuse or their survival. No confession seems out of the realm of possibility.

The publicness of trial on/by TV presents a particularly complicated narrative for feminists. Rape trials like Mike Tyson's or William Kennedy's call forth feminists' condemnation of rape at the same time that race and class privilege act to co-opt the analysis. Instead of seeing the intersections, each is served up against the "other."

Lyle and Eric Menendez's defense for murdering their parents relied upon the discourse of sexual abuse. But the discourse was used with no recognition of its originary feminist content. Sexual abuse becomes disembodied and depoliticized, part of the mass-culture market.

Lorena Bobbitt spoke of sexual battery while explaining why she cut off her husband's penis. She cried and appeared very much a victim while her husband, the aggressor, also became the victim. And feminists were asked to clarify that they do not condone cutting off body parts.

Susan Smith killed her two young sons, then accused a black man of kidnapping them, and was spared the death penalty on the basis of her own sexual abuse as a teenager. The trial was not televised, but the unrelenting media attention created a spectacular viewing of the seamy side of abusive family life.

Televised trials and talk shows allow for a continuous public viewing of these private/sexual issues that were originally publicized by feminists working against domestic violence. The O. J. Simpson trial is a fantasmatic viewing of spousal abuse and domestic violence through a racially charged lens. It is the perfect media event because it displaces the intersections between racial and gender identity. As such, it becomes a spectacle meaning everything about race and sex, *and* nothing at all.

The Simpsons were an interracial couple. The defense team was interracial; the prosecutorial team was interracial and of mixed gender. So were the witnesses for both sides. This complicates the racial/gender viewing. Black witness is challenged by black counsel. White witness is challenged by black counsel. White witness is challenged by white counsel. Women are interrogated by men, and men are interrogated by women. Both Nicole Simpson's years of domestic violence and the Rodney King beating by the los angeles police department haunted the proceedings.

To complicate matters further, the Simpson trial was not just about O. J. As one cab driver said: "So many black men have been hung, lynched, and killed for things they didn't do, that it's time for a black man to get off for something he did do." Or from a somewhat different angle, Nick Charles, writing for the *Village Voice*, says that some blacks hope that the "system may betray its own agenda and vindicate a black man. And by extension vindicate us."[27] Black women seem to get the short shrift or are almost absent here, like O. J.'s first wife. They are caught in between sexual abuse and their color. And white women are placed in a complicated position as the lynching trope is reactivated.

O. J.'s maneuvers are similar to those of Clarence Thomas. Thomas also claimed that Hill's accusations exposed him to unconscionable racism, "a high-tech lynching." His charge of racism was used to deflect the sexual-harassment claim. Thomas tried to cover up one with the other, and in part he succeeded.[28]

Race is always an issue in a color-coded society, so it is significant that black men are used to publicly symbolize the problems of sexual harassment and domestic violence. When they then choose racism as their defense they encode black women's lives with an aura of unreality. And the representations and meanings float alongside whatever else attaches to them.

VICTIMIZING FEMINISM AND
NATIONALIZING THERAPY

Media/pop-culture feminism markets the ideas it thinks will sell. Dissent is even made part of this culture. So, in the end, women are made victims of their fear, be it rape or other sexual violence. And therapy, rather than politics, is presented as the answer. Or, as Hans Magnus Enzensberger says, "it is therapy, rather than the means of production, that has been nationalized."[29]

The mass media domesticates male violence. The National Rifle Association (NRA) takes this full circle as it uses feminist language to sell its guns to women. Their ads read: "Refuse to be a victim." The NRA represents the threat of violence as originating from outside the family: the burglar, the rapist on the street. Women can use semiautomatic rifles to protect themselves and their families.[30]

These advertisers encourage women to buy guns by using women's sense of vulnerability while publicizing the violence against women. Their goal is to sell guns, not stop violence against women.[31] However, the commercialization of this feminist concern cannot be completely co-opted because daily violence is exacerbated by the marketing of sexual fear.

Mass culture/pop feminism succeeds because it feminizes and individualizes feminism for privatized times. While pop/mass-media feminism advertises the victim status of women, the radical critique of male privilege is sanitized; feminist politics is effaced by market individualism. And the anxiety is displaced to the unruly borders of feminism.

This anger toward feminists is found among some who say they are feminist. These women blame feminism for overly identifying women *as* victims. This "feminist" critique of feminism laments the takeover of opportunity/equity feminism by radical feminists who see battery and victimization everywhere. Some lament that feminists are too busy trying to protect women from rape, pornography, and sexual abuse, and they say that women can take care of themselves. Others say they are sick of being frightened, or being told that they need to be careful.[32] They would do better to recognize the place of transnational capital in creating victim status, or the AIDS epidemic in defining a protectionist sexuality, rather than blaming feminists. Anyway, feminists come in all sizes and shapes. Some like to envision the possibility of anti-sexist porn, others are anti-porn, others think domestic violence is the key issue facing women today, others do not.

This anger directed at feminists is a bit curious. I wish feminism had the power being attributed to it. I'm not saying that there aren't aspects of feminism that elicit protectionist stances.[33] The indictment of masculinist privilege can overstate women's powerlessness, their victim status. But feminism *as part of* popularized culture is both defined by victimization and a lens on it. It cannot help but get contaminated to some degree.

Feminism is neither innocent nor guilty here. Instead it is held hostage by the mass media's packaging of victimized women *while* it condemns the violence toward women. Feminism theorizes that wherever there is a victim there is a struggle over power, and that the potential for resistance always exists.[34] But the market does not theorize resistance for us.

The individualism of feminism that underwrites the significance of women as a larger community also makes feminism highly susceptible to being marketed; sexual violence can be reduced to its individual experiences; consciousness raising to an individual therapeutic moment. Political solutions are shunted aside.

Naomi Wolf says it is now time to focus on "power" feminism rather than victim feminism. She writes: "Women are fed up with reminders of their own oppression." She says we should not form our identity from our powerlessness.[35] The problem is that victimization is a popular identity today; even our president markets himself as a "survivor." It is a status assigned to feminism by the pop-culture industry more than it is a chosen politics.

Much of the feminist critique of feminism is aimed at regulating the radicalism of feminism. The radicalism indicts the structural privileges of masculinity; it ties the personal and sexual to the racialized class meanings of identity. Feminism is different from a talk-show confessional which exposes the privileges of masculinity and then leaves them pretty much as they were before.

Vulnerability/victimhood is real. It gets more real as the globalization of capital complicates the dislocations due to transnational capital flight. Victimization works as a marketing strategy for translating fear into depoliticized venues while the u.s. struggles to find its way in the global market. The therapeutic model and self-help books construct a paternalist individualism that assists the new boundaries of transnationalism. One must depend on oneself and one's family, and not politics or the government for help.

The hierarchical gender borders questioned by feminism only unsettles the global change further. This is why the market tries to isolate women from feminism and renegotiate gender at the same time.

FEMINISM, NATION BUILDING, AND HILLARY

Nations need reconstructing when their contours change. With economic borders defined transnationally, and family structures challenged by multicultural/racial meanings, gender and racial borders become grist for the political mill. Hillary Rodham Clinton represents one icon of this process. It is not unimportant that as first lady she is supposed to symbolize the nation at its best. She stands as a metaphor for national politics, and no one metaphor seems to work well. Hence, her constant rewriting.

I have argued that women supply the icons for stabilizing the nation. Women populated the military and sanitized the gulf war as the "mother" of all wars.[36] Hillary Clinton serves her country; she is simultaneously wife and mother and civic servant and contested symbol of "power-feminism."[37]

As an icon, Hillary Clinton embodies the crisis of "the" nation. As a woman, she symbolizes the gender borders of the nation. As first lady she is supposed to represent a fantasmatic unity and stabilize boundaries. Instead, she unsettles them. She seems to be too independent, to feel too comfortable with power. This is not the kind of wife a shaky nation needs.

Hillary Rodham has made accommodations given her husband's job. She has done this because the nation needs this of all of its wives. But for some people, this is not enough. Hillary represents feminism to these people because she is not a homemaker. She enters a nationwide cookie-baking contest, but she does not gain much here. Instead, she becomes the cookie monster.[38]

Hillary Clinton does not readily identify with the women's movement.[39] She says little about most feminist issues: child care, abortion, prenatal care for poor women, etc., etc. Her silences inscribe a significant distance from the feminist movement.[40]

But the label sticks to her, whether she wants it or not. When Kathleen Gingrich, Newt's mother, called Hillary a bitch on national TV and then explained that Hillary was always taking over and won't be able to do that "with Newty there," few came to the rescue.[41] We are once again served up Hillary as domineering and pushy, the flip side of mass-market victim feminism. There are no apologies from Kathleen. Despite this, Hillary invites Newt and his mom to the White House the next day and performs as the forgiving woman/mother/wife. The gesture was a sign of unity.

With no private identity allowed, Hillary becomes the scapegoat for men and women who fear feminism—whatever they think it is. She unsettles sex/gender borders because she collides the symbolization of women with her presence. She provokes hostility because she is a wife first but not just a wife. She creates fear and hate because she is both stereotypic of feminism and not enough of a feminist. In this sense she is like any other woman because there is never a perfect fit between gender as we live it and its imaginary.

So some hate her because she is too much like them and is supposed to be different. She stays with a man who has told us all, in so many words, that he "betrayed" her, and he uses her skills to protect himself. Her marriage is supposed to sustain the nation, but it appears shaky. Her marriage looks too much like the rest of the country's: a contract of convenience. People do not want to be reminded that marriage is a sham. The nation does not need this right now.

The problem is that the Clintons are a bit too unsettling for unsettled times. Hillary represents the gender disorder that the nation needs to forget. This is all too much to handle. On the other hand, Bill's marital infidelities humanize Hillary as the suffering wife even if they democratize her a bit too much for everyone's liking. The aggressive bitch is refeminized while Bill the wimp is remasculinized.

Throughout the Gennifer Flowers episode Bill said little, and it was clear to anyone who *wanted* to read his silence that his private actions were his and Hillary's business. Hillary practiced avoidance and spoke protectively for Chelsea. When Hillary appeared with Bill for a TV interview to set the Flowers allegations straight she said she was no "stand-by-your-man woman." But to many watching, she sure did look like one. Victim-feminism looks a lot like power-feminism here.

Powerful women receive little support in our country.[42] Feminism also receives little support from powerful people. Feminism is not necessarily about powerful women, and powerful women are very often not feminist. So it should be no surprise that women working with Clinton say that he "likes the same white-male comfort zone that president George Bush did."[43] Hillary does and does not count in this viewing because she has no official position in the administration. She did not step in to save press secretary Dee Dee Myers her job because it would have crossed over the boundaries of her role as dutiful wife to Bill and "the" nation. Speaking on behalf of Myers, and questioning the white-male comfort zone is too subversive, like feminism, for the racial/gender borders of the nation.

Before becoming first lady, Hillary Rodham Clinton was a committed advocate for children's rights.[44] Despite her book *It Takes a Village,* there is little sign of this commitment now, while the attack against poor women and their children dominates the news. Such advocacy would position Hillary with a feminism that questions the privatizing of the state and the enforcement of traditional familial relations.

If she would speak on behalf of women it would be easier for feminists to let their fortunes be tied up with her. But as a mass-marketed icon of feminism, women lose if she loses, and we do not necessarily gain when she does. And she continues to accommodate power rather than use it on behalf of women.

One day we see her, then for weeks we don't. Then we see her poised and posed in a full-length spread in Vogue; her head is back, and she is wearing a long black dress with shoulders showing.[45] This public wooing of her husband is more than a little embarrassing. It contrasts with the symbolic polka-dot 1950s dress with big neck bow that she wore to unveil the start of her health-care plans. This time the wooing is a total domesticated mommy look; no sleek model or professional woman is in sight here. One wonders how many writings one body can absorb.

When Hillary presented the outlines of the health-care package on capitol hill she did so always positioned vis-à-vis a male patriarch: as a wife, a mother, and a daughter. She said she was "proud to serve her country." We are presented yet another viewing here: domesticated professional woman for the twenty-first century. She is wife and mother for the post–cold war nation.

This time Hillary subtextually advocates a "power-feminism" from her position as a devoted citizen with market appeal. According to Tamar Lewin of the *New York Times,* she focuses on what women can do, not on what they are kept from doing. She shows "no rage at men, no rhetoric about oppression or empowerment, not even a whisper of a Ms."[46] While on capitol hill we are shown her competence, her intelligence, her fortitude. She is "the feminist," recoded and neutralized as citizen-mother in a changing transnational and multicultural world.

Several months later she looks different and talks different, again. The health plan failed, and Hillary the professional is disciplined; she is domesticated back to her family, once again. Gender is rewritten on her body: her hair, her clothes, and her voice are rescripted. She tells a group of women reporters that she does not know who the woman is that she reads about in the news. She says she is sorry for making a mess of health care and will take the blame. She says she must work harder at being good.

So who is this? And why "women" reporters, anyway? The doublespeak of pop/market feminism reads: "I am 'just' a woman and will speak with others like me to make clear to the public that I will try harder to be like the woman they want me to be."

Hillary is speaking the language of personalized co-dependency on a national level while allegations of impropriety in the White House Travel Office firings and Whitewater investments swirl around her.

By March 1995, she has started to stress women and children's issues as she travels abroad. It is interesting to see how her focus shifts once she leaves the country. Once outside u.s. borders she speaks quite readily on behalf of poor women in india. She finds a new voice in which to read a young girl's poem in new delhi, titled "Silence." The clearly feminist poem asks for an end to women's silences.[47]

While in india Hillary meets with the Self-Employed Women's Association, which assists women in the largely invisible and informal economy of self-employed women.[48] She is very taken with their organization and praises its results in addressing women's poverty. From this space outside the u.s. Hillary criticizes the "rampant materialism and consumerism" of western countries.[49]

However, Hillary Clinton reinscribes the east/west divide in her depiction of women's lives in southeast asia. She states: "When I think about the women who've been imprisoned, tortured, discouraged, barred from involvement in education or professional opportunity—what any of us in America go through is minor in comparison."[50] Though Hillary means to highlight and condemn the official, state-mandated torture of women in other countries, she inadvertently slights the gross inequities affecting many women in the west. She legitimates (even if unwillingly) the quieting of feminist voices at home.

So Hillary leaves the country in order to speak as a feminist in other countries, and at united nation conferences on women. She takes feminism, as an export, abroad. She defines the backwardness of india as the backdrop for her concerns with "girls and women," which becomes a "human rights" issue.[51] Strangely enough, because she is speaking about children, some in the media now call her a traditional first lady. Wrong again.

Hillary has been called just about everything because the nation does not know what she needs to be.[52] Hillary merely em*bodies* the changing familial structures of the nation during globalization of the market while the nation needs more fluid borders than the racial/gender structure can easily deliver.

The "triumph of the image"[53] makes it impossible to see Hillary as she really is, whatever that means. And if this is true for Hillary, it is of course true for Bill. The two, as a presidential couple, are defined by each other. Hillary is too domineering; Bill waffles. Bill runs and has thunder thighs and loves junk food; Hillary likes vegetables. Bill talks too much and too long and is too empathetic. Hillary is short and curt. Bill is a womanizer, a survivor of an alcoholic and abusive father. Hillary knows how to cope.

People say they complement each other; he's feminized, and she is masculinized. They together represent opportunity discourse: she's a working mom. But the feminizing of Bill and masculinizing of Hillary problematize equality because it is pretty obvious that she could make as good a president as Bill, and yet she's just his wife. Meanwhile, we must pretend that she couldn't.[54] If this is equality, who needs it?

Bill and Hillary are the post–modern therapeutic couple. They know how to survive. They are willing to change, again and again. Their adaptability is their politics for the twenty-first century. They know how to redefine gender borders without dismantling them.

FUCKING WOMEN AND BUILDING NATIONS

Constructions of masculinity and femininity build nations, and masculinity depends a great deal on silencing and excluding women. Why? Because women upset the imagined femininity, more often than they do not.

So Hillary Clinton destabilizes the contours of politics as usual, simply by being a female who wants to actively participate. Golda Meir and Margaret Thatcher were hardly pacifist-woman types, but they visually destabilized the political as male. All the other heads of state were men. Gender borders are fragile and cannot take too much shaking up.

This fragility is why masculinity has to be continually positioned against homosexuality in the military, on the job, wherever. Once the heterosexist man/woman divide is denaturalized, the race/sex/gender contours of the nation seem as flexible as international capitalist loyalties. Clinton's early attempts to realign the sexual borders in the military, similar to his attempts to modernize the economic borders of the north american global network, were easily subverted. He did not stand his ground on the military. It was as though he did not understand the significance of what he challenged: the very orderliness of militarism and the nation. His own feminized status as a draft dodger only further highlighted the sex/gender militarist boundaries that his policy called into question.

Little good came from the entire exchange he initiated on gays in the military. Other than clarifying, for those who did not already know it, that gays can serve the military and the nation in patriotic ways, little has changed. Instead, the anti-gay militarist stance has been *re*newed for the post–cold war global era.

Pretense is important because people's sexual identities are too complex to railroad, and pigeonhole, even within militarist masculinism. Susan Faludi details this complexity when she describes several cadets at the Citadel—a military academy where nationhood is in the making. She describes the cadets' fascination with drag queens who hang out at a local bar. One of the drag queens says she makes her Citadel lover wear his military cap when they have sex. "It's manhood at its most."[55]

The men at the Citadel can opt into positions of submission that they would misogynistically associate with women if women were admitted. By keeping women out, they are able to enjoy homoerotic and sadomasochistic relations, as if these relations were consistent with what they regard as "normal masculinity."[56]

If sex/gender lines are so flexible and open, the creation of gender hierarchies becomes essential. It is why administrators at the Citadel want girls kept from cadet rank. They make clear that plenty of women occupy positions on the campus already. But being a cadet is being *like a man*, and the nurturing of this masculinity requires exclusivity.

Shannon Faulkner was admitted initially to the Citadel when the admissions board assumed she was a man. When they found out she was a woman, she was denied admittance. Then she demanded entry as an individual who happens to be a woman.[57]

It is hard to imagine why Shannon Faulkner wanted into the Citadel other than to test the waters of equality feminism: she has the (equal) right to join. But equality, meaning the sameness of treatment, does not do well by her. At first it meant that as a cadet, her hair would be shaved like a man's, and that she would stay in the barracks with no special protections. But a shaved woman's head is not the same as a man's: he is empowered by a short crop of hair while she is ostracized by it. So the Citadel decided that she need not be shaved; she need only cut her hair short. The school built her a private bathroom, along with video surveillance outside her room, to "protect" her from her newly won equality as a single (vulnerable) female among only males. Equality cannot and should not mean sameness here.

In her first week at the Citadel heat sickness overtook Shannon Faulkner and landed her in the infirmary for most of Hell Week. Then, after all she struggled through to get in, she announced that she was leaving. She said that life at the Citadel was too hard, and that she was too alone.

Of course she was too alone. The Citadel is about the making of men and not about letting women act like they are men. Every taunt a cadet hears equates him with women as objects of contempt: bitch, dyke, whore, lesbo. Lesbians are the worst.[58] A woman with no man is something to fear, hate, or lust after.

Military life supposedly creates the unity of family life. Men take care of each other and care about each other as though they are family. No women or gays are to be present to ruin the role "playing." Women would unmask the mother; gays would unveil the sexuality.

Pluralized sexual/gendered meanings and desires deeply challenge the homogeneous viewing of masculinity/femininity. These naturalized constructions of manliness become more important when economic nations are in transition. The transnational global economy and its multicultural web leave the protectors of the dwindling nation groping for what once worked for them.

Nation building at the Citadel sounds a bit like nation building in bosnia. Written on one of the men's rooms during Shannon Faulkner's appeal for equal entrance was: "Let her in...then fuck her to death."[59] It is an amazing statement of hatred from those she seeks to join. It makes the rules of entry clear: once you are in, we will teach you that you still are only a woman.

The Citadel, and bosnia, and gays in the military share the problem of nationalism in the context of militarism. Racial, gendered, and sexual boundaries are guarded so carefully in the world's militaries as a way of encoding the nation itself as masculine.

The hatreds expressed toward feminisms and people of color and gays bind the nation. Post–cold war nationalisms are obviously rooted in many of these old stories. As economies criss-cross and nations are carved geographically anew, race and its genders and gender and its races become re-naturalized and biologized. But not all is smooth here. The newly emerging transnationalized global relations need to write gender and race on the globe for the twenty-first century, when there is no neat or simple fit. So feminism is depoliticized in its pop/market export form while its feminist content remains subversive to the masculinist aspects of global capital.

The west publicizes sex *and* feminism of the west for export to the global market. The newly transnationalized economies are not necessarily ready to absorb this. Nor are third-world countries of the south and east. But western feminism for export has begun a dialogue of its own with women of these countries. Even the pope is worried about this dialogue. So in his 1995 papal letter on women, he apologized for those in the church "who have contributed to the oppression of women." And he acknowledged the need to "achieve real equality in every area: equal pay for equal work, protection for working mothers, fairness in career advancements, equality of spouses with regard to family rights."[60] He does all this *in order* to speak against abortion.

A transnational discussion among women is the most hopeful sign yet that it might be possible to think—together—through the nation and beyond transnational capital.

FEMINISMS OF THE

GLOBAL SOUTH AND EAST

Because I am of "the" west and north, my awareness and naming of feminisms across the globe can be only partial. Recognizing this, I go forward cautiously.

I look for any signs of women's actions within and against the nation poised against colonialism and global capitalism. And I do this while feminism of the west as export renegotiates the multiracial aspects of the globe for transnational capital.

Cosmopolitan magazine runs a lead story, "The State of Women in the World," in which it condemns the veiling of women in islam, child brides in india, sex clubs in thailand, and circumcision in egypt as contributory to "sexual slavery, female infanticide and wife abuse" across the globe.[1] The pop/market victim trope threads with the multiracialism of the globe to distance "east" from "west." In Walt Disney's *Aladdin*, one of its most profitable films to date, islamic gender, in the character of Jasmine, represents islamic culture in general. The european reading of the medieval persian story is presented in refigured cartoon form for post–gulf war america.[2]

Feminism of the west, as export, operates colonially and imperialistically in third-world countries of the south and east. And then it brings these women back to the west as foreigners. So women in these countries must find their way out of this complex situation on their own terms, needing a non-colonialist feminism to challenge the patriarchalism of third-world nationalisms.

There are many ways to think this dilemma through. Some women in iran who wear the veil support women's rights; others do not. Some women in algeria who identify as feminist mean that they support women's right to education; others mean the right to a good job. Some women in egypt, slovakia, and iran believe in these very issues, yet say they are not feminist. Some muslim women believe deeply in women's need to control their fertility but do not speak their views within their islamic communities. Some women in russia see abortion as a necessity and wish it weren't.

Many women in eastern europe, northern africa, and islamic countries want a dialogue between north and west *and* south and east. The u.s. itself is already home to many of these cultures. Women of poland, romania, the former soviet union, algeria, egypt, and so on, have histories that women in the west can learn from. Women in these countries often already know the westernized feminism exported globally. But they also need to know the more dissident western feminisms, particularly those of western women of color.

At this "post-modern" moment, particularly as it has affected feminist dialogue, the very idea of *woman* and her identity as *feminist* has been called into serious question. The arguments run as follows: that the category *woman* does not exist as such; that the categories of feminism regulate more than they free; that feminism is totalizing and homogenizing; that it misrepresents more than it represents.[3] I take each of these claims as a warning of what I do not want to do as I look for transnational, transcultural meanings for women in the global economy.

Although post-modernism's anti-essentialism is crucial to making a space for radically multicultural/racial feminisms, it also can destroy the willingness to build a politics that can recognize women. I am not arguing that there is one kind of feminism, or woman, or one kind of equality. Rather, I am saying that the debate should focus on recognizing different feminisms rather than questioning their theory. Let us use the dialogues between feminisms to build connections between these communities of women.

Feminism recognizes and names women as a collectivity. It is, in part, fantasy, an imaginary construction. It imagines beyond the differences between women to a community that respects diversity and radical pluralism. This pluralism recognizes a sharedness among women that is not a given, but is, rather, a possibility. Sometimes the conflicts are too great, and other allegiances overwhelm the possibility of feminist identities.

By naming women *at the start*, so to speak, I mean to call attention to their absences and silences in the "isms" of the twenty-first century. I want to denaturalize and denormalize the borders of sex, gender, family, and nation that women invisibly make visible. So I look at women and their lives as they struggle through post-'89 revolutionary moments and the aftermath of the gulf war.

The fall of communism has affected the entire globe, with particular penalties for women. The new nationalisms and the global economy are having devastating effects on women worldwide. Illiteracy, hunger, poor health, and childbirth circumscribe women's lives simply because *they are female*. Even the united nations has recently recognized the special global "plight" of women.[4]

I will strive to avoid falsely homogenizing women, as nationalism does, albeit for different purposes. And I will try to be inclusive while knowing that one can never be fully so. My inclusivity embraces radical differences in order to see expansive, transcultural, multiracial feminisms.   CHOOSE GENDER, RECREATE, PASS ON GENDER

FEMINISM, COLONIALISM, AND NATIONALISM

There is no one feminism. No one nationalism. No one patriarchy. No one colonialism. They take different shapes, are defined in and through different contexts, and have different histories. Anne McClintock, writing of women's struggles within the anti-apartheid movement in south africa, describes the historic women's anti–pass-book march in the 1950s demanding an end of state surveillance.[5]

South african black women asked white women, as mothers, how they could tolerate apartheid: "A mother is a mother, black or white. Stand up and be counted with other women."[6] McClintock argues that a transformed african discourse on feminism has emerged in which black women fashion feminism to their own needs. In 1990 the African National Congress embraced the emancipation of women, recognizing the independence of feminism and its misrepresentation in third-world countries.[7]

Feminism, as western export, is marketed as part of the promissory of western democracy and as contradictory to traditionalist islamic and patriarchal nationalisms. The challenge is not, however, to the masculinist privilege of islamic states and third-world nations, but to the way the gendered borders of these traditional discourses hinder the global market and marketing of women.

Countries of the south and east are depicted as backward. Just look at "their" women: they are veiled from head to toe, bound by traditionalism. Women in the west and north are modern and free: they even dressed in military khaki during the gulf war.[8]

These wrongly homogenized depictions of women's lives create multiple and unexpected responses. Although some aspects of western-export feminism delegitimize feminism in general in third-world nationalist movements and post-communist societies, this exported feminism also advertises the fantasmatic of the west's freedom, which is not completely co-optable.

The cultural flow charts are messy: the skepticism in eastern european countries of a feminism that sounds too similar to communist statist rhetoric about women's equality; the criticism of what Leila Ahmed calls "colonial feminism,"[9] which remains patriarchal at its core but also uses western women's position to undermine arab cultures; and the complicated dynamics of anti-colonialist nationalisms and the feminisms they create. As Margot Badran clarifies for women in egypt: their struggles against colonialism involved women in a "nationalist militancy" that was also tied to women's advancement.[10]

The complex mix in the global south and east derives from the uneven intersections of statist feminism—the state's abuse of equality discourse; colonialist feminism—western hegemony's symbolization of its women as representative of equality and modernity; pop/market western feminism—the mass-marketed view of u.s. women as sexy and free; and third-world anti-colonialist feminist discourses. Women in every region of the globe must interpret their particular set of historical and cultural meanings.

Women of the south and east also confront the white privilege of euro-american-centrism in western/liberal feminism. Their experience in their own countries is one of shadings of color: browns, light browns, dark browns, black-browns, etc. Corporatist multiculturalism does not renegotiate the white center for the globe, but adds differences around it. Racialized gender continues to operate here in the construction of border crossings. This is so even while "color" is often unacknowledged in many of these countries. I do not mean to impose color on those who disavow it as an issue, but I do wish to bring it to the foreground of global capital.

Western feminism is used by the global telecommunications networks—TV, e-mail, CNN news—as well as the film industry to define a colonialist/imperialist narrative that reconfigures barriers between women across the globe. Yet this same feminism is subversive to the patriarchal aspects of eastern european masculinism and arab/muslim male traditionalism. Western feminism, even in this pop/market export version, is promissory of a real equality for women. Global communications can reveal the redundancy of male privilege across and through racialized differences and masculinist nationalisms. As the world gets smaller it gets less equal, and easier to see. Women's plight is worsening worldwide.

Marnia Lazreg, writing of algerian women, says that we must *write* across cultures without assuming oppression. That one should not give arab women, middle eastern women, or algerian women an "identity that may not be theirs." She worries that categories over-categorize. She is hesitant about the phrase *women of color*, fearing that it reinscribes race rather than challenges the constraints of race.[11]

Leila Ahmed explains the complex relations between feminism and patriarchal colonialism, which, she argues, uses the language of feminism. Patriarchal colonialism "captures" feminism as such and uses "women's position in Islamic societies as the spearhead of the colonial attack on those societies."[12]

Statist communist regimes also reconfigured the feminist language of "equality" for their own purposes. This "capture" of women's needs by colonialism and statist communism creates a major dilemma for women in these parts of the globe. The misuse of feminist promises by these governments has created skepticism and cynicism. Transnational capital only complicates this further as it promises freedom for all.

Valentine Moghadam argues that the misrepresentation of islam through the symbolization of its "backward" women misrepresents islam as conflated with patriarchy *and* falsely homogenizes islamic women.[13] The world seems to have taken islamic fundamentalists to be representative of all muslims—a crucial error, Moghadam argues. According to her, islam is no more, nor less, patriarchal than any other religion. After all, "islam provided women with property rights for centuries while women in Europe were denied the same rights."[14]

Nevertheless, Moghadam also believes that middle eastern feminists have a difficult road to walk. To embrace gender equity, they have to embrace a national identity that celebrates its home culture but reject the patriarchal traditions of this nationalism.[15] As a result, a westernized woman is identified by nationalist discourse as part of imperialist culture. According to Badran, this is why many women who are pro-feminist shy away from the feminist label. However, this does not keep these women from gender activism alongside women who readily identify as feminist *or* islamist.[16]

In algeria, most young women do not wear a veil today, although many more of these women wore the hijab in the early 1990s. Darima Bennoune says that "wearing blue jeans has become an act of defiance" against islamic traditionalism. Many algerian women's groups acted together to force the abolition of algeria's 1984 Family Code, which legalized polygamy. Algerian writer Aicha Lemsine says: "Women are now the stake and symbol for the future course of Algeria."[17]

In this struggle, algerian women are being shot to death by islamic fundamentalists for holding jobs or choosing not to wear the veil. Since the violence began, at least forty-eight algerian women have been killed in the latest attempts by religious fundamentalists to take over the government. According to Youssef Ibrahim in the *New York Times*, by spring '94 a campaign had been launched "to kill wives, daughters and other women related to police and army personnel unless fundamentalist women were freed from Algerian prisons."[18]

As the economy creates new instability in turkey, islamic fundamentalists are gaining new legitimacy. The *New York Times* represents this unstable process pictorially: women in traditional dress walk on a street in istanbul, and the caption under the picture reads, "as a 'sign' of rising Islamic fundamentalism."[19]

Meanwhile, Nawal El Saadawi was imprisoned until 1981 in egypt for her feminist stances. She has been banished for her founding of the Arab Women's Solidarity Association and now lives in the u.s.[20] Taslim Nasrin, a bangladeshi writer who was forced into exile after questioning the role of women in the islamic world, writes: "I know if I ever go back I'll have to keep silent, stay inside my house. I'll never lead a normal life in my country, until my death."[21] Despite this, she has returned home.

Women—some of whom spoke as feminists, others not—transformed the worldwide discussion at the 1994 United Nations Conference on Population and Development in cairo. Documents from the conference strongly argue that population control cannot take place without the improvement of the status of women. This changed status requires women's control over their bodies and fertility,[22] and the women at the conference, many of whom were from the third-world-south and -east, demanded greater involvement in their own reproductive health.

The pope said no.[23] But many muslim countries said yes. Despite the pope, the "general powerlessness suffered by millions of women" was identified as a major world problem. There was widespread agreement that, as Wang Jiaxiang said, "women all over the world have a lot of things in common"[24]—simple as it may sound. The new official discourse of the UN recognizes the right of women to make their own decisions regarding their own fertility. The United Nations Fourth World Conference on Women, held in beijing in 1995, further elaborated this position and began to articulate a new and yet undefined notion of sexual rights for women.[25]

Equating the language of the cairo conference with westernized feminism was easy because of the identification of "rights." Masculinist islamic nationalisms had an easy time depicting the conference as a western conspiracy against the catholic church and islam that endorsed homosexuality, sex outside of marriage, and abortion. To the extent the conferences were associated with western feminism, it was easy to call forth the anti-family/rampant individualist underside of mass-market feminism. But to the extent that reproductive rights issues are not simply western, the assault was not wholly successful. Though some governments, such as egypt's, chose to align themselves with the vatican's position, many did not.

Women also crossed national borders and spoke collectively—even while disagreeing—at the World Conference on Human Rights in vienna, in 1993. Human-rights activists from across the globe demanded a recognition of the "acute human rights abuses suffered by women because they are women."[26] As Charlotte Bunch wrote, "the physical territory of this political struggle over what constitutes women's human rights is women's bodies."[27] Other writers, such as Alice Walker, Awa Thiam, and Nahid Toubia, have spoken out directly against female genital mutilation, claiming this territory as one of everyday torture and terrorism.[28]

Rosalind Petchesky, international coordinator of the International Reproductive Rights Research Action Group, says that the desire for women to know their bodies and be in control of them is overwhelming, and not solely western in origin. The definitions of these desires, whether in brazil, egypt, indonesia, malaysia, mexico, nigeria, philippines, or the u.s., reappear over and over again, even though they may be formulated differently.[29]

If one recognizes these desires, the tensions between various "isms"—third-world nationalisms and imperialism, traditionalism and globalism, westernized feminism and feminisms of "the" east and south—get reconfigured. Islamic nationalists choose to cover up these tensions, precluding new choices for women in the process.[30] This assists the equation between the nation and the invisibility of gender, as woman is symbolized *as* the nation. Muslim feminists ask for another scenario in its place: let feminism develop along with anti-imperialist and nationalist struggles.[31] Let those struggles create "their own symbolic universe,"[32] one that would eliminate what Badran calls "the persistence of indigenous patriarchal domination."[33]

If patriarchal nationalism is a counter to patriarchal colonialism, women in "the" east and south still must struggle to be seen and heard. Muslim women of third-world countries exist between and through multiple identities. Kumkum Sangari and Sudesh Vaid write that women in india face patriarchal ideologies in the constructs of tradition and modernity alike because both have been defined by colonialism.[34] These women experience their lives through the intersections of globalism, colonialism, nationalism, and multiculturalism. Each of these identities is threaded through traditionalist masculinism. For the women who feel constrained by these cross-pressures, they must rename for themselves a kind of feminism.

POST–GULF WAR GLOBALISM AND THE VEIL

The gulf war was a post–cold war phenomenon. It aligned new enemies to stand in for old hatreds. The u.s. fought against arab terrorism to protect democracy. It is not clear how kuwait represents democracy, but that concern gets lost along with everything else as the images of war triumph over the war the u.s. actually fought.[35]

The war was pictured on women's bodies. Women in military uniforms and chadors represented the north/west-south/east divide. This juxtaposition asks us to forget that many of these women in the gulf dress western, have university educations, practice medicine in women-only hospitals, etc. We are also asked to forget that many women in the u.s. military are there because it's the only job they could get or the only way they could finance their educations. Freedom *and* equality is a bit hard to come by on either side of the north/west-east divide. As Cynthia Enloe argues, "women of both countries are being turned into the currency with which men attempt to maintain the unequal relations between their societies."[36]

Many of the iraqi and kuwaiti women had little or no choice in this war. Tens of thousands of them died, along with their children. Those who survived still walk a tightrope between the patriarchalism of their own societies and the westernized feminism of cultural imperialism.[37]

Deniz Kandiyoti argues that western orientalists use women's status to indict islamic culture, while islamic law (shari'a) is somewhat ambivalent on the issue. Carla Makhlouf Obermeyer says that the ambiguities of religious text could be used to enhance women's status. The constraints on women are not inherently islamic because egalitarian elements exist in the Koran. Islam can be reformist or reactionary, and political context matters as much, if not more, than religious text. This was evident in the iranian islamist revolution of 1989, when national birth control policy expanded women's reproductive options so that abortions were no longer strictly forbidden.[38]

Muslim women must critique islamic practices, their place in the global economy, *and* the possibilities of transnational feminisms. They find this more difficult, according to Deniz Kandiyoti, when women are used "to symbolize the progressive aspirations of a secularist elite."[39] This secularization of the family code in turkey, as well as the enfranchisement of women, was part of the broader struggle that Kandiyoti describes as creating "a new legitimising state ideology."[40] Then, cultural authenticity is positioned against feminism, and feminism against religious fundamentalism. But this is not always the case. At times, feminism has been used by middle-eastern and asian male nationalist reformers to emblemize modernization.

Islamic modernism, contrasted with traditionalism, will invoke feminist concerns with sexual equality. For the nation to advance women must progress.[41] This stance has suited egypt at different historical moments, as the veil has at others, although the notion of equality does not usually extend into the private sphere. Most arab men do not believe that women should have equality in the home; women have not gained new rights inside the family based on their work outside. Obedience to husband is still expected in the muslim family, although this contrasts with the needs of market colonialism.[41] Nawal El Saadawi says that although most arab men do not reject the idea that a woman should have the right to work outside the home, they do not accept women's participation in other public activities.[43]

Some muslim feminists retreat into the protective certainties of religious conservatism. Others use fundamentalism in active ways for their own protection. These women do not simply submit to religious demands but try to mold the constraints to their own purposes.[44] So some arab/muslim women wear the veil to protect themselves from unwanted intrusion; they find they have more freedom to move about when they wear it. According to Kandiyoti, in egypt a woman can choose to not wear the veil; or she can wear it (mitdayyinan) and be "formidable, untouchable and silently threatening."[45] However, in iran, western-style women are identified with former Shah Pahlavi, so the veil represents cultural authenticity against western colonialism.[46]

According to Valentine Moghadam, "the massive participation of women was vital" to the success of the iranian revolution against the shah in the late 1970s. The many women who wore the veil as a protest symbol against Pahlavi and the west "did not expect hijab (veiling) to become mandatory." After, when the Ayatollah Khomeini said that he preferred traditional islamic dress for women, many women felt betrayed. These women were betrayed again in 1980 when wearing the veil became compulsory.[47]

The iranian women's movement during this period was split. Some supported Khomeini, others did not. Ideas varied about women's rights and the veil. Some women sought protection in the veil; others did not. Moghadam argues, however, that compulsory veiling was not about protecting women but "signaled the (re)definition of gender rules, and the veiled woman came to symbolize the moral and cultural transformation of society."[48]

There is about as much agreement in islam on the meaning of the veil as there is agreement in the u.s. about the meaning of pornography. As Hafidha, an egyptian civil engineer who yearns to design high-tech factories says of her fundamentalist lifestyle, "I don't have to behave like a European or American to be a scientist....I can very well be an eminent scientist or engineer and wear my hijab!"[49] Badran adds to the complexity while noting that in egypt muslims, jews, and christians all wear veils.[50]

The veil speaks a particular history of colonialism and patriarchy. According to Ahmed, western eyes see the veil as the most visible sign of the "differentness and inferiority of Islamic societies." And this sign symbolizes the "oppression of women" and the "backwardness of Islam" simultaneously.[51] Now that chastity is located in the veil, and sexuality is demonized as western, women of "the" south and east are presented as de-eroticized.[52]

The french removed algerian women's veils as part of colonialism; islamic fundamentalists have reveiled them as part of third-world nationalism.[53] Frantz Fanon wrote of the veil as allowing women "to see without being seen." The veil stood against the conversion to western ways. It was a form of demarcation of both algeria and its feminine component. It protected because it was a uniform that did not tolerate modification by the west.[54]

The varied dialogues about the veil express multiple feminisms among women inside the third-world south and east. Some militant turkish women who "demand the right to veil"[55] do not view women or their rights differently from women who choose not to wear the veil. Yet, the struggle over the veil reflects women's opposition to forced veiling. Fatima Mernissi says that "if fundamentalists are calling for the return to the veil, it must be because women have been taking off the veil."[56]

The veil depicts gender borders as geographical at the same time that it crosses the borders of third-world south and east. The veil alludes to the uncontrollable sexuality of women at the same time that it bespeaks their unavailability.

Veils hide faces, and some women feel protected and safer when hidden. But the veil exposes exactly what it also hides. Unavailability and respectability are the flip side of the forbidden.[57]

This last message is complicated because the veil, in its asexual reading, frees women from their reproductivity. Woman, as virgin, must be something other than her (reproductive) body.[58] But islamic law and culture endorse women's sexuality and their right to sexual pleasure in marriage.

The fall of communism and the gulf war have had far-ranging effects on the four hundred fifty million muslim women in arab countries and eastern europe. As market capitalism thunders into eastern europe, we see porn and prostitution alongside the new-old nationalisms *and* the veil.

WOMEN IN POST-COMMUNIST NATIONALISMS

Whereas the revolutions of '89 were depicted by the western media as a victory for capitalist democracy, exclusionary nationalisms now dominate the landscape. Women in eastern and central europe have had a troubled status in statist communism, which makes them exceedingly important and yet particularly vulnerable to the process of nationalizing identity (ies). Gender boundaries are being redefined by global markets and state rollbacks. Yet no matter how punishing the new markets have been for women, women still hope for the freedoms that these markets promise. State services and supports for women have been cut everywhere. The privatized markets have transnational gendered effects.[59] And the bosnian war represents the ugliest side of the underbelly of post-communism. There is no one scenario to uncover in women's lives in poland, russia, the czech republic, and bosnia. Circumstances vary broadly from country to country, yet they tell a similar story.

The new economies in eastern europe have displaced majorities of women in the labor force. These women have worked in the market for a long time and did not welcome their forced unemployment. Many of these women's children, now also in the market, have been reared in state day-care centers. They have had access to abortion for several decades now. Their individual histories, their exhaustion, their desires, the assaults against them, and the existence of dispersed and uncoordinated women's actions are part of the feminist story starting to unfold. It is a story of new markets, new kinds of poverty, leftovers of statist communism, and nationalist wars.

Privatization and new markets are redefining the relationships between states and their economies, families and public/private life, and political and cultural life. Because these renegotiations retranslate masculinist privilege, women have a particular interest in affecting these changes. Agitation on the part of women in these post-communist societies is not new, and yet, it is also not simply like western feminism. After all, "feminism has no particular ethnic identity."[60] The transnational privatization of the globe creates new possibilities for a crossover dialogue among women in the east, and between the east and west.

The transnational presence of feminisms stand counter to the nationalisms of russia, poland, bosnia, etc. Without these feminisms' criticism of gender privilege, nationalism will remain "a repository of male hopes, male aspirations, and male privilege."[61] This misogyny does not stand alone, according to Christina Thurmer-Rohr, a berlin professor and psychologist. She argues that misogyny is so intertwined with racism and anti-semitism that western feminists should reject the white, middle-class woman as their model. She insists on a feminism that is explicitly anti-racist.[62]

Early on, the revolutions of '89 "imagined" religious freedom, political freedom, and sexual freedom. The hope was for a freedom for the "private" self. Slavenka Drakulic, a feminist from zagreb, croatia, captures this sense of privacy when describing the lack, under communism, of such consumer goods as toilet paper and tampons.[63] Many of her concerns with privacy are tied to bodily/sexual needs, which were much ignored under the old regime. At home, Drakulic is treated as a traitor because of her feminism and her anti-nationalist views.[64]

Equality, and most particularly sexual equality, had a bad name with women living in statist communist regimes. Sexual equality was identified with forced work, low pay, abortion as the main method of contraception, and triple days of labor (home, job, and shopping). It also was associated with entitlements such as state day care, pregnancy leaves, child subsidies, etc., which were sporadic and contradictory in their effect. Even though few women are happy about losing their jobs *and* their state entitlements to global capital, fewer yet, at least up to this point, would want to return to the old regimes.

Liberal democrats, as the philosphers of capitalism, and marxists, as the theorists of communism, totalize "the" economy. Communism was to end class conflict and all other conflict with it. Communist theorists did not envision a gender hierarchy within the economy. Gorbachev, and Yeltsin, as well as Vaclav Havel, make the same mistake; women are not imaged in their nations as active citizens. Gorbachev even promised that *perestroika* would allow women to return to their homes and be feminine again.[65]

Women are *made* absent in discussions of the '89 revolutions and their aftermath. Little is said about how many czech dissidents were women. Little is said about the way women kept civil society alive as a counter to the totalitarianism of the various regimes. Tatiana Bohm of the german democratic republic says that the revolutionary changes in eastern and middle europe would never have been possible without the widespread participation of women.[66]

One also hears very little of the women in ex-yugoslavia who fight against the war. Sonia Licht of belgrade says women have built a peace movement, helped organize the May 1992 demonstration of one hundred thousand people against the bombing of sarajevo, and maintained a candlelight vigil for victims of the war from October '91 to February '92. She tells of the "women in black," the Crisis Line, and Centers for Raped Women in belgrade—all of which are actions by women to stop the war.[67] One hardly hears mention in the media of *Viva Zena*, an anti-nationalist women's magazine published in sarajevo, or the women's therapy center in multiethnic tuzla and medica, or the mixed ethnic women's therapy project in zenica. These women stand against masculinist nationalism and tell a different story.[68]

PHALLOCRATIC MARKETS AND TRANSNATIONAL CAPITAL

Statist communism's rhetoric bespoke a sexual equality that overburdened women with multiple responsibilities as wage earner, mother, and domestic drudge.[69] The rhetoric was largely sexless. Although abortion was available, the *assembly-line* way in which it was performed was humiliating and, often, medically unsafe. Zarana Papic says that yugoslav women were so overworked and humiliated that they were effectively silenced by the rigors of everyday life.[70] Marina Blagojevic calls this drudgery of the everyday the "tyranny of triviality" and "self-sacrifice."[71]

Before world war II, women in yugoslavia were very often restricted to domesticity within a confining patriarchal culture. After world war II, with the coming of socialism women were granted the right to vote, the right to abortion, and equal pay for equal work.[72] This came to mean forced emancipation (working dreary jobs), protective legislation (which assisted women while creating "mommy politics"), and the necessity of abortion (given that it was the main form of contraception)—all of which was thoroughly paternalistic.

The concern with women's equality was manipulated for the purposes of patriarchal communism throughout eastern europe. The state functioned in interventionist, paternalistic ways to create a form of egalitarian patriarchal privilege that served the state above all else. Men and women suffered in this process, but women suffered more. Crude ideological manipulations encouraged women to bear children they did not want. Special legislation for women was then used to provide a minimal amount of relief from their triple burden.[73] This was quite different from the state's promise. If socialists had wanted to emancipate women they would have figured out a way to socialize housework and transform the family.

Post-communism has been no kinder to women. They have been the first to lose their jobs in the economic restructuring. Daycare subsidies and welfare entitlements have been cut, thus straightjacketing women's options. The editor of a new woman's journal— *One Eye Open/Jednim Oken*—in the czech republic states that although capitalism provides new opportunities for women it also has been responsible for major cuts in funding for women's projects.[74]

Alongside the market changes and increased levels of unemployment and poverty, there is rampant crime, drug abuse, prostitution, and excessive levels of violence, particularly in the former soviet union, Tatyana Mamonova says. Anything seems to go. There is "brazen insolence," from beauty contests to porn to rape.[75]

New markets in poland have brought Slim-Fast, the american diet product. Plastic surgeons are supposedly doing a brisk new business in breast enlargements and liposuction. Cosmetics are more easily available if you have the money, but *most women, experiencing a new poverty*, do not.

Many polish women now find the catholic church more oppressive and constricting than the old communist party.[76] This criticism of the new regimes is also made by women in the czech republic, bulgaria, and albania, where they compose 60 percent of the unemployed. In romania, women make up 85 percent of the unemployed.[77]

Seventy-three percent of russia's unemployed are women. Half of these women have higher educations, and more than 40 percent of these women are under the age of 30. Some russian women say that their politicians act more like religious fundamentalists than like democrats. It shows how women in diverse contexts are reconfiguring "fundamentalism" as being about gender, power, and tradition, and less about religion. Russian feminists readily critique the lack of democracy for women amid the new changes. The traditionalism is made clear by Gennady Melikyan, russia's labor minister. When asked about labor practices, he said: "Why should we employ women when men are unemployed? It's better that men work and women take care of children and do the housework."[78]

In the former soviet union commercialization of the female body is a central element of the transition to market relations. Once again we see the marketing of gender for masculinist purposes. Since *glasnost*, films more readily depict sexual violence against women. The new right to freedom of speech has been used by politicians, the western media, and even some feminists to defend the pornography industry.

Clearly *perestroika* and the revolutions of '89 were written with men, not women, in mind.[79] The new markets have instigated and nurtured a nostalgia for pre-communist patriarchal society that post-communist nationalisms capitalize on. And nostalgic masculinism constructs the contours of the new national identities. A transnational nationalist stance within eastern and central europe marks similarities among women beyond national borders. This traditionalist patriarchal domesticity stands in stark contrast to the wage-earning domesticity of former communist regimes.

The de-industrialized service economies of western first-world countries have necessitated that a majority of married women enter the labor force, although never to the degree that communist regimes such as poland, the soviet union, or yugoslavia did. Liberal democratic rhetoric never argued that it was woman's duty to work, nor was sexual equality ever tied to women's labor. In the 1950s, u.s. women were depicted as "housewives" while women in eastern europe were traipsing off to work in the factories in the name of sexual equality. In the 1990s, a majority of u.s. white women have joined women of color in the labor force while their eastern european counterparts are losing their jobs. Transnational global markets may change this yet again, as the u.s. competes alongside eastern europe for jobs in this global marketplace.

Neither statism—communist or nationalist—nor capitalist markets, per se, are friends to women. Both statist communism and global capitalism are patriarchal and paternalist. Statist communism forced eastern european women into the centrally planned economy. Globalized capitalist markets and the nationalistic responses they trigger in eastern and central europe reignite the conflicts surrounding women's domesticity. The process of transition from communism to capitalism is not all even and smooth. The same global market that necessitates an increase in women's unemployment in some regions also promises new freedoms; and these freedoms run counter to traditionalist nationalisms of "the" east or west. This same global market demands that women enter the market as the cheapest of cheap labor in central america and southeast asia without the promise of much of anything.

A new politics *may* emerge in eastern europe to stem the nationalist rhetoric of domesticity after half a century of enforced "sexual equality." There is new history to be written out of this postcommunist nationalist repositioning of women as women respond to the few options afforded them by the global market. Women's oppositions will be charted through the maze of tensions between statist communism's enforced equality, a new domesticity enforced by racialized nationalisms and global capital, and the promissory freedom of the market itself.

Since '89, gender-specific labor has been structurally reinforced by new market restrictions. Enforced domesticity within a failing market for women who themselves are products of state day care holds out new possibilities for feminist identity. Because today's women in eastern europe are the daughters of women who were in the labor force, their model differs from the western, white, middle-class trajectory of housewifery. So, Ol'ga Lipovskaia says, "most feminist activity and the development of feminist ideas will be located in the family,"[80] as women are sent there.

Western women and women in eastern europe face similar dilemmas with different histories. Eastern european women have had state entitlements and social welfare policies that most women in the west have not had. Women in the west have been defined by the liberal democratic discourse of freedom of choice, rather than communist statist equality. Western women can learn from eastern european women's experience how entitlements such as protective legislation on the job or state-run day-care centers can remain patriarchal in purpose. Women in eastern europe can learn from women in the west that individual freedom is not enough and must be accompanied by sexual equality.

BODILY RIGHTS AND POST-COMMUNIST TRANSNATIONAL NATIONALISMS

The euphoria of *glasnost* and *perestroika* was short-lived. Economic reforms did not achieve the promise for most working people. Reductions in government subsidies and increases in consumer prices dashed the hopes for most of an easy transition to a market economy. Soon there was rationing of sugar, salt, soap. The queues got longer.[81] Just putting food on the table became a major feat. As Tatyana Mamonova says: "Whereas communism meant waiting in line an hour to buy bread, capitalism means waiting a year to be able to afford it."[82]

Masculinism is written all over the new economy. The markets are very skewed by what men want to buy. Women know that infant formula and contraceptive products will never become a priority consumer item as long as men continue to dominate the market. In short order women have been left with gynoglasnost and catastroika.[83] According to Anastasia Posadskaya, men who have benefited from the market "want to spend their money on flats and foreign cars, on night clubs... and they want their wives to stay home and take care of the kids." It is no surprise that predominantly middle-aged and older russian men voted for the right-wing, "pro-family" nationalist Vladimir Zhirinovsky.[84]

The new hardships of privatized markets affect women's "duties" the most directly as more and more responsibility is relegated to the home. More foods are grown in home gardens. More canning is done in the home to avoid high prices at the store. Women migrate back to home labor, while men hold several low-paying jobs.[85] The similarities to working- and middle-class women in the u.s., created by transnational capital, are significant.

The backdrop out of which eastern european women come— the state support and subsidies—also make the global market harder to adjust to. These women are used to getting meals at canteens where they work and having their children in day-care centers. As they lose their jobs, they become responsible for meals and child care.[86] At the same time, state-sponsored pro-family campaigns are under way, summed up in the draft form of "The Law on the Protection of the Family."

Women have been quickly removed from industrial jobs in this transition.[87] This has happened in economies where full-time domesticity is not a real alternative because of low (male) wages.[88] The single-parent family headed by a woman is substantially on the rise everywhere.[89] In former east germany women over the age of fifty and women with college degrees have the highest rate of unemployment.[90]

Besides the staggering joblessness, east german women have lost their year's paid leave for a first child; their four to eight week paid leave for the care of sick children; their subsidized public day care; their job guarantees; their free contraceptives. Add to this the attacks on abortion in just about all the countries mentioned so far. These developments do not hold out much promise for a liberatory domesticity.

Many women in the former soviet union say that if money were no issue, they would like to cut their work hours to part-time. Interestingly, when asked, men also expressed this wish. Approximately 66 percent of men surveyed said they would like to cut back on their work in some way. The figure for women was 83.3 percent.[91] Many women in hungary expressed the same desire.[92] A 1989 study in the former czechoslovakia found that many female industrial workers wanted more flexibility in their working hours (44.4 percent) and better support services (33.3 percent). Fewer numbers expected equal pay or status (16 percent).[93]

Meanwhile, the division of home from market, and private from public spheres, sets the contours of transnational markets against what was formerly communist statism. Women are intrigued by the newness of these relations and the freedom for the "private" self. "To say that anything is 'western' is a form of legitimation."[94] So wealthy women wear flashy fur coats, high-heeled boots, and lots of mascara.

The fantasmatic of "being free" captures women throughout eastern europe, much as it does elsewhere. But the freedom seems more extraordinary when positioned against a history of communism. Many women see porn as an emancipation from the desexualization of life under communism.[95] They are therefore hesitant to criticize the sexually exploitative side of the market, including the porn industry. Such policing reminds them of a politics of old. Even if the marketing of sex is not exactly what they want, it is better than no sex at all. The freedom—to express one's sensuality through consumer goods—is intoxicating. Zarana Papic, in belgrade, says that no one can imagine how attractive consumer culture appears to people who have not been allowed to have any of it.[96]

Still, many of these same women think it is impossible to be sexually free when contraception is in extremely short supply. In October 1992, one russian newspaper reported that there were only three condoms available per year for each russian man and that the supply of oral contraceptives can only satisfy 2 percent of the demand.[97]

Many of these women *also* say that the "sexual swaggering and bullying" at work and the new sense of permissiveness tied to porn videos, casinos, and beauty contests make life very difficult for them in this changing economy. Valentina Konstantinova, a researcher at the russian Center for Gender Studies, says that democracy "has mainly freed the male libido."[98]

Women's bodies—their commodification *and* their control— are at issue as the new markets take hold. The new markets have brought, on the one hand, the sex and porn market, *and*, on the other, attempts to restrict abortion and reproductive choice. The same market that popularizes sex videos seems uninterested in condoms and other contraceptives.

Masculinism is remapped on the economy *and* women's bodies in the struggles over abortion in poland, croatia, and germany. Even in russia, where abortion is the main form of birth control, a small right-wing assault is developing. Although it is still rare to find somebody in russia who speaks against abortion, anti-abortion forces held their first major conference in early '94.[99]

Under communism, abortion was tied to the necessity of women's availability for wage labor. State-sanctioned abortion was integral to communism's labor policy. As such, abortion was viewed as a necessity of the market rather than a woman's right. Women viewed it as an unwanted necessity; they wished for contraceptive options that would make abortions less frequent. It is only since the fall of communism, and the contestation surrounding abortion for the new market, that the protection of the unborn has been positioned against a woman's right to choose.[100]

The December '90 constitution of slovenia states that the "constitution originates from the sanctity of life." The croatian constitution initially declared that every unborn child has a right to life, and then was revised to read that every human being has this right.[101] Renata Salecl writes from slovenia in fall '95 that the right wing is pushing for mandatory three-year pregnancy leaves.[102]

In poland, although 95 percent of the population identifies itself as catholic, more than half do not agree with the church on birth control and abortion.[103] Nevertheless the March 1993 abortion law instigated by the church made abortion criminal except in cases of rape, incest, and preserving the life of the woman. It maintained that the right to life starts at conception and must be protected by law. Doctors who perform abortions are subject to imprisonment. The law was passed even though only 11 percent of polish women use modern contraceptives.[104] As stated by a member of the polish senate: "We will nationalize those bellies."[105] Maybe the senate cannot do much about the economy, but it can domesticize women and reassert control by men.

The new freedom in poland is marked by pinups everywhere, alongside the assault against abortion. Polish women responded to these developments by voting the communists back into office in the fall '93 elections. Meanwhile, The Fatherland Catholic Election Coalition was unable to garner any parliamentary seats.[106] By July '94 the polish senate narrowly voted to ease its abortion law: abortion would be allowed for "difficult marital conditions or a demanding personal situation."[107] Lech Walesa vetoed the revisions even though more than 75 percent of poles say they favor freedom of choice.[108]

Attacks against abortion rights continue throughout eastern and central europe, as well as in the u.s. Although abortion was readily accessible in the former czechoslovakia, along with free contraception—except for condoms—the new slovakia passed a bill titled "The Law on the Protection of Human Life,"[109] which was supposedly to greatly curtail the availability of abortion.

But it was the unification of germany that created the most publicly contested debate over abortion. Establishing control over women's bodies was key to establishing the unified nation, but east and west could not agree. Initially, no solution to the abortion issue could be found.

Article 31 of the Unity Treaty tried to find a compromise between the west's fetal-protection stance and the east's access to and overuse of abortion. Separate laws remained for a two-year period until an "Interim Law" was finally agreed upon which straddled the two countries' former abortion positions. Then germany's highest court ruled in May '93 that the unified country's compromise abortion law violated a constitutional provision requiring the state to protect human life. Although abortion is now illegal, the state does not prosecute women who undergo abortions in the first three months of pregnancy, or their doctors.[110]

German abortion law also states that abortion is not a general right of women in the first twelve weeks of pregnancy and therefore requires obligatory counseling. The state must "encourage" pregnancy unless it "exceeds the reasonable boundaries of sacrifice." The legislature was asked to generate a new abortion law that will conform to the court's restrictions.

Along with this ruling there have been cuts in the "birth benefit" paid to all women after delivery from 1,000 east marks to 150 west marks. Significantly, there has been a 50 percent drop in the east german birth rate and a 500 percent increase in sterilization since 1991.[111] The sluggish economy and the lack of support for child rearing makes having children a luxury that many german women do not feel free to choose today.

But an illicit gynecological network appears to be developing in poland and germany.[112] The network grows out of a unique consciousness that has developed in reaction to the constraints of statist communism's pro-natalist *and* pro-emancipation rhetoric *and* limited contraceptive possibilities and supplies. Although the sexual equality discourse of the communist period has been discredited as flawed and "imposed" from above and has created *an allergic reaction* to the rhetoric of the communist past, pro-abortion women in these countries see abortion as an utter necessity.[113]

The continued disputes over the borders and parameters of choice express the transnational dispute over women's bodily autonomy. All of the transitional market societies attempt to redefine and re-encode masculinist and patriarchal family structures to enhance the options for men in the new markets. Post-communist society rearticulates traditional familial fantasies in the hopes of bringing order to a very disorderly economy. Such fantasies, however, require a refutation of statist equality *and* economies that support patriarchal familialism, which necessitates male wages capable of supporting wives and children. Transnational capital in eastern europe is unable to subsidize these nationalist fantasies as these countries become a part of the new globalized third world.

POST-COMMUNIST/POST-NATIONALIST WOMEN'S MOVEMENTS AND IDENTITIES

The legacy of forced collectivism and universalism encircles any and all possibilities for developing feminist politics in eastern europe.[114] Many eastern european women remain highly critical and skeptical of the deformed gender equality espoused in hypocritical ways by their former regimes. Communism's version of sexual equality meant standardization, weariness, sameness, and dreariness. For these women, democracy represents the promise of a new freedom of individual expression: political, economic, and sexual. In this scenario, equality and freedom are constructed as opposites.

Women, as a transnational category, with all their racial, ethnic, sexual, bodily, religious differences, can reveal the inadequacy of false homogeneity as a standard, either in relation to themselves or to men. These differences necessitate a revisioning of equality discourse—both communist and liberal democratic style. Like communist discourse, liberal democratic notions of equality also assume likeness and similarity of a male standard. To be treated equal is to be treated *like* a man, but not exactly. Women are expected to have a job, but it won't be as well-paid. Pregnancy is treated like a disability a man might have, even though it is completely female.

No wonder so many russian women have loudly insisted that they are not interested in being treated *like* men any longer. And they are not interested in western feminism if it is limited to this equality rhetoric. They are tired of their triple day of labor. They have yet to experience the forced domesticity of the 1950s that white, western, middle-class feminists critiqued. Their wariness is quite similar to the position of women-of-color feminists in the west during the 1970s. These women, already in the labor force and experiencing its race/gender ghettoes, imagined beyond likeness to an equality rich in diversity.[115]

Alena Heitlinger argues interestingly that human rights discourse may hold more promise than western feminism for eastern european women simply because women's rights, as a politics, is overly identified with the former communist regimes. The Global Campaign for Women's Rights takes this tact. It uses the human rights aspects of specific gender issues to call attention to the transnational violence against women.[116] Human rights discourse is used to erode the public/private division that conceals the everyday familial violence of women's lives. This focus transforms and relocates the meaning of human rights through a gendered lens.

The global violence toward women—the sexual torture of dissidents, sexual violence toward prisoners and refugees, rape in war, etc.—is set against the backdrop of human rights instead of women's rights. As Charlotte Bunch states: "significant numbers of the world's population are routinely subject to torture, starvation, terrorism, humiliation, mutilation, and even murder simply because they are female." Human rights discourse can be used to unveil the transnational sexual violence without getting caught in the east/west feminist divide.[117]

The theorized visibility of women—the naming of women as a collectivity with the possibility of shared transnational identities as "sisters"—is always absent in the ruminations of nationalism and post-communism. In contrast, feminism names women and the possibility of their shared identities.

Eastern european feminisms are beginning to address this lack. How they will name and speak and write their situation will slowly emerge. The process is complicated by the fact that women are not named politically; things need a name to be seen, and seeing is in part being able to name. Or as Rey Chow says: "Only when things are *put in the bold*, so to speak, can a thorough dismantling of the habits of seeing be achieved."[118]

Feminists in the west need to see women's oppositions in eastern europe within their own territory and histories. Gayatri Spivak might call this a translation that recognizes "the terrain of the original."[119] The eastern european women I meet with ask me to see their unique struggles as they exist, but to not see difference when it does not exist. Renata Salecl says the "feminism of differences" has competing and conflicting results. She warns that westerners see easterners as too different, and that easterners then insist on the notion of difference when it is of advantage to keep intact their traditional patriarchal structures.[120]

The various expressions of women's resistance and oppositions are defined by what Chandra Mohanty calls the politics of location.[121] Barbara Einhorn warns that many women in dissident movements in eastern europe were and remain politically active and yet publicly invisible.[122] This activism on the part of women—which does not mimic that of men—takes place outside traditional political avenues.

Czech and slovak women who took an active part in the subversion of the socialist state are not now a part of the new governments. These women argue that their exclusion is in part their choice. Their notion of politics remains highly critical of bureaucratic statism and its required political obedience. These women say they are not interested in holding office and desire a politics of a different sort, one rooted in democratic everyday life processes. These women built an opposition civil society under communism that may begin to define a particularly post-communist feminism.

This post-communist feminism will remain skeptical of what Anastasia Posadskaya calls years of "forced solidarity" that was never "real."[123] The new ways of thinking about political participation may rely on what looks like traditional female qualities and activities. Julia Szalia of hungary argues that women's refusal to participate in bureaucratic state formations reflects a particular embrace of their oppositional familial role. Under communism, the family safeguarded a restricted measure of private liberty vis-à-vis the totalitarian state, a kind of civilian autonomy. She therefore sees women's widespread retreat from arenas of the state as a desire for autonomy, rather than an embrace of traditionalism.[124]

Similar sentiments are expressed by many russian women. "The Russian kitchen was a front of massive resistance to the totalitarian regime.... One was surrounded by intimacy, publicity, and intellectual creativity."[125] "Kitchen talk" was a form of resistance; the home was a different kind of political space. It was where people gathered, *after* work, and against the state. Einhorn argues that the private realm offered a space for renewal, a kind of a "haven" from state surveillance and the publicness of one's life.

Transnational markets are changing this status. Today, as global capital privatizes the public, the home space is no longer a site of anti-state, civil status.[126] As the home loses its "resistance" value, women are being sent there from the market. And they are sent there poorer than before, without jobs. This framing of domesticity is similar to white middle-class women's experiences—their exclusion from the bourgeois market of the eighteenth and nineteenth centuries—in the west/north. They, however, were kept from entering the market, whereas in eastern europe today, women, having already entered, are being kicked out.

There is also a new sense of personal privacy that was impossible under communism. According to Mita Castle-Kanerova, "Openness about family matters, about sexual roles and relationships, belong positively to the sphere of society that is coming alive."[127] Still unclear is how personal and familial life will be woven into post-communist feminisms; and whether transnational capital will subvert this feminist domesticity by its own excesses: female poverty alongside domestic drudgery.

I remain skeptical about the possibilities for a democratic domesticity. I worry about the patriarchal presence that infiltrates family life, no matter how insurgent family life might be. Rethinking family life as an anti-politics[128] has its problems because it does not cite the family as a politics.

Women-of-color feminists in the u.s. have long viewed the family as a place of everyday political struggle and integrity.[129] For them the family is a location of resistance and power, as well as oppression and violence. Feminist politics, defined through personal life, locates feminist struggles in the community and neighborhood; in food boycotts and protests against food shortages; in underground abortion clinics. These forms of resistance are neither merely personal nor domestic.

This dialogue criss-crosses geographical, racial/ethnic, and national divides. In the west and north, industrial capitalism initially distinguished public and private life, wage labor and non-wage domestic labor. White, middle-class married women were relegated to the home. Women of color worked for wages, often as domestics. In the east and south, arab/muslim women have been defined by a family that de-emphasizes public life while allowing them to work outside the home. Now global capital once again redefines a public/private divide for new third-world countries, privileging the market against the labor-intensive domesticity of the home and an absent state. Meanwhile, deindustrialization in first-world countries writes new divides out of increasing privatization. What once was the public purview of the state is privatized by neocons, so individuals must now take care of themselves.

Global capitalism demands these new realignments. So eastern european women lose their jobs while privatization displaces the public arena. Muslim fundamentalists, in partial reaction to global capital, demand the return of women to the home and the veil. Meanwhile, transnational capital turns women into poverty-wage workers in mexico, korea, and indonesia.[130] Global capital privatizes more and more of the globe, and women and young girls "man" the factories and/or are forced into prostitution. In the free-trade-zone factories in central america and the caribbean, maquiladora workers slave away for 38 cents an hour, in fifteen-hour-a-day shifts. The workers are mainly girls, some as young as fourteen. They make garments for The Gap, and Eddie Bauer, and the Banana Republic.[131]

Amid the economic uncertainties, the nationalist horror stories, the ferocious fears, a large number and range of women's informal groups have emerged. By 1990 the czech republic was home to numerous women's groups and parties of all varieties. The Political Party of Women and Mothers formed a national network to encourage political participation and provide information on women's rights.

Because many women view established political groups with much suspicion, many of the women's informal groups remain disparate and haphazard. Very often the groups consist of "anonymous" women who take initiatives into their own hands because national politics still carry a stigma of "top-down authoritarianism."[132] Many women prefer to identify individually rather than politically. Jana Hradilkova, a czech woman, states: "Feminism smells like an ideology, and people have had their fill of ideology here."[133] Any "ism" remains suspect.[134] At the same time, many women say they will not let anyone push them back to the home—or anywhere, for that matter.

The new economy in russia, despite its negative consequences for women, has opened up opportunities for independent women's organizations to challenge state-sponsored women's groups and forge a new feminist politics. Some of these women's groups are openly feminist, while others are not; still others might become feminist. The feminist possibilities are many stemming from: "women in small business, mothers of soldiers, women in defense conversion, women's environmental groups, women's soup kitchens, women's centers, etc."[135]

Tatyana Mamonova says that a women's movement in russia "is alive and well, though not always conscious." It is still developing and is expressed in many forms. Sometimes a women's movement is conspicuous; sometimes it operates quietly within women's homes. Every once in a while one can see its presence, as in the first lesbian and gay pride demonstrations, which took place in 1991 and '92. The placards read "turn red squares into pink triangles."[136] It is also true that patriarchal fundamentalism is thriving amidst the economic deterioration. It should be no surprise that feminist actions and imaginings ebb and flow with the difficulty of the moment.

Many women say that they are not feminists because feminists hate men and they do not; others say they are not feminists because they are already tired of their so-called emancipation; others say their struggle is not against men, but against society. Most of their dialogue seems positioned against the man-hating demonization they have seen in western feminism.

Few would argue that there is a mass feminist movement in eastern europe today. Fewer yet would say that western feminism has taken root in poland, russia, the czech republic, or bosnia. But Laura Busheikin argues that there is already a western-style backlash before there is a western-style feminism.[137] In the czech newspaper the *Prague Post,* Josef Skvorecky caricatures western feminism as lesbian and radically anti-male. He launches his attack against man-hating "lesboid feminism."[138]

Feminism, as export, is beamed across the globe. So it exists even where it has no local roots. Anyone can see it if they have a TV, watch hollywood films, listen to worldwide news, or use e-mail. The feminism they see is affluent and consumerist.[139] But in spite of this capture by the western/global networks, feminism is not entirely contained by its advertisers. Feminism makes women as "female" visible, even if its partial viewing makes women in the south and east less visible than those in the north and west.

Local feminisms and women's oppositions can emerge through and in dialogue with this transnational communications network. The telecommunications global web potentially allows communication across the very divides that transnational capital constructs. Women can see themselves, across the globe, in ways that were just not possible before.

Communism's collapse means both more and less freedom for women across the globe. It also means less equality for all women, especially for those of the third-world east and south.

My specifying women in post-communist nationalisms and in transnational capitalism pushes us to imagine a democracy that includes infant formula, contraceptives, reproductive freedom, decent jobs, and a creative and peaceful non-heterosexist home life. Feminism(s) as transnational—imagined as the rejection of false race/gender borders and falsely constructed "others"—is a major challenge to masculinist nationalism, the distortions of statist communism *and* "free"-market globalism. It is a feminism that recognizes individual diversity, and freedom, and equality, defined through and beyond north/west and south/east dialogues. It recognizes the necessity of entitlements, and is yet cautious about statist interventionism, rejects privatization by global capital, and moves beyond masculinist nationalisms.

Such a feminism is poised between communism and capitalism, between collectivism and individuality, between publicness and privacy, between sameness and differences, and between women's different imaginings. This demands feminisms beyond nationalism and global capitalism.

I began to believe such a feminism is possible, in spite of the tremendous odds against it, on my visit to belgrade in May 1995.[140] As a part of the new serbia, belgrade is also home to feminists who daily reach out beyond the horrific borders of this struggling new nation. They shun the safety of their birthing and instead speak against the war, and for their sisters in sarajevo, zepa, bihac, and gorazde.

WOMEN IN BELGRADE AND SARAJEVO

The nationalisms in bosnia bespeak the horrors of race/gender warfare. Serb nationalism uses and violates women as it nationalizes identity along bloodlines. In this scenario motherhood has national meaning, and so does rape. Rape destroys "others" and establishes serbia at the same time.[141] In an interview, two bosnian muslim rape survivors—one a lawyer, the other a judge—say that by killing/raping older women, history is erased; by killing/raping young women, the future is wiped away.[142] And so a serb nation is built. Nevertheless, women in the refugee camps were "resisting the temptation to hate."[143]

This is the backdrop for women's actions throughout the war zone of bosnia.

Everyone I met wanted the war to end. They identified more readily as yugoslav than as serb. They were desperate for an end to the slaughter in sarajevo but saw no end in sight. Many of the women I spoke with said that they lived in an immoral situation in belgrade; that they were free of bombs, while friends and family were killed elsewhere. Not one woman I met in belgrade would call herself a nationalist. Many identified as feminists, and were desperately concerned for the fate of women, especially those in sarajevo.

Many people tried to leave belgrade because they could not stand to live there while others died so close by. Others came to belgrade as refugees from sarajevo and mostar. It is a city steeped in loss and tension.

While there I met with women who were both victims and survivors, who had no hope but who still hope, who search for candles and cans of food to send to sarajevo, who were deeply torn between guilt about the war and activism against it. They wish the profiteers of the war would be stopped. They wished that they could get everyone out of sarajevo, especially the women and children.

Feminists in belgrade traveled to sarajevo whenever they could. After one visit, the feminists in belgrade wrote to the women in sarajevo: "We are writing to you with the knowledge about the complexity of the fact of where each of us comes from.... We came back changed more than ever. We are full of traces of your testimonies and our deep feelings that life is far more difficult for you than you wanted to show us. We have seen your different women's groups. We have taken your papers, and statements to share with others. We will let others know what is happening to you. We are supporting you totally and ceaselessly. We will repeat ten thousands times how you are courageous. We will come to you again, as soon as possible. Drinking coffee with you in sarajevo touches our souls."[144]

Lepa Mladjenovic, from the "women in black" and the "autonomous women's center" in belgrade, says that the women from belgrade and sarajevo are "very different" and "not so different," and that they must "keeping moving through the differences."[145] Jasna, a friend of Lepa's, and a feminist from sarajevo, says that each one of the women from both cities "must be dignified for the position she occupies." They must deal with their different wartime realities in order to meet each other's needs. She says that the packages sent from the women in belgrade "were equal to a dream." "We would all sit around the table and open a box slowly and put each item out one by one and look, and not know whether to cry or feel joy; if we should just look at the food, or eat it." Jasna argues that she could "have never received these packages if the women in belgrade were not precisely in belgrade" to send them. And Lepa sadly acknowledges that "we precisely could only send packages and do nothing else from belgrade."[146] These women in belgrade and sarajevo refused to let the war turn them into enemies. But this refusal required them to know their own painful locations. Their connections to each other are fragile and tenuous, yet hopeful.

The "women in black" demonstrated in belgrade in hopes that the world would hear and see that they "are against the serbian regime, against militarism and war violence, against the raping of our sisters of all nationalities from all sides.... We are also against killing the treasure of differences that we have been living with for centuries, enjoying the differences, feeling more rich with them and really being rich from them."[147]

The warriors in croatia, and serbia, and bosnia-herzegovina should have listened to these women earlier. And feminists across the globe must be witness to their ability to move through and beyond deadly difference.

IMAGINING TRANSNATIONAL FEMINISMS

Given the epistemological and political construction of feminism—that it starts from the self and moves outward; that it is personal as well as political; that it is at one and the same time individualist and collectivist; that it requires an understanding of individual women as part of a larger complex community which is permeated by differences of color, ethnicity, economic class, colonialism, and nationhood—it stands counter to the masculinist nationalist constructions of separatism and false universalisms.

My feminist imaginings allow me a counter to global privatization and masculinist nationalisms. They elicit the possibility of a feminist network made up of women of different ethnicity, religion, color, and economic class. And they come together to demand the importance of their personal, bodily boundaries, while rejecting racialized nationalist border constructions.

Or said in a slightly different way by Antoinette Fouque: "each according to her own uniqueness, together."[148] We can reinvest feminism with new meanings that speak people's different histories, cultures, bodies, etc. The "we" here is imagined; it is not *not* islamic; and it is not *not*-western, even though mass-marketed western feminism dominates the global discourse. As Chela Sandoval says of u.s. third-world feminists, "we" also must move between ideologies.[149]

The "we" will represent a cacophony of particular selves who *share* female bodily borders. The "we" of feminism identifies a commitment to build a solidarity among and between women transnationally and multiracially. As such it must recognize but also subordinate differences. The imagined "we" must see and not see; must see how differently we live all over the globe and not see only the differences; must see the differences and not see them as barriers; must see likeness and not see it only. If feminisms across the globe can see through and beyond the barriers of colonialism, racism, nationalism, and transnational capital, they may be able to limit the hatreds that threaten to engulf the twenty-first century.

NOTES TO THE INTRODUCTION

1. Nelly S. Toll, *Behind the Secret Window: A Memoir of a Hidden Childhood During World War Two* (New York: Dial Books, 1993).

2. Mary E. Lyons, *Letters From A Slave Girl, The Store of Harriet Jacobs* (New York: Charles Scribner's Sons, 1992).

3. For a full explication of the engendering of race and the racializing of sexuality see my *The Color of Gender* (Berkeley: University of California Press, 1994).

4. Dean MacConnell, Afterword, in *Empty Meeting Grounds* (New York: Routledge, 1992), p. 309, n. 5.

5. Geoffrey Bennington, "Postal Politics and the Institution of the Nation," in Homi Bhabha, ed., *Nation and Narration* (New York: Routledge, 1990), p. 122.

6. Ella Shohat and Robert Stam, *Unthinking Eurocentrism* (New York: Routledge, 1994), pp. 13, 15.

7. Chris Hedges, "Arabs, Too, Play the Ethnic Card," *New York Times*, March 5, 1995, p. E4.

8. Manning Marable, "History and Black Consciousness: The Political Culture of Black America," *Monthly Review*, vol. 47, no. 3 (July/August 1995), p. 85.

9. Kathy Ferguson, *Kibbutz Journal* (Pasedena: Trilogy Books, 1995), p. 53.

10. Kevin Fedarko and Mark Thompson, "All For One," *Time*, vol. 145, no. 25 (June 19, 1995), pp. 21–26.

11. Ira Berkow, "Dear Mickey: Messages and Prayers for an American Hero," *New York Times*, June 25, 1995, p. S9.

NOTES TO CHAPTER 1

1. Slavoj Zizek, *The Sublime Object of Ideology* (London: Verso, 1989), p. 118.

2. Jean-Paul Sartre, *Anti-Semite and Jew* (New York: Schocken Books, 1948), pp. 17, 69.

3. Homi K. Bhabha, *The Location of Culture* (New York: Routledge, 1994), p. 82.

4. Aijaz Ahmad, *In Theory, Classes, Nations, Literatures* (London: Verso, 1992).

5. Julia Kristeva, *Strangers to Ourselves*, trans. by Leon Roudiez (New York: Columbia University Press, 1991), p. 195. See also: *Nations Without Nationalism*, trans. by Leon Roudiez (New York: Columbia University Press, 1993).

6. Michael Taussig, *Mimesis and Alterity* (New York: Routledge, 1993), p. xvi.

7. See the fabulous discussion of the unspeakability of hate in Shoshana Felman and Dori Laub, *Testimony* (New York: Routledge, 1992).

8. As quoted in Robert D. McFadden, "Islam Speaker in New Tirade Against Jews," *New York Times*, February 28, 1994, p. B1. See also The Nation of Islam, *The Secret Relationship Between Blacks and Jews*, vol. 1 (Boston: Latimer Associates, 1991); and Tony Martin, *The Jewish Onslaught* (Dover, Mass.: The Majority Press, 1993).

9. As quoted in Roger Cohen, "Sarajevo Girl Killed, Yet Serbs Suffer," *New York Times*, April 26, 1995, p. A8.

10. James Brooke, "Boom! Suddenly, The Children See Life Starkly," *New York Times*, July 27, 1994, p. A4.

11. James Brooke, "Car Bomb Outside the Israeli Embassy in London Wounds 13," *New York Times*, July 27, 1994, p. A8.

12. Sergei Kovalev, "Death in Chechnya," *New York Review of Books*, vol. XLII, no. 10 (May 11, 1995), p. 12.

13. Christoper Hitchens, "Minority Report," *The Nation*, vol. 260, no. 20 (May 22, 1995), p. 711.

14. Mark Thompson, "The Final Solution of Bosnia-Hercegovina," in Rabia Ali and Lawrence Lifschultz, eds., *Why Bosnia? Writings on the Balkan War* (Connecticut: The Pamphleteer's Press, 1993), p. 164.

15. Jacqueline Rose, *Why War?* (Oxford: Blackwell, 1993), pp. 5, 10.

16. Mikkel Borch-Jacobsen, *The Freudian Subject* (Stanford: Stanford University Press, 1988), pp. 5, 4, 2.

17. Ronald Takaki, *Iron Cages, Race and Culture in 19th Century America* (New York: Alfred Knopf, 1979), pp. 13, 148.

18. Jacqueline Rose, p. 33.

19. Wilhelm Reich, *The Mass Psychology of Fascism* (New York: Farrar, Straus and Giroux, 1970), pp. 41, 20. Also see: Lee Baxandall, ed., *Sex-Pol, Essays*, 1929–34 (New York: Vintage Books, 1966).

20. T.W. Adorno, Else Frenkel-Brunswik, Daniel Levinson, and R. Nevitt Sanford, *The Authoritarian Personality* (New York: W.W. Norton and Co., 1950), p. 976.

21. Frantz Fanon, *Black Skin, White Masks* (New York: Grove Press, 1967), pp. 92, 93.

22. Paul Gilroy, *There Ain't No Black in the Union Jack: The Cultural Politics of Race and Nation* (London: Hutchinson, 1987), p. 12.

23. Jonathan Rutherford, "A Place Called Home: Identity and the Cultural Politics of Difference," in Jonathan Rutherford, ed., *Identity, Community, Culture, Difference* (London: Lawrence & Wishart), pp. 11, 13.

24. Michael Kimmelman, "Constructing Images of the Black Male," *New York Times*, November 11, 1994, p. C1.

25. Judith Butler, "Endangered/Endangering: Schematic Racism and White Paranoia," in Robert Gooding-Williams, ed., *Reading Rodney King, Reading Urban Uprising* (New York: Routledge, 1993), p. 19.

26. Frantz Fanon, pp. 159, 162.

27. Adolf Hitler, *Mein Kampf* (New York: Reynal & Kitchcock, 1940), pp. 26, 111.

28. Wilhelm Reich, pp. 101–103.

29. Michael Ignatieff, *Blood and Belonging* (New York: Farrar, Straus and Giroux, 1993), pp. 5, 246.

30. Danilo Kis, "On Nationalism," in Ali and Lifschultz, eds., *Why Bosnia?* p. 126.

31. As quoted in Alan Riding, "From Sarajevo, A Girl and A Diary," *New York Times*, January 6, 1994, p. A1. See also Zlata Filopovic, *Zlata's Diary: A Child's Life in Sarajevo* (New York: Viking/Penguin, 1994).

32. Zizek, *The Sublime Object of Ideology*; and his *For They Know Not What*

They Do; Enjoyment as a Political Factor (London: Verso, 1991).

33. Zlatko Dizdarevic, *Portraits of Sarajevo* (New York: Fromm International Pub. Corp., 1994), p. 96.

34. Steven Holmes, "You're Smart If You Know What Race You Are," *New York Times*, October 23, 1994, p. E5.

35. Julia Kristeva, *Powers of Horror: An Essay on Abjection* (New York: Columbia University Press, 1982); and her *Desire in Language: A Semiotic Approach to Literature and Art* (New York: Columbia University Press, 1980).

36. Zizek, *The Sublime Object of Ideology*, p. 47.

37. *Ibid.*, pp. 29, 118, 123, 126.

38. Anna Marie Smith, *New Right Discourse on Race and Sexuality*, Britain 1968–90 (New York: Cambridge University Press, 1994).

39. Bruno Bettelheim, "The Ignored Lesson of Anne Frank," in *Surviving and Other Essays* (New York: Alfred Knopf, 1979), p. 250.

40. Zizek, *The Sublime Object of Ideology*, p. 33.

41. Alison Owings, *Frauen: German Women Recall the Third Reich* (New Brunswick, N.J.: Rutgers University Press, 1993), pp. 440, 460, 473, 340, 213.

42. *Ibid.*, pp. 22, 23, 213.

43. Hannah Arendt, *Eichmann in Jerusalem: A Report on the Banality of Evil* (New York: Penguin, 1963), p. 233.

44. *Ibid.*, pp. 174, 458.

45. *Ibid.*, p. 133.

46. Jacques Lacan, *Speech and Language in Psychoanalysis*, trans. by Anthony Wilden (Baltimore: Johns Hopkins Univ. Press, 1968); Anike Lemaire, *Jacques Lacan*, trans. by David Macey (New York: Routledge & Kegan Paul, 1977); Juliet Mitchell and Jacqueline Rose, eds., *Feminine Sexuality: Jacques Lacan and the Ecole Freudienne* (New York: W.W. Norton, 1982); and Zizek, *The Sublime Object of Ideology*.

47. Maria Lugones, "Purity, Impurity and Separation," *Signs: Journal of Women in Culture and Society*, vol. 19, no. 2 (Winter 1994), p. 469. See also Gloria Anzaldua, *Borderlands, La Frontera* (San Francisco: aunt lute books, 1987).

48. Douglas Crimp, "Right on, Girlfriend," in Michael Warner, ed., *Fear of a Queer Planet* (Minneapolis: University of Minnesota Press, 1993), p. 316.

49. Lauren Berlant and Elizabeth Freeman, "Queer Nationality," in Warner, ed., *ibid.*, p. 205.

50. Anna Marie Smith, *New Right Discourse on Race and Sexuality*, p. 40.

51. Renate Bridenthal, Atina Grossmann, and Marion Kaplan, *When Biology Became Destiny: Women in Weimar and Nazi Germany* (New York: Monthly Review Press, 1984), p. xiv.

52. See: Judith Butler, *Bodies That Matter* (New York: Routledge, 1993), especially chapter 2, for an interesting discussion of the lesbian phallus.

53. Kristeva, *Strangers to Ourselves*, pp. 103, 117, 66, 1, 170, 192.

54. Jeanine Amber, "Brothers and Sisters: One Woman Faces the Nation," in *Village Voice*, vol. xxxix, no. 7 (February 15, 1994), p. 28.

55. Sigmund Freud, "The Taboo of Virginity," James Strachey, ed. and trans., *The Standard Edition of the Complete Psychological Works of Sigmund Freud* (London: Hogarth Press, 1953, 74), vol. 11, p. 199. Also see vol. 21, chapter 5, "Civilization and Its Discontents," p. 114.

56. Michael Ignatieff, pp. 21–28.

57. Klaus Theweleit, *Male Fantasies,* vol. 1 (Minneapolis: University of Minnesota Press, 1987), p. 434.

58. Julia Kristeva in Toril Moi, ed., *The Kristeva Reader* (New York: Columbia University Press, 1986), p. 312.

59. Kathleen Canning, "Feminist History after the Linguistic Turn: Historicizing Discourse and Experience," *Signs: Journal of Women in Culture and Society*, vol. 19, no. 2 (Winter 1994), p. 369.

60. Alice Walker and Pratibha Parmar, *Warrior Marks: Female Genital Mutilation and the Sexual Blinding of Women* (New York: Harcourt Brace & Co., 1993), pp. 110, 12, 10.

61. Dorinda Outram, *The Body and the French Revolution* (New Haven: Yale University Press, 1989), p. 1.

62. Judith Butler, *Bodies That Matter*, p. 234.

63. Mary Douglas, *Purity and Danger: An Analysis of the Concepts of Pollution and Taboo* (New York: Routledge, 1991), p. 4.

64. Kristeva, *Powers of Horror*, pp. 71, 59, 77.

65. Sandra Lee Bartky, "Foucault, Femininity, and the Modernization of Patriarchal Power," in Irene Diamond and Lee Quinby, ed., *Feminism and Foucault* (Boston: Northeastern University Press, 1988), p. 71.

66. Zillah Eisenstein, *The Female Body and the Law* (Berkeley: University of California Press, 1988), p. 80.

67. Leslie A. Adelson, *Making Bodies, Making History* (Lincoln: University of Nebraska, 1993), p. 19.

68. *Ibid.,* pp. 1, 2, 34.

69. See Linda Nicholson, "Interpreting Gender," *Signs*, vol. 20, no. 1 (Autumn 1994), pp. 70–103, for a provocative discussion of the meanings of sex, gender, and bodies.

70. Frantz Fanon, pp. 117, 116.

71. Lisa Jones, *bulletproof diva* (New York: Doubleday, 1994), p. 296.

72. William Schmidt, "Refugee Missionaries From Rwanda Speak of Their Terror, Grief and Guilt," *New York Times*, April 12 1994, p. A6.

73. See the discussion by Judith Lewis Herman, *Trauma and Recovery* (New York: Basic Books, 1992).

74. Dorinda Outram, p. 23.

75. Mikhail Bakhtin, *Rabelais and His World*, trans. by Helene Iswolsky (Bloomington: Indiana University Press, 1984), p. 26.

76. Kristeva, *Powers of Horror*, p. 72.

77. Michel Foucault, *Discipline and Punish: The Birth of the Prison*, trans. by Alan Sheridan (New York: Vintage Books, 1979); and his *Power/Knowledge: Selected Interviews and Other Writings 1972–77*, ed. by Colin Gordon (New York: Pantheon, 1972).

78. Dorinda Outram, pp. 21, 1.

79. Elizabeth Grosz, "Inscriptions and body-maps: representations and the corporeal," in Terry Threadgold and Anne Cranny-Francis, *Feminine, Masculine and Representation* (London: Allen & Unwin, 1990), pp. 62, 73, 64, 69.

80. Elaine Scarry, *The Body in Pain* (New York: Oxford University Press, 1985), pp. 3, 14–18, 23, 27, 28.

81. Karen Remmler, "Sheltering Battered Bodies in Language, Imprisonment Once More?" in Angelika Bammer, ed., *displacements* (Bloomington: Indiana University Press, 1994), p. 224.

82. Judith Lewis Herman, pp. 37, 51, 52.

83. Shoshana Felman and Dori Laub, pp. 109, 160.

84. W. E. B. Du Bois, *The Souls of Black Folk* (New York: Signet Classic, 1969), p. 94.

85. Ali & Lifshultz, eds., *Why Bosnia?*, p. 113.

86. Mary Douglas, *Natural Symbols* (New York: Pantheon, 1982), p. vii.

87. David Theo Goldberg, *Racist Culture* (Oxford: Blackwell, 1993), pp. 81, 80.

88. Etienne Balibar, "Racism and Nationalism," in Etienne Balibar and Immanuel Wallerstein, *Race, Nation, Class* (London: Verso, 1991), p. 37.

89. Shirlee Taylor Haizlip, *The Sweeter the Juice* (Simon & Schuster, 1994), p. 266.

90. Etienne Balibar, "Is There a 'Neo-Racism'?" in Balibar and Wallerstein, p. 23.

91. Arendt, *Eichmann in Jerusalem*, pp. 113, 169.

92. Roger Cohen, "Bosnian Foes Gaze at History's Mirror and See a Jew," *New York Times*, October 2, 1994, p. E3.

93. Lisa Jones, p. 31.

94. As quoted in Sharon Begley, "Race Is Not Enough," *Newsweek*, vol. CXXV, no. 7 (February 13, 1995), p. 68.

95. Shirlee Taylor Haizlip, pp. 14, 30.

96. Sander L. Gilman, *Jewish Self-Hatred* (Baltimore: Johns Hopkins, 1986), p. 207.

97. W. E. B. Du Bois, p. 54.

98. Etienne Balibar, "Is There a 'Neo-Racism'?" and "Racism and Nationalism," in Balibar and Wallerstein, pp. 40, 37, 26.

99. *Ibid.*, p. 21.

100. W. E. B. Du Bois, "Fifty Years After" edition of *The Souls of Black Folk* (New York: Blue Heron Press, 1953) and reprinted in *Monthly Review*, vol. 45, no. 7 (December 1993), p. 34.

101. Richard Herrnstein and Charles Murray, *The Bell Curve: Intelligence and Class Structure in American Life* (New York: The Free Press, 1994).

102. Zlatko Dizdarevic, *Sarajevo, A War Journal* (New York: Fromm International, 1993), p. 21.

103. Edward W. Said, *Orientalism* (New York: Vintage Press, 1978), pp. 311–12.

104. Winthrop D. Jordan, *White Over Black: American Attitudes Toward the Negro, 1550–1812* (New York: W.W. Norton, 1968), pp. 238, 151.

105. Calvin C. Hernton, *Sex and Racism in America* (New York: Grove Press, 1965), p. 245.

106. Sander L. Gilman, *Freud, Race, and Gender* (Princeton: Princeton University Press, 1993), pp. 36–58.

107. Faisal Fatehali Devji, "Hindu/Muslim/Indian," *Public Culture*, vol. 5, no. 1 (Fall 1992), p. 12.

108. As stated in Partha Chatterjee, *Nationalist Thought and the Colonial World* (Minneapolis: Univ. of Minnesota Press, 1993), p. 54.

109. Sander Gilman, *Freud, Race, and Gender*, pp. 49, 172, 163.

110. *Ibid.*, p. 38–39.

111. Ali & Lifshultz, eds., *Why Bosnia?*, p. xix.

112. Paul Hockenos, *Free to Hate: The Rise of the Right in Post-Communist Eastern Europe* (New York: Routledge, 1993), pp. 25, 27.

113. Sander Gilman, *Freud, Race, and Gender*, p. 19–20.

114. Alison Owings, p. 341.

115. Ali & Lifshultz, eds., *Why Bosnia?*, p. 56.

116. *Ibid.*, p. 123.

117. Bridenthal, Grossmann, and Marion Kaplan, p. 272. Also see: Cornelie Usborne, *The Politics of the Body in Weimar Germany* (Ann Arbor: University of Michigan Press, 1992).

118. George L. Mosse, *The Crisis of German Ideology* (New York: Schocken Books, 1981), p. 141.

119. Bridenthal, Grossmann, and Kaplan, pp. 24, 272, 288.

120. Sandra Lee Bartky, pp. 62, 64.

121. Faisal Devji, p. 9.

122. Fatima Mernissi, *The Veil and the Male Elite*, trans. by Mary Jo Lakeland (New York: Addison-Wesley, 1987), pp. 93, 195.

NOTES TO CHAPTER 2

1. "Culture, Nationalism, and the Role of Intellectuals: An Interview with Aijaz Ahmad," *Monthly Review*, vol. 47, no. 3 (July/August 1995), p. 48.

2. Susan Jeffords and Lauren Rabinovitz, "Seeing through Patriotism," in Susan Jeffords and Lauren Rabinovitz, eds., *Seeing Through the Media: The Persian Gulf War* (New Brunswick, N.J.: Rutgers University Press, 1994), p. 207.

3. Judith Butler, noting Ruth Gilmore, in "Endangered/Endangering: Schematic Racism and White Paranoia," in Robert Gooding-Williams, ed., *Reading Rodney King, Reading Urban Uprising* (New York: Routledge, 1993), p. 16.

4. I am grateful to Joy James for helping me to clarify this point of differential privilege within the nation.

5. Salman Rushdie, *The Satanic Verses* (Dover, Del.: The Consortium, 1988), p. 469.

6. Hans Magnus Enzensberger, *Civil Wars: From L.A. to Bosnia* (New York: The New Press, 1994), pp. 20–21.

7. Jacqueline Rose, *Why War?* (Oxford: Blackwell, 1993), pp. 16, 17.

8. See Benedict Anderson, *Imagined Communities: Reflections on the Origin and Spread of Nationalism* (New York: Verso, 1983, 1991) for a full accounting of this idea.

9. See William Pfaff, *The Wrath of Nations* (New York: Simon & Schuster, 1993), p. 40, for a discussion of nation as a collectivity.

10. Edgar Morin, quoted in Geoffrey Bennington, "Postal Politics and the Institution of the Nation," in Homi Bhabha, ed., *Nation and Narration* (New York: Routledge, 1990), p. 121.

11. William Pfaff, p. 137.

12. Gayatri Chakravorty Spivak, *Outside in the Teaching Machine* (New York: Routledge, 1993), p. 55.

13. For a full discussion of state privatization see Zillah Eisenstein, *The Color of Gender: Reimaging Democracy* (Berkeley: University of California Press, 1994).

14. Hans Magnus Enzensberger, p. 107.

15. Hannah Arendt, *The Origins of Totalitarianism* (New York: Meridian Books, 1951), p. 185.

16. Hannah Arendt, *Eichmann in Jerusalem* (New York: Penguin, 1977), p. 60.

17. Edward Said, *The Question of Palestine* (New York: Vintage, 1979, 1992), pp. xxi, 87.

18. Paul Gilroy, *"There Ain't No Black in the Union Jack," The Cultural Politics of Race and Nation* (London: Hutchinson, 1987), p. 46.

19. David Theo Goldberg, *Racist Culture* (Oxford: Blackwell, 1993), p. 79.

20. As quoted by Gina Dent, "Black Pleasure, Black Joy: An Introduction," in Gina Dent, ed., *Black Popular Culture* (Seattle: Bay Press, 1992), p. 9.

21. David Theo Goldberg, p. 81.

22. Yale Strom, *Uncertain Roads: Searching for the Gypsies* (New York: Four Winds Press, 1993), p. 50.

23. Introduction to Andrew Parker, Mary Russo, Doris Sommer, and Patricia Yaeger, eds., *Nationalism and Sexualities* (New York: Routledge, 1992), p. 8.

24. Stuart Marshall, "The Contemporary Political Use of Gay History: The Third Reich," in Bad Object Choices, eds., *How Do I Look? Queer Film and Video* (Seattle: Bay Press, 1991), p. 86.

25. Phyllis Bennis, "Command and Control: Politics and Power in the Post–Cold War United Nations," in Phyllis Bennis and Michel Moushabeck, eds., *Altered States: A Reader in the New World Order* (New York: Olive Branch Press, 1993), p. 48.

26. Chris Hedges, "War Turns Sarajevo Away From Europe," *New York Times*, July 28, 1995, p. A4.

27. Faisal Fatehali Devji, "Hindu/Muslim/Indian," *Public Culture*, vol. 5, no. 1 (Fall 1992), pp. 3, 7.

28. James Snead, "European Pedigrees/African Contagions: Nationality, Narrative, and Communality in Tutuola, Achebe, and Reed," in Homi K. Bhabha, ed., *Nation and Narration* (New York: Routledge, 1990), p. 245.

29. James Kurth, "The Post-Modern State," *The National Interest*, no. 28 (Summer 1992), p. 32. Also see: Samuel Huntington, "The Clash of Civilizations?" *Foreign Affairs*, vol. 72, no. 3 (Summer 1993), pp. 22–49; and his "If Not Civilizations, What?" *Foreign Affairs*, vol. 72, no 5 (December 1993), pp. 186–194; "Comments; Responses to Samuel Huntington's 'The Clash of Civilizations,'" *Foreign Affairs*, vol. 72, no. 4 (September/October 1993), pp. 2–26; and Bruce Porter, "Can American Democracy Survive?" *Commentary*, vol. 96, no. 5 (November 1993), pp. 37–40.

30. E.J. Hobsbawm, *Nations and Nationalism Since 1780* (New York: Cambridge University Press, 1990), pp. 185, 187.

31. George Soros, "Bosnia and Beyond," *New York Review of Books*, vol. XL, no. 13 (October 7, 1993), p. 15. See also Robert Block, "Killers," *New York Review of Books*, vol. XL, no. 19 (November 8, 1993), p. 9; and Misha Glenny, "Bosnia: The Tragic Prospect," *New York Review of Books*, vol. XL, no. 18 (November 4, 1993), pp. 38–49.

32. Renata Salecl, "Nationalism, Anti-Semitism, and Anti-Feminism in Eastern Europe," *New German Critique*, no. 57 (Fall 1992), p. 54. Also see her *The Spoils of Freedom* (New York: Routledge, 1994).

33. For an interesting discussion of the continual redefinition of racial

and sexual discrimination see Immanuel Wallerstein, "The Ideological Tensions of Capitalism: Universalism versus Racism and Sexism," in Etienne Balibar and Immanuel Wallerstein, *Race, Nation, Class, Ambiguous Identities* (New York: Verso, 1991), p. 34.

34. Paul Gilroy, "It's a Family Affair," in Gina Dent, ed., *Black Popular Culture*, pp. 306, 311, 310.

35. Angela Davis, "Black Nationalism: The Sixties and the Nineties," in Gina Dent, ed., *ibid*., p. 324.

36. Shireen Hassim, "Family, Motherhood and Zulu Nationalism: The Politics of the Inkatha Women's Brigade," *Feminist Review*, no. 43 (Spring 1993), pp. 17, 20.

37. I am indebted to conversations with Rosalind Petchesky for clarification of this point.

38. Stephen Kinzer, "The War Memorial: To Embrace the Guilty, Too?" *New York Times*, November 15, 1993, p. A4.

39. Sylvia Walby, "Woman and Nation," *International Journal of Comparative Sociology*, vol. xxxiii, nos. 1–2 (January/April 1992), p. 83.

40. Virginia Woolf, *The Three Guineas* (London: Harcourt, Brace and World, 1938), p. 109.

41. Anannya Bhattachardee, "The Habit of Ex-Nomination: Nation, Woman, and the Indian Immigrant Bourgeoisie," *Public Culture*, vol. 5, no. 1 (Fall 1992), pp. 20, 30, 31.

42. Ernest Gellner, *Nations and Nationalism* (Ithaca: Cornell University Press, 1983), p. 15. Also see Partha Chatterjee, *Nationalist Thought and the Colonial World* (Minneapolis: University of Minnesota Press, 1986, 1993); and Homi K. Bhabha, *The Location of Culture* (New York: Routledge, 1994).

43. Benedict Anderson, *Imagined Communities*, pp. 6, 22, 36, 144.

44. *Ibid*., pp. 16, 6, 15.

45. *Ibid*., pp. 141–54. For critiques of Anderson's treatment of race and nation, see Homi K. Bhabha, *The Location of Culture*, pp. 248–250; and David Theo Goldberg, p. 79.

46. W. E. B. Du Bois, *The Souls of Black Folk* (New York: Signet, 1969), p. 51.

47. Floya Anthias and Nira Yuval-Davis, *Racialized Boundaries* (New York: Routledge, 1992), p. 22.

48. Geraldine Heng and Janadas Devan, "State Fatherhood: The Politics of Nationalism, Sexuality, and Race in Singapore," in *Nationalisms and Sexualities*, p. 356.

49. George Mosse, *Nationalism and Sexuality* (Madison: University of Wisconsin Press, 1985), p. 1.

50. Geraldine Heng and Janadas Devan, p. 349.

51. Greta N. Slobin, "Revolution Must Come First: Reading V. Arsenov's Island of Crimea," *Nationalisms and Sexualities*, p. 249.

52. Anne McClintock, "'No Longer in a Future Heaven': Women and Nationalism in South Africa," *Transition*, 51 (1991), p. 104.

53. Patricia Hill Collins, "Learning to Think for Ourselves: Malcolm X's Black Nationalism Reconsidered," in Joe Wood, ed., *Malcolm X, In Our Own Image* (New York: St. Martin's Press, 1992), pp. 78–79.

54. Judith Butler, *Bodies That Matter* (New York: Routledge, 1993), p. 191.

55. I do not mean to make this all too simple. The use of familial symbolisms have been successfully used to mobilize women in the support of the nation. Women in the Ku Klux Klan circulated racial, religious, and national bigotry. See Kathleen Blee, *Women of the Klan* (Berkeley: University of California Press, 1991), p. 3.

56. See Anna Marie Smith, *New Right Discourse on Race and Sexuality* (New York: Cambridge University Press, 1994) for an interesting discussion of the common-sense realities of fictive imagery.

57. Anna Quindlen, "Barbie at 35," *New York Times*, September 10, 1994, p. A19.

58. Natalini Natarajan, "Woman, Nation, and Narration in *Midnight's Children*," in Inderpal Grewal and Caren Kaplan, eds., *Scattered Hegemonies* (Minneapolis: University of Minnesota Press, 1994), pp. 79, 88, 83, 85.

59. See the "Introduction" in Valentine M. Moghadam, ed., *Gender and National Identity* (London: Zed Press, 1994).

60. Lata Mani, "Contentious Tradition: The Debate on Sati in Colonial India," in Kumkum Sangari and Sudesh Vaid, eds., *Recasting Women* (New Brunswick, N.J.: Rutgers University Press, 1990), p. 118.

61. Uma Chakravarti, "Whatever Happened to the Vedic Dasi?" in *ibid.*, p. 79.

62. Karima Bennoune, "Algerian Women Confront Fundamentalism," *Monthly Review*, vol. 46, no. 4 (September 1994), pp. 26–49.

63. I am indebted to conversations with Linda Zerilli for clarification of this discussion.

64. Edward Said, *Orientalism* (New York: Vintage Books, 1978), p. 54.

65. *Ibid.*, pp. 312, 43, 5, 55, 73.

66. Julia Kristeva, *Nations Without Nationalism* (New York: Columbia University Press, 1993), p. 35.

67. Nancy Chodorow, "Gender as a Personal and Cultural Construction," *Signs*, vol. 20, no. 3 (Spring 1995), pp. 518, 536, 541.

68. Marianne Hirsch, "Pictures of a Displaced Girlhood," in Angelika Bammer, ed., *Displacements* (Bloomington: Indiana University Press, 1994), p. 75.

69. Julia Kristeva, *Desire in Language: A Semiotic Approach to Literature and Art* (New York: Columbia University Press, 1980), pp. 136, 137.

70. For further discussion, see Juliet Mitchell and Jacqueline Rose, eds., *Feminine Sexuality: Jacques Lacan and the Ecole Freudienne* (New York: W.W. Norton & Co., 1983); and Renata Salecl, *The Spoils of Freedom*.

71. George Mosse, *Nationalism and Sexuality*, pp. 132–34.

72. Mark Gevisser, "Who is a South African?" *New York Times*, April 26, 1994, p. A23.

73. Craig Charney, "Democracy Won," *New York Times*, April 27, 1994, p. A17.

74. Rey Chow, *Woman and Chinese Modernity* (Minnesota: The University of Minnesota Press, 1991), pp. xiii, 3.

75. Zarana Papic, "Nationalisms, Patriarchy and War," pp. 6, 8. Paper delivered at the Network of East-West Women Public Policy Forum: "Gender and Nationalism: The Impact of the Post-Communist Transition," October 26–27, 1993, Washington, D.C. Also see her unpublished paper "Nationalism, War and Gender: Ex-Feminity and Ex-Masculinity of Ex-Yugoslavian Ex-Citizens," Faculty of Philosophy, Dept. of Sociology, Belgrade.

76. Michael Schmidt, *The New Reich: Violent Extremism in Unified Germany and Beyond* (New York: Pantheon Books, 1993). Also see Czeslaw Milosv, "Swing Shift in the Baltics," *New York Review of Books*, vol. XL, no. 18 (November 4, 1993), pp. 12–16; and Craig Whitney, "Germans Begin to Recognize Danger in Neo-Nazi Upsurge" *New York Times*, October 21, 1993, p. A1.

77. Stephen Kinzer, "News Media in Belgrade Mute Their Nationalism," *New York Times*, July 8, 1995, p. A5.

78. Zlatko Dizdarevic, *Portraits of Sarajevo*, (New York: Fromm International, 1994), pp. 49, 54.

79. Schmidt, *The New Reich*, pp. 215, 217. Also see: Paul Hockenos, *Free to Hate, The Rise of the Right in Post-Communist Eastern Europe* (New York: Routledge, 1993); Paul Lewis, "Stoked by Ethnic Conflict, Refugee Numbers Swell," *New York Times*, November 10, 1993, p. A6; and the *Report of the United Nations Commissioner for Refugees*, October 1993.

80. Milica Antic, "Yugoslavia: The Traditional Spirit of the Age," in Chris Corrin, ed., *Superwomen and the Double Burden* (Toronto: Second Story Press, 1992), p. 178.

81. Lydia H. Liu, "The Female Body and Nationalist Discourse: Manchuria in Xiao Hong's *Field of Life and Death*," in Angela Zito and Tani E. Barlow, eds., *Body, Subject and Power in China* (Chicago: University of Chicago, 1994), pp. 161–62.

82. Wilhelm Reich, *The Mass Psychology of Fascism* (New York: Farrar, Straus and Giroux, 1970), p. 57.

83. Ruth Seifert, "War and Rape: A Preliminary Analysis," in Alexandra Stiglmayer, ed., *Mass Rape, The War Against Women in Bosnia-Herzegovina* (Lincoln: University of Nebraska Press, 1994), p. 65.

84. Julie Mertus, "Women Warriors," in *The Village Voice*, vol. xxxii, no. 40 (October 5, 1993), p. 20.

85. Mita Castle-Kanerova, "Czech and Slovak Federative Republic: The Culture of Strong Women in the Making," in Chris Corrin, ed., *Superwomen and the Double Burden* (Toronto: Second Story Press, 1992), p. 102.

86. Normal Cigar, *Genocide in Bosnia* (College Station: Texas A&M University Press, 1995); and Jasminka Udovicki and James Ridgeway, eds., *Yugoslavia's Ethnic Nightmare* (New York: Lawrence Hill Books, 1995).

87. Ann Jones, *Next Time She'll Be Dead* (Boston: Beacon Press, 1994). See also Emily Love, "Equality in Political Asylum Law: For a Legislative Recognition of Gender Based Persecution," pp. 133–56; and Elizabeth A. Pendo, "Recognizing Violence Against Women: Gender and Hate Crimes Statistics Act," pp. 157–84, both in *The Harvard Women's Law Journal*, vol. 17 (Spring 1994).

88. Catharine MacKinnon, "Turning Rape into Pornography: Postmodern Genocide," in *Mass Rape*, p. 184.

89. Slavenka Drakulic, "Women Hide Behind a Wall of Silence," *The Nation*, vol. 256, no. 8 (March 1, 1993), pp. 253–72; Jeri Laber, "Bosnia: Questions About Rape," *New York Review of Books*, vol. XL, no. 6 (March 25,

1993), pp. 3–6; Paul Lewis, "Rape Was Weapon of Serbs, U.N. Says," *New York Times*, October 20, 1993, p. A1; Alan Riding, "European Inquiry Says Serbs' Forces Have Raped 20,000," *New York Times*, January 9, 1993, p. A1; Laura Pitter and Alexandra Stiglmayer, "Will the World Remember? Can the Women Forget?" *Ms. Magazine*, vol. 3, no. 5 (March/April 1993), pp. 19–22; and "Serbia's War Against Bosnia and Croatia," *Off Our Backs*, vol. xxiii, no. 5 (May 1993), pp. 4–6.

90. Julie Mertus, "Women Warriors," p. 20. Also see: Rachel Pine and Julie Mertus, "Meeting the Health Needs of Women Survivors of the Balkan Conflict," pamphlet (New York: The Center for Reproductive Law and Policy, 1993). For a different viewing of the issue of rape in its more generalized statement of gender violence, see Catharine MacKinnon, "Turning Rape Into Pornography: Postmodern Genocide," *Ms. Magazine*, vol. 4, no. 1 (July/August 1993), pp. 24–30.

91. Correction in *New York Times*, October 23, 1993, p. A1. This was a revision of Paul Lewis's, "Rape Was Weapon of Serbs, U.N. Says," *New York Times*, October 20, 1993, p. A1.

92. Rhonda Copelon, "Surfacing Gender: Reconceptualizing Crimes Against Women in Time of War," in *Mass Rape*, p. 205.

93. Ruth Seifert, *Mass Rape*, p. 65. Also see Mandy Jacobson's film *War Crimes Against Women*, Bowery Productions, Community Television, tel. no. 212–219–1385.

94. Inger Agger, *The Blue Room* (London: Zed Books, 1994), p. 106.

95. *Ibid*, pp. 7–8, 21, 106.

96. Ruth Seifert, *Mass Rape*, p. 55.

97. Alexandra Stiglmayer, "The Rapes in Bosnia-Herzegovina," in *Mass Rape*, p. 85.

98. Discussions with John Borneman first alerted me to this reality. Also see Victoria Stegic, "Des Milliers d'hommes victimes de violences sexuelles dans les camps en ex-Yougoslavie?" *La Presse*, Montreal, March 9, 1995, p. 25.

99. John Borneman, "Towards a Theory of Ethnic Cleansing: Territorial Sovereignty, Heterosexuality and Europe," in *Working Papers on Transitions from State Socialism*, Mario Einaudi Center for International Studies, Cornell University, April 1994.

100. *Ibid.*, p. 57.

101. Frantz Fanon, *The Wretched of the Earth* (New York: Grove Press, 1963), pp. 254–59.

102. Donatella Lorch, "Wave of Rape Adds New Horror to Rwanda's Trail of Savagery," *New York Times*, May 15, 1995, pp. A1, A6.

103. As discussed in Laura Palmer, "Her Own Private Tailhook," *New York Times Magazine*, May 28, 1995, pp. 22–25.

104. The "women in black" take their name from the israeli women who are anti-war and committed to building bridges with palestinian women.

105. Timothy Brennan, "The national longing for form," in Homi K. Bhabha, *Nation and Narration*, p. 46.

NOTES TO CHAPTER 3

1. Hazel V. Carby, The Multicultural Wars," in Gina Dent, ed., *Black Popular Culture* (Seattle: Bay Press, 1992), p. 190.

2. Floya Anthias and Nira Yuval-Davis, *Racialized Boundaries* (New York: Routledge, 1992), p. 38.

3. Arthur M. Schlesinger Jr., *The Disuniting of America* (New York: W.W. Norton, 1992), pp. 17, 40, 41.

4. Benjamin Schwarz, "The Diversity Myth: America's Leading Export," *The Atlantic Monthly*, vol. 275, no. 5 (May 1995), p. 60.

5. Salman Rushdie, *Imaginary Homelands* (London: Granta Books, 1991), p. 137.

6. For interesting discussions or radical revisioning of the way we "view," see Russell Ferguson, Martha Gever, Trinh T. Minh-ha, and Cornel West, eds., *Out There: Marginalization and Contemporary Cultures* (Cambridge: MIT Press, 1990); and Gayatri Chakravorty Spivak, *Outside in the Teaching Machine* (New York: Routledge, 1993).

7. Marsha Sinetar, *Developing a 21st Century Mind* (New York: Villard Books, 1991).

8. From an autobiographical text by Isak Samokovlija, cited in Rabia Ali and Lawrence Lifschultz, eds., *Why Bosnia? Writings on the Balkan War* (Connecticut: The Pamphleteer's Press, 1993), p. 245.

9. "We Are All Neighbors," a Granada video film, presented by anthropologist Tone Bringa; available from Globalvision, 1600 Broadway, Suite 700, New York, N.Y., 10019.

10. Quoted in David Firestone, "U.S. Immigrants Make Christmas Their Very Own," *New York Times*, December 26, 1993, p. 36.

11. Dale Maharidge, "Can We All Get Along?" *Mother Jones*, vol. 18, issue 6 (November/December 1993), p. 23.

12. David Lyons, "The Balance of Injustice and the War for Independence," *Monthly Review*, 45, no. 11 (April 1994), pp. 17–25; Howard Zinn, *A People's History of the United States* (New York: Harper & Row, 1980). See also Roy Rosenzweig, Steve Brier, and Josh Brown, *Who Built America?* (New York: Voyager, 1993), CD-ROM, MacIntosh.

13. Robert S. Boynton, "The New Intellectuals," *The Atlantic Monthly*, vol. 275, no. 3 (March 1995), p. 70.

14. Ronald Takaki, *Iron Cages: Race and Culture in 19th Century America* (New York: Alfred Knopf, 1979), p. 79.

15. Kimberle Crenshaw, "Mapping the Margins: Intersectionality, Identity Politics, and Violence Against Women of Color," *Stanford Law Review*, 43, no. 6 (July 1991), pp. 1241–99.

16. Richard Barnet and John Cavanagh, *Global Dreams* (New York: Simon & Schuster, 1994), p. 308.

17. Annette Kolodny, "Setting an Agenda for Change: Meeting the Challenges and Exploring the Opportunities in Higher Education," *Transformations*, vol. 4, no. 2 (Fall 1993), p. 5.

18. Sam Roberts, "Hispanic Population Outnumbers Blacks in Four Cities as Nation's Demographics Shift," *New York Times*, October 9, 1994, p. A34.

19. Report 878, "Employment in Perspective: Minority Workers," 2nd quarter, 1994; U.S. Dept. of Labor, Bureau of Labor Statistics, p. 1.

20. Dale Maharidge, "Can We All Get Along?" *Mother Jones*, vol. 18, issue 6 (November/December 1993), pp. 19, 22. Also see "Americans in 2020: Less White, More Southern," *New York Times*, April 22, 1994, p. A16.

21. David Rieff, *Los Angeles: Capital of the Third World* (New York: Touchstone Book, 1991), p. 57.

22. Lois Foster and David Stockley, *Multiculturalism: The Changing Australian Paradigm* (England: Multilingual Matters, 1984), pp. 8, 19, 57.

23. Gayatri Chakravorty Spivak, *Outside in the Teaching Machine* (New York: Routledge, 1993), p. 80.

24. Sneja Gunew, "Multicultural Writers: Where Are We Writing from and Who Are We Writing For?" in *Writing in Multicultural Australia 1984: An*

Overview, compiled by the multicultural literature program (North Sydney: Australia Council for the Literature Board, 1985), p. 20.

25. George Michelakakis, "Literature and the Greek Migrants in Australia," in *ibid.*, p. 62.

26. Edward W. Said, *The World, the Text, and the Critic* (Cambridge: Harvard University Press, 1983), p. 11.

27. Sneja Gunew, "Denaturalizing Cultural Nationalisms: Multicultural Readings of 'Australia,'" in Homi K. Bhabha, ed., *Nation and Narration* (New York: Routledge, 1990), p. 100.

28. For a more detailed discussion of this process, see Zillah Eisenstein, *The Color of Gender* (Berkeley: University of California Press, 1994), especially chapters 2 and 3.

29. Arthur Schlesinger, *The Disuniting of America*, pp. 13, 38. Also see Andrew Hacker, "'Diversity' and Its Dangers," *New York Review of Books*, vol. XL, no. 16 (October 7, 1993), pp. 21–25; and his "The Crackdown on African-Americans," *The Nation*, vol. 261, no. 2 (July 10, 1995), pp. 45–49.

30. Mary Antin, *The Promised Land* (New York: Houghton Mifflin, 1911), p. 187.

31. David Rieff, *Los Angeles: Capital of the Third World*, p. 174.

32. Gloria Anzaldua, *Borderlands/La Frontera* (San Francisco: aunt lute books, 1987), p. 53.

33. For related discussion see Anna Marie Smith, *New Right Discourse on Race and Sexuality*, Britain 1968–90 (New York: Cambridge University Press, 1994), pp. 32, 34.

34. David Rieff, *Los Angeles: Capital of the Third World*, p. 136.

35. Sneja Gunew, "Denaturalizing Cultural Nationalisms," Bhabha, p. 110.

36. Gloria Anzaldua, *Borderlands/La Frontera*, p. 78.

37. Trinh T. Minh-ha, "Not You/Like You: Post-Colonial Women and the Interlocking Questions of Identity and Difference," in Gloria Anzaldua, ed., *Making Face, Making Soul: Haciendo Caras* (San Francisco, aunt lute books, 1990), pp. 371–73.

38. Jeffrey Weeks, "The Value of Difference," in John Rutherford, ed., *Identity, Community, Culture, Difference* (London: Lawrence & Wishart, 1990), p. 98.

39. See Zillah Eisenstein, *The Color of Gender*, especially chapter 7, for

elaboration of radical pluralist identities.

40. Jeffrey Weeks, "The Value of Difference," in Rutherford, p. 88.

41. Andrea Stuart, "Feminism:.Dead or Alive," in Rutherford, p. 41.

42. Interview with Homi Bhabha, "The Third Space," in Rutherford, pp. 211, 208.

43. Ella Shohat and Robert Stam, *Unthinking Eurocentrism* (New York: Routledge, 1994), p. 359.

44. Lisa Jones, *Bulletproof Diva* (New York: Doubleday, 1994), p. 54.

45. Jose Vasconcelos, *La Raza Cosmica* (Los Angeles: A Centro de Publicaciones Edition, California State University, 1925, 1979), p. 37.

46. Henry Louis Gates Jr., *Colored People* (New York: Alfred Knopf, 1994), p. xv.

47. Stuart Marshall, "The Contemporary Political Use of Gay History, The Third Reich," in Bad Object Choices, ed., *How Do I Look?* (Seattle: Bay Press, 1991), p. 86.

48. Susan Bordo, "Feminism, Postmodernism, and Gender-Skepticism," in Linda Nicholson, ed., *Feminism/Postmodernism* (New York: Routledge, 1990), pp. 133–54.

49. Stuart Marshall, "Political Use of Gay History," p. 92.

50. Vinita Srivastava, "Brown and Out in New York," *The Village Voice*, vol. xl, no 26 (June 27, 1995), pp. 38, 39.

51. Zillah Eisenstein, *The Female Body and the Law*, especially chapter 6.

52. Homi K. Bhabha, *The Location of Culture* (New York: Routledge, 1994), pp. 4, 58, 207–209; and an interview with Homi Bhabha, "The Third Space," in Rutherford, pp. 207–221.

53. Julia Kristeva, *Strangers to Ourselves* (New York: Columbia University Press, 1991), pp. 122, 132.

54. Eric Alterman, "Who Speaks for Me?" *Mother Jones*, 19, no. 1 (January/February 1994), p. 62.

55. Partha Chatterjee, *Nationalist Thought and the Colonial World* (Minneapolis: University of Minnesota Press, 1993), p. 76.

56. David Rieff, *Los Angeles: Capital of the Third World*, p. 239.

57. Sneja Gunew, "Denaturalizing Cultural Nationalisms," in Homi Bhahba, ed., *Nation and Narration*, p. 112.

58. Homi Bhabha, *The Location of Culture*, p. 224.

59. James Wilton, "From 'Culotta' to Castro: The Migrant Presence in

Australian Writing," in *Writing in Multicultural Australia 1984*, p. 28.

60. Robert Boynton, "The New Intellectuals," p. 68.

61. Betsy Sharkey, "Beyond Tepees and Totem Poles," *New York Times*, June 11, 1995, p. H1.

62. "The Diversity Challenge," a special advertising supplement to the *New York Times*, October 23, 1994, p. 15.

63. "The Diversity Challenge," a special advertising supplement to the *New York Times*, May 7, 1995, pp. 4, 7.

64. *Ibid.*, p. 4.

65. "The Diversity Challenge," October 23, 1994, p. 27.

66. John Rutherford, "A Place Called Home: Identity and the Cultural Politics of Difference," in Rutherford, ed., *Identity*, p. 11.

67. Lisa Jones, *Bulletproof Diva*, p. 149.

68. James Hannaham, "Deep Disney, Gay Day in the Magic Kingdom," *The Village Voice*, vol. xl, no. 26 (June 27, 1995), p. 34.

69. Salman Rushdie, *The Satanic Verses* (Dover, Del.: The Consortium, 1988), pp. 61, 63.

70. Henry A. Giroux, *Living Dangerously: Multiculturalism and the Politics of Difference* (New York: Peter Lang, 1993), p. 70.

71. Stanley Fish, "Reverse Racism, or, How The Pot Got To Call The Kettle Black," *The Atlantic Monthly* 272, no. 5 (November 1993), pp. 128–36.

72. Peter Kilborn, "White Males and the Manager Class," *New York Times*, March 17, 1995, p. A17.

73. William Honan, "Unity to be Theme of Town Meetings," *New York Times*, January 16, 1994, p. A22.

74. Larry Rohter, "Florida Opens New Front in Fight on Immigrant Policy," *New York Times*, February 11, 1994, p. A14. See also B. Drummond Ayres Jr., "California Governor Seeking Identification Cards for All," *New York Times*, October 27, 1994, p. A1; Ashley Dunn, "In California, the Numbers Add Up to Anxiety," *New York Times*, October 30, 1994, p. E3; and Joel Kotkin, "Hotheads in California," *New York Times*, October 27, 1994, p. A29.

75. Elizabeth Kadetsky, "Bashing Illegals in California," *The Nation*, special issue "The Immigration Wars," vol. 259, no. 12 (October 7, 1994), p. 416.

76. David Cole, "Five Myths About Immigration," in *ibid.*, p. 410.

77. Sam Howe Verhovek, "Legal Immigrants Seek Citizenship in Record

Numbers," *New York Times*, April 2, 1995, p. A1.

78. Leslie Marmon Silko, "The Border Patrol State," *The Nation*, "The Immigration Wars," pp. 413–14.

79. Felix Rohatyn, "What Became of My Democrats?" *New York Times*, March 31, 1995, p. A31.

80. Major Garrett, "Beyond the Contract," *Mother Jones*, vol. 20, issue 2 (March/April 1995), pp. 52–62; David Shipler, "My Equal Opportunity, Your Free Lunch," *New York Times*, March 5, 1995, p. E1.

81. See the interesting discussion by Nancy Fraser and Linda Gordon, "A Genealogy of Dependency: Tracing a Keyword of the U.S. Welfare State," *Signs*, vol. 19, no. 2 (Winter 1994), pp. 323, 327. See also Isabel Wilkerson, "An Intimate Look at Welfare: Women Who've Been There," *New York Times*, February 17, 1995, p. A1.

82. Dale Maharidge, "Walled Off," *Mother Jones*, vol. 19, issue 6 (November/December 1994), p. 31.

83. Richard Sennett, "The Identity Myth," *New York Times*, January 30, 1994, p. E17.

84. Henry Giroux, *Living Dangerously*, p. 102.

85. James Fallows, "Looking at the Sun," in *The Atlantic Monthly*, 272, no. 5 (November 1993), p. 78. See also his *More Like Us* (Boston: Houghton Mifflin, 1989).

86. Samuel P. Huntington, "If Not Civilizations, What?" *Foreign Affairs*, 72, no. 5 (November/December 1993), p. 190. See also his "The Clash of Civilizations?" *Foreign Affairs*, 72, no. 3 (Summer 1993), pp. 22–49.

87. Andrew Hacker, "'Diversity' and Its Dangers," p. 21.

88. Michael Kinsley, "The Spoils of Victimhood," *The New Yorker*, vol. LXXI, no. 5 (March 27, 1995), p. 64.

89. *Ibid.*, p. 69.

90. (AP), "Reverse Discrimination of Whites is Rare, Labor Study Reports," *New York Times*, March 31, 1995, p. A23.

91. Charles Murray and Richard Herrnstein, *The Bell Curve: Intelligence and Class Structure in America* (New York: The Free Press, 1994).

92. Charles Lane, "The Tainted Sources of 'The Bell Curve,'" *New York Review of Books*, vol. XLI, no. 20 (December 1, 1994), p. 14.

93. Herbert Gans, letter to the *New York Times Book Review*, November 13, 1994, section 7, p. 3.

94. Steven Fraser, ed., *The Bell Curve Wars* (New York: Basic Books, 1995).

95. Richard Berke, "Defections Among Men to G.O.P. Helped Ensure Rout of Democrats," *New York Times*, November 11, 1994, p. A1.

96. Felicia Lee, "Cuts Set Off Debate on Helping Homeless With AIDS," *New York Times*, March 21, 1995, p. B1.

97. John Guillory, *Cultural Capital* (Chicago: University of Chicago Press, 1993).

98. For an important sampling of feminist multicultural writings see Gloria Anzaldua, ed., *Making Face, Making Soul*; Cherrie Moraga and Gloria Anzaldua, eds., *This Bridge Called My Back* (Watertown, Mass.: Persephone Press, 1981); Trinh T. Minh-ha, *Woman, Native, Other* (Bloomington: Indiana University Press, 1989); and Gayatri Chakravorty Spivak, *In Other Worlds: Essays in Cultural Politics* (New York: Routledge, 1988).

NOTES TO CHAPTER 4

1. Paul Kennedy, *Preparing for the Twenty-First Century* (New York: Random House, 1993), p. 151.

2. Ellen Meiksins Wood, "What is the 'Postmodern' Agenda? An Introduction," *Monthly Review*, vol. 47, no. 3 (July/August 1995), p. 11.

3. G.A. Elmer Griffin, "Word Bullets," *Transition*, issue 66, vol. 5, no. 2 (Summer 1995), p. 58.

4. Terry Eagleton, "Where do Postmodernists Come From?" *Monthly Review*, p. 64.

5. Kwame Anthony Appiah, "The Color of Money," *Transition*, p. 81.

6. Geoffrey Wisner, "Abuses of Haiti," *Transition*, p. 41.

7. Richard Barnet and John Cavanagh, *Global Dreams: Imperial Corporations and the New World Order* (New York: Simon & Schuster, 1994), especially chapter 2. Also see: Richard Barnet, "Lords of the Global Economy," *The Nation*, vol. 259, no. 21 (December 19, 1994), pp. 754–60.

8. *Ibid.*, pp. 17, 69, 272, 279.

9. "The Diversity Challenge," a special advertising supplement to the *New York Times*, October 23, 1994, p. 3.

10. Barnet and Cavanagh, *Global Dreams*, p. 14.

11. *Ibid.*, p. 280.

12. *Ibid.*, p. 235.

13. Inderpal Grewal and Caren Kaplan, "Introduction: Transnational Feminist Practices and Questions of Postmodernity," in Inderpal Grewal and Caren Kaplan, eds., *Scattered Hegemonies* (Minneapolis: University of Minnesota Press, 1994), pp. 7–22.

14. Edward Thompson, "The End of Cold War: A Rejoinder," in Robin Blackburn, ed., *After the Fall* (London: Verso Press, 1991), p. 105.

15. Tim Weiner, "Finding New Reasons to Dread the Unknown," *New York Times*, March 26, 1995, p. E1.

16. Eric Hobsbawm, "Goodbye to All That," in *After the Fall*, p. 122.

17. Michael Tanzer, "The International Oil Industry: Recent Changes and Their Implications for Mexico," *Monthly Review*, vol. 46, no. 4 (September 1994), pp. 2, 3.

18. Philip Shenon, "On Saigon's Day of Defeat, Glitter of Rebirth," *New York Times*, April 30, 1995, p. A1.

19. Paul Gilroy, *The Black Atlantic* (Cambridge: Harvard University Press, 1993), p. 15.

20. Ishmael Reed, "What's American about America? Toward Claiming Our Multicultural Heritage," *Utne Reader*, no. 32 (March/April 1989), p. 102.

21. John Borneman, "Emigres as Bullets/Immigration as Penetration Perceptions of the Marielitos," *Journal of Popular Culture*, vol. 20, no. 3 (1986), p. 84.

22. Clovis Maksoud, "Redefining Non-Alignment: The Global South in the New Global Equation," in Phyllis Bennis and Michel Moushabeck, eds., *Altered States, A Reader in the New World Order* (New York: Olive Branch Press, 1993), p. 35.

23. Aijaz Ahmad, *In Theory: Classes, Nations, Literatures* (New York: Verso, 1992), pp. 103, 313, 316–18.

24. Richard Bryan, "The State and the Internatiolization of Capital: An Approach to Analysis," *Journal of Contemporary Asia*, vol. 17, no. 3 (1987), pp. 253–75.

25. Robert Reich, *The Next American Frontier* (New York: Penguin, 1983), pp. 260, 264.

26. Robert Reich, *The Work of Nations* (New York: Vintage, 1991), pp. 131, 305. See also his "The Fracturing of the Middle Class," *New York Times*, August 31, 1994, p. A19.

27. *Ibid.*, pp. 105, 111–13.

28. Joel Bleifuss, "The Death of Nations," *In These Times*, June 27, 1994, pp. 12–13.

29. As quoted in Louis Uchitelle, "The Rise of the Losing Class," *New York Times*, November 20, 1994, p. E1.

30. Jeremy Brecher and Tim Costello, *Global Village or Global Pillage* (Boston: South End Press, 1994), especially chapter 2.

31. Emily Martin, *Flexible Bodies* (Boston: Beacon Press, 1994), especially the introduction.

32. Leslie Camhi, "Imaginary Jews," *The Village Voice*, vol. xl, no. 28 (July 11, 1995), p. 29.

33. Ralph Nader, "Introduction: Free Trade and the Decline of Democracy," in *The Case Against "Free Trade"* (San Francisco: Earth Island Press, 1993), pp. 15, 1, 13.

34. Jeremy Brecher and Tim Costello, *Global Village or Global Pillage*, p. 27.

35. Robert Scheer, "Trilateral Pass," *The Nation*, vol. 260, no. 24 (June 19, 1994), p. 874.

36. Larry Rohter, "Cuba, In Ideological Retreat, To Lay Off Many Thousands," *New York Times*, May 13, 1995, p. A1.

37. Jeremy Brecher and Tim Costello, *Global Village or Global Pillage*, especially chapter 8.

38. As quoted in Louis Uchitelle, "U.S. Corporations Expanding Abroad at a Quicker Pace," *New York Times*, July 25, 1994, p. D4.

39. Roger Rouse, "Thinking Through Transnationalism: Notes on the Cultural Politics of Class Relations in the Contemporary U.S.," *Public Culture*, vol. 7 (1995), p. 366.

40. Keith Bradsher, "Gap in Wealth in U.S. Called Widest in West," *New York Times*, April 17, 1995, p. A1. See also Kevin Phillips, *The Politics of Rich and Poor* (New York: Random House, 1991); and his *Boiling Point* (New York: Random House, 1993).

41. Graham Button, "The Billionaires," *Forbes*, vol. 156, no. 2 (July 17, 1995), pp. 110, 111.

42. G.J. Meyers, "Dancing with Headhunters," *Harper's Magazine*, vol. 291, no. 1742 (July 1995), pp. 38, 48, 50.

43. Ronald Takaki, *A Different Mirror: A History of Multicultural America* (Boston: Little, Brown and Co., 1993), p. 11.

44. Reed, "What's American About America?" p. 104.

45. Takaki, *A Different Mirror*, p. 2.

46. Patricia Braus, "What Does Hispanic Mean?" *Race and Ethnic Relations 94/95*, ed., John A. Kromkowski (Guildord, Ct.: Dushkin Pub., 1994), p. 94.

47. Angelika Bammer, Introduction, in Angelica Bammer, ed., *Displacements* (Bloomington: Indiana University Press, 1994), p. xi.

48. Barbara Crossette, "This Is No Place Like Home," *New York Times*, March 5, 1995, p. E3. Also see Matthew Connelly and Paul Kennedy, "Must It Be the Rest Against the West?" *The Atlantic Monthly*, vol. 274, no. 6 (December 1994), pp. 72–75.

49. Philip Martin and Elizabeth Midgley, "Immigration to the U.S.: Journey to an Uncertain Destination," *Population Bulletin* (Washington, D.C.: Population Reference Bureau), vol. 49, no. 2 (September 1994), pp. 26–28.

50. Amartya Sen, "Population: Delusion and Reality," in *The New York Review of Books*, vol. XLI, no. 15 (September 22, 1994), pp. 62, 63.

51. Jorge G. Castañeda, "Mexico and California, The Paradoxes of Tolerance and Dedemocratizations," in Lowenthal and Burgess, eds., *The California-Mexico Connection* (Stanford: Stanford University Press, 1993), pp. 35, 42, 43.

52. Takaki, *A Different Mirror*, p. 393.

53. Gloria Anzaldua, *Borderlands/La Frontera: The New Mestiza* (San Francisco: aunt lute books, 1987), p. 79.

54. Gabriel Szekely, "California and Mexico, Facing the Pacific Rim," in Lowenthal and Burgess, eds., *The California-Mexico Connection*, p. 116.

55. David Rieff, *Los Angeles: Capital of the Third World* (New York: Touchstone Books, 1991).

56. Katrina Burgess and Abraham Lowenthal, "Challenges from the South, Enhancing California's Mexico Connection," in Lowenthal and Burgess, eds., *The California-Mexico Connection*, p. 274.

57. Denise Dresser, "Exporting Conflict, Transboundary Consequences of Mexican Politics," in Lowenthal and Burgess, eds., *The California-Mexico Connection*, p. 112.

58. Elaine Bernard, "What's the Matter with NAFTA?" *Radical America*, vol. 25, no. 2 (April/June '91, published '94), pp. 19, 20. See also Jack D. Forbes, "Native Intelligence: NAFTA is Unconstitutional," in Elaine Katzenberger, ed., *First World, Ha, Ha, Ha!* (San Francisco: City Lights, 1995),

pp. 183–88.

59. Medea Benjamin, "Interview: Subcomandate Marcos," in Katzenberger, ed., *First World, Ha Ha Ha!*, p. 67.

60. Peter Rosset, "Understanding Chiapas," in *ibid.*, p. 158.

61. Andrew Pollack, "U.S. Supports Asia-Pacific Free Trade but Questions Timing," *New York Times*, November 12, 1994, p. A1.

62. Elaine Bernard, p. 20.

63. Herbert Schiller, "Manipulating Hearts and Minds," in Hamid Mowlana, George Gerbner, and Herbert Schiller, eds., *Triumph of the Image* (Boulder CO: Westview, 1992), p. 28. See also Susan Jeffords and Lauren Rabinovitz, eds., *Seeing Through the Media* (New Brunswick N.J.: Rutgers University Press, 1994).

64. Noam Chomsky, "The Media and the War: What War?" in *Triumph of the Image*, pp. 51–63. See also Zillah Eisenstein, *The Color of Gender* (Berkeley: University of California Press, 1994), pp. 85–89; and Michael Albert, "Lessons of the Gulf War," in Cynthia Peters, ed., *Collateral Damage* (Boston: South End Press, 1992), pp. 387–412.

65. Holly Sklar, "Brave New World Order," in Cynthia Peters, ed., *Collateral Damage*, pp. 3–46.

66. Fouad Ajami, "The Summoning," in Comments, *Foreign Affairs*, 72, no. 4 (September/October 1993), pp. 3, 7.

67. Samuel Huntington, "The Clash of Civilizations?" *Foreign Affairs*, 72, no. 3 (Summer 1993), pp. 22–49. Also see his "If Not Civilizations, What?" *Foreign Affairs*, 72, no. 5 (November/December 1993), pp. 186–94.

68. Huntington, "If Not Civilization, What?" p. 194.

69. See the Chinese Exclusion Case: Chae Chan Ping v. United States, 130 U.S. 581 (1889).

70. See the *Immigration and Nationality Act*, Pub. L. No. 89–236, 201, 79 Stat. 911, 920 (1965). See also Michael Scaperlanda, "Polishing the Tarnished Golden Door," *Wisconsin Law Review* 965 (1993), pp. 965–1032.

71. Thomas Alexander Aleinikoff and David A. Martin, *Immigration, Process and Policy*, 2d ed., and the companion *Immigration and Nationality Laws of the U.S., 1992*, American Casebook Series (St. Paul, Minnesota: West Pub. Co., 1991). Also see Takaki, *Iron Cages* and *A Different Mirror.*

72. John F. Kennedy, *A Nation of Immigrants* (New York: Harper and Row, 1964, 1986), p. 67.

73. *Ibid*.

74. Stephen R. Graubard, ed., *Australia: The Daedalus Symposium* (Australia: Angus and Robertson Pub., 1985).

75. Louis Uchitelle, "The New Faces of U.S. Manufacturing," *New York Times*, July 3, 1994, p. F1.

76. Eric Alterman, "Who Speaks for Me?" *Mother Jones* 19, no. 1 (January/February 1994), p. 60.

77. Barbara Crossette, "U.N. Study Finds a Free Eastern Europe Poorer and Less Healthy," *New York Times*, October 7, 1994, p. A13.

78. Daniel Singer, "Of Lobsters and Poles," *The Nation*, vol. 257, no. 21 (December 1993), p. 765.

79. Michael Specter, "Russia Fights a Rising Tide of Infection," *New York Times*, October 2, 1994, p. A9.

80. Michael Specter, "Russia's Declining Health: Rising Illness, Shorter Lives," *New York Times*, February 19, 1995, p. A1.

81. Jeremy Brecher and Tim Costello, *Global Village or Global Pillage*, p. 27.

82. Quoted in Michael Specter, "Russia Fights a Rising Tide of Infection," p. A9.

83. Jane Perlez, "G.E. Finds Tough Going in Hungary," *New York Times*, July 25, 1994, p. D1.

84. Serge Schmemann, "Russia Lurches Into Reform But Old Ways Are Tenacious," *New York Times*, February 20, 1994, p. A14.

85. Steven Erlanger, "To Be Young, Russian and Middle Class," *New York Times*, July 23, 1995, p. A1.

86. Jeremy Brecher and Tim Costello, "Taking on the Multinationals," *The Nation*, vol. 259, no. 21 (December 19, 1994), p. 757.

87. Leo Panitch, "Globalisation and the State," in Ralph Miliband and Leo Panitch, eds., *Between Globalism and Nationalism: Socialist Register, 1994* (London: Merlin Press, 1994), p. 69.

88. Sylvia Nasar, "The Bureaucracy: What's Left to Shrink?" *New York Times*, June 11, 1995, p. E1.

89. Thomas L. Friedman, "When Money Talks, Government Listens," *New York Times*, July 24, 1994, p. E3.

90. Barnet and Cavanagh, *Global Dreams*, pp. 25, 169, 36.

91. Grewal and Kaplan, eds., *Scattered Hegemonies*, introduction, p. 13.

92. Barnet and Cavanagh, *Global Dreams*, p. 171.

93. I am grateful to discussions with Patricia Zimmerman about the transnational media empire.

94. Benjamin Barber, "From Disney World to Disney's World," *New York Times*, August 1, 1995, p. A15.

95. Ella Shohat and Robert Stam, *Unthinking Eurocentrism* (New York: Routledge, 1994), p. 7.

96. Pat Aufderherde, "The Media Monopolies Muscle In," *The Nation*, vol. 258, no. 1 (January 31, 1994), pp. 1–21.

97. Fred Halliday, "The Ends of Cold War," in Robin Blackburn, ed., *After the Fall*, pp. 78–99.

98. Arjun Appadurai, "Disjuncture and Difference in the Global Cultural Economy," *Public Culture*, vol. 2, no. 2 (Spring 1990), p. 7.

99. John Rockwell, "The New Colossus: American Culture As Power Export," *New York Times*, January 30, 1994, p. H1.

100. Arjun Appadurai, "Disjuncture and Difference," pp. 16, 17.

101. James Kurth, "The Post-Modern State," *The National Interest*, no. 28 (Summer 1992), pp. 26–35.

102. U.N. Center on Transnational Corporations, *World Investment Report 1992: Transnational Corporations as Engines of Growth* (New York: United Nations, 1992), pp. 1, 34.

103. Robert Reich, *The Work of Nations*, p. 250.

104. *Ibid.*, p. 285.

105. E.J. Hobsbawm, *Nations and Nationalism Since 1780* (New York: Cambridge University Press, 1990), especially chapter 6.

106. Zbigniew Brezinski, "The Great Transformation," *The National Interest*, no. 33 (Fall 1993), p. 10.

107. I am indebted to Julie Mostov's discussion in her "Do Women Have Something to Fear?": Nationalism in Eastern Europe," presented at Cornell University, November 14, 1993, for eliciting the idea of an "outsider" economy.

108. Cited in Steven Holmes, "A Rights Leader Minimizes Racism as a Poverty Factor," *New York Times*, July 24, 1994, p. A18. Also see his Keynote Address, National Urban League Convention, July 24, 1994, Indianapolis, Indiana.

109. Cynthia Enloe, "The Globetrotting Sneaker," *Ms. Magazine*, vol. V,

no. 5 (March/April 1995), p. 12. Also see her *The Morning After* (Berkeley: University of California Press, 1993).

110. Barbara Ehrenreich and Annette Fuentes, "Women in the Global Factory" (Boston: South End Press Pamphlet, 1984).

111. As cited in Jeremy Brecher and Tim Costello, *Global Village or Global Pillage*, p. 23.

112. Lourdes Beneria, "Gender and the Global Economy," in Arthur MacEwan and William Tabb, eds., *Instability and Change in the World Economy* (New York: Monthly Review Press, 1989), pp. 241–50.

NOTES TO CHAPTER 5

1. I identify western feminism as a mix of liberal and radical feminism. See Zillah Eisenstein, *The Radical Future of Liberal Feminism* (Boston: Northeastern University Press, 1981, 1993).

2. I do not hold to a neat division between popular, meaning of the people, and mass, meaning of the market; the two realms of culture collide too often. See Ella Shohat and Robert Stam, *Unthinking Eurocentrism* (New York: Routledge, 1994), pp. 240–342 for clarification of the distinction.

3. Margot Badran, "Letter to the Editor," *The Women's Review of Books*, vol. VII, no. 9 (June 1995), p. 4.

4. Jennifer Gonnerman, "The Femi-Newtics," *The Village Voice*, vol. XL, no. 5 (January 31, 1995), pp. 18–19.

5. Felicity Barringer, "Hillary Clinton's New Role: A Spouse or a Policy Leader?" *New York Times*, November 16, 1992, p. A1; Connie Bruck, "Hillary the Pol," *The New Yorker*, vol. LXX, no. 15 (May 30, 1994), pp. 56–96; Maureen Dowd, "Hillary Rodham Clinton Strikes New Pose and Multiplies Her Images," *New York Times*, December 12, 1993, p. E3; Alessandra Stanley, "A Softer Image for Hillary Clinton," *New York Times*, July 13, 1992, p. B1.

6. See the original radical feminist writings of: Ti Grace Atkinson, *Amazon Odyssey* (New York: Links, 1974); Shulamith Firestone, *The Dialectic of Sex* (New York: Bantam, 1970); Kate Millett, *Sexual Politics* (New York: Doubleday, 1970); Robin Morgan, ed., *Sisterhood is Powerful* (New York: Vintage, 1970); and Redstockings, *Feminist Revolution* (New York: Redstockings Inc., 1975).

7. David Brock, *The Real Anita Hill* (New York: The Free Press, 1993); Robert Chrisman and Robert Allen, eds., *Court of Appeal* (New York: Ballantine Books, 1992); Jill Abramson and Jane Mayer, *Strange Justice: The Selling of Clarence Thomas* (New York: Houghton Mifflin, 1994); Toni Morrison, ed., *Race-ing Justice, En-gendering Power* (New York: Pantheon, 1992); and Kathleen Sullivan, "The Hill-Thomas Mystery," *The New York Review of Books*, vol. XL, no. 14 (August 12, 1993), pp. 12–16.

8. See Zillah Eisenstein, *The Color of Gender* (Berkeley: California University Press, 1994), especially pp. 79–85.

9. Richard Goldstein, "Hooked!" *The Village Voice*, vol. XL, no. 28 (July 11, 1995), p. 8.

10. For a discussion of the complex relations of real/ideal and how this is embodied in liberal law, see Zillah Eisenstein, *The Female Body and the Law* (Berkeley: University of California Press, 1988), especially chapters 1 and 2.

11. See Zillah Eisenstein, *The Radical Future of Liberal Feminism*.

12. Caryn James, "What Are They Really Saying?" *New York Times*, January 15, 1995, p. E4.

13. Cynthia Enloe, *The Morning After* (Berkeley: University of California Press, 1993).

14. I am indebted to discussions with Mary Katzenstein about how the military has mainstreamed feminist ideas, as well as to her manuscript in process, *Liberating the Mainstream*, which studies the military and catholic church's use of feminist discourse.

15. Eric Schmitt, "Aspin Moves to Open Many Military Jobs to Women," *New York Times*, January 14, 1994, p. A22.

16. Eric Schmitt, "White House Split Over Legal Tactics on Gay Troop Plan," *New York Times*, December 19, 1993, p. A1.

17. Gewn Ifill, "Clinton Chooses Two and Deplores Idea of Cabinet Quotas," *New York Times*, December 22, 1992, p. A1.

18. Zillah Eisenstein, *The Color of Gender*, chapter 2.

19. Lani Guinier, *The Tyranny of the Majority: Fundamental Fairness in Representative Democracy* (New York: The Free Press, 1994).

20. Lani Guinier, "Democracy's Conversation," *The Nation*, vol. 260, no. 3 (January 23, 1995), pp. 85–90.

21. Lani Guinier, "Lani Guinier's Day in Court," *New York Times Magazine*,

February 27, 1994, Section 6, pp. 38–66; and Peter Applebome, "Guinier Ideas, Once Seen as Odd, Now Get Serious Study," *New York Times*, April 3, 1994, p. E5.

22. For a full discussion of performative see Judith Butler, *Bodies That Matter* (New York: Routledge, 1993).

23. Jennifer Gonnerman, "Angry White Women," *The Village Voice*, vol. XL, no. 28 (July 11, 1995), pp. 17–19.

24. Katherine Q. Seelye, "Gingrich's 'Piggies' Poked," *New York Times*, January 19, 1995, p. A20.

25. Richard J. Herrnstein and Charles Murray, *The Bell Curve: Intelligence and Class Structure in American Life* (New York: The Free Press, 1994). See also Charles Lane, "The Tainted Sources of 'The Bell Curve,'" *New York Review of Books*, vol. XLI, no. 20 (December 1, 1994), pp. 14–19.

26. Todd Purdum, "President Shows Fervent Support for Goals of Affirmative Action," *New York Times*, July 20, 1995, p. A1.

27. Nick Charles, "The O.J. Papers," *Village Voice*, vol. XXXIX, no. 44 (November 1, 1994), p. 23. See also Terry McMillan, "An Icon, But Not a Hero," *New York Times*, June 25, 1994, p. A23; and Seth Mydans, "In Simpson Case, an Issue for Everyone," *New York Times*, July 22, 1994, p. A16.

28. See Toni Morrison, Introduction to *Race-ing Justice, En-gendering Power*, pp. vii–xxx; and Kimberle Crenshaw, "Whose Story Is It Anyway? Feminist and Antiracist Appropriations of Anita Hill," in Morrison, ed., *Race-ing Justice, En-gendering Power*, pp. 402–440. See also Nell Irvin Painter, "Who Was Lynched?" *The Nation*, vol. 253, no. 16 (November 11, 1991), pp. 576–77.

29. Hans Magnus Enzensberger, *Civil Wars* (New York: The New Press, 1994), p. 32.

30. Katharine Q. Seelye, "Two Sides in the Gun Debate Duel with Personal Stories," *New York Times*, April 1, 1995, p. A26.

31. Ann Jones, "Living With Guns, Playing with Fire," *Ms. Magazine*, vol. IV, no. 6 (May/June 1994), p. 40. See also Melinda Henneberger, "The Small-Arms Industry Comes On To Women," *New York Times*, October 24, 1993, p. E4.

32. A few popular versions of this feminist anti-feminism are found in Elizabeth Fox-Genovese, *Feminism Without Illusions* (Chapel Hill: The University of North Carolina Press, 1991); Wendy Kaminer, "Feminism's

Identity Crisis," *The Atlantic Monthly*, vol. 272, no. 4 (October 1993), pp. 51–68; Karen Lahrman, Off Course," *Mother Jones*, vol. 18, issue 5 (September/October 1993), pp. 45–68; Katie Roiphe, *The Morning After* (New York: Little, Brown and Co., 1993); Christina Hoff Sommers, *Who Stole Feminism?* (New York: Simon & Schuster, 1994); and Naomi Wolf, *Fire with Fire* (New York: Random House, 1993).

33. See my critique of the protectionist framework of some anti-pornography feminists in *The Female Body and the Law*. For classic discussions of the protectionist feminist stance, see Catherine MacKinnon, *Feminism Unmodified: Discourses on Life and Laws* (Cambridge: Harvard University Press, 1987); and Andrea Dworkin, *Pornography, Men Possessing Women* (New York: Perigee, 1979).

34. For an influential discussion of the non-protectionist politics of radical feminism as distinguished from cultural feminism, see Alice Echols, *Daring to be Bad: Radical Feminism in America 1967–1975* (Minneapolis: University of Minnesota Press, 1989).

35. Wolf, *Fire with Fire*, pp. 37, 135.

36. Cynthia Enloe, *The Morning After*, especially chapter 6.

37. Tamar Lewin, "A Feminism that Speaks for Itself," *New York Times*, October 3, 1993, p. E1.

38. Karen Lehrman, "Beware the Cookie Monster," *New York Times*, July 18, 1992, p. A23.

39. Judith Arner, *Hillary Clinton, The Inside Story* (New York: Signet Books, 1993). See also *The Hillary Clinton Quarterly*, published quarterly since 1993, Maracom, 128C North State St., Concord, NH 03301.

40. Nina Martin, "Who Is She?" *Mother Jones*, vol. 18, issue 6 (November/December 1993), pp. 34–43.

41. Richard Goldstein, "Yoo-hoo, Mrs. Gingrich!" *Village Voice*, vol. XL, no. 3 (January 17, 1995), p. 8.

42. Frank Rich, "Jo Rodham March," *New York Times*, January 15, 1995, p. E17.

43. Maureen Dowd, "Amid a Debate on White House Women, Hillary Clinton Tries to Push On," *New York Times*, September 29, 1994, p. A18.

44. Gary Wills, "H. R. Clinton's Case," *New York Review of Books*, vol. XXXIX, no. 5 (March 1992), pp. 3–5.

45. Julia Reed, "The First Lady," *Vogue*, vol. 183, no. 12 (December 1993),

pp. 228–233.

46. Tamar Lewin, "A Feminism that Speaks For Itself," *New York Times*, October 3, 1993, p. 2E.

47. Todd Purdum, "Hillary Clinton's Trip: Women's Voice," *New York Times*, March 30, 1995, p. A6.

48. (AP), "Hillary Clinton Talks to Poor Working Women's Group in India," *New York Times*, March 31, 1995, p. A7.

49. Todd Purdum, "First Lady Holds Forth, Long Distance," *New York Times*, March 20, 1995, p. A13.

50. As quoted in "Hillary Clinton Talks to Poor Working Women's Group in India," p. A7.

51. Todd Purdum, "Hillary Clinton, A Traditional First Lady Now," *New York Times*, April 6, 1995, p. A1.

52. Michael Kelly, "Saint Hillary," *New York Times Magazine*, May 23, 1993, pp. 22–66.

53. Hamid Mowlana, George Gerbner, and Herbert Schiller, eds., *Triumph of the Image* (Boulder, CO: Westview Press, 1992).

54. For a discussion of living "as if," see Slavoj Zizek, *The Sublime Object of Ideology* (London: Verso, 1989).

55. Susan Faludi, "The Naked Citadel," *The New Yorker*, vol. LXX, no. 27 (September 5, 1994), p. 81. Much of my discussion is indebted to her astute article.

56. I am indebted to Anna Marie Smith for clarification of this point.

57. (AP) "State Offers Alternative to Women at Citadel," *New York Times*, June 7, 1995, p. B10; and, (AP) "Woman May Live in Barracks," *New York Times*, June 8, 1995, p. A25.

58. Susan Faludi, "The Naked Citadel," p. 81.

59. *Ibid*., p. 75.

60. As quoted in: "The Papal Letter: To the Women of the World, An Affirmation of 'Feminine Genius,'" *New York Times*, July 14, 1995, p. E7.

NOTES TO CHAPTER 6

1. Jan Goodwin, "The State of Women in the World," *Cosmopolitan Magazine*, vol. 218, no. 3 (March 1995), pp. 225–27.

2. Erin Addison, "Saving Other Women from Other Men," *camera*

obscura, vol. 31 (January/May 1993), pp. 5, 6, 19.

3. A small sample of this vast literature includes Judith Butler, *Gender Trouble: Feminism and the Subversion of Identity* (New York: Routledge, 1990); and her *Bodies That Matter* (New York: Routledge, 1993); Laura Lee Downs, "If 'Woman' is Just an Empty Category, Then Why am I Afraid to Walk Alone at Night? Identity Politics Meets the PostModern Subject," *Comparative Studies in Society and History* 35, no. 2 (1993), pp. 414–37; Suad Joseph, "Gender and Relationality Among Arab Families in Lebanon," *Feminist Studies*, 19, no. 3 (Fall 1993), pp. 465–86; Teresa de Lauretis, ed., *Feminist Studies/Critical Studies* (Bloomington: Indiana University Press, 1986); and Elizabeth Weed, ed., *Coming to Terms: Feminism, Theory, Politics* (New York: Routledge, 1989).

4. United Nations Conferences held in cairo, egypt, in 1994 and in Copenhagen, Denmark, in 1995 recognized the international plight of women. The "Women and United Conference" held in new york city, March 1995, did so as well. See the pamphlet "The Cairo Conference, A Programme of Action for Reproductive Rights?" from the Center for Reproductive Law and Policy, 120 Wall St., New York, N.Y. 10005.

5. Anne McClintock, "'No Longer In A Future Heaven': Women and Nationalism in South Africa," *Transition* 51 (1991), p. 121.

6. *Ibid.*, quoting Albertina Sisulu, p. 116.

7. *Ibid.*, p. 119.

8. Cynthia Enloe, "The Gendered Gulf," in *Seeing Through the Media: The Persian Gulf War*, ed. Susan Jeffords and Lauen Rabinovitz (New Brunswick, N.J.: Rutgers University Press, 1994), p. 217.

9. See Leila Ahmed, *Women and Gender in Islam; Historical Roots of a Modern Debate* (New Haven: Yale University Press, 1992).

10. Margot Badran, *Feminists, Islam, and Nation* (Princeton: Princeton University Press, 1995), pp. 13, 77.

11. Marnia Lazreg, *The Eloquence of Silence; Algerian Women in Question* (New York: Routledge, 1994), pp. 2, 7, 9. See also Haleh Afshar and Mary Maynard, eds., *The Dynamics of "Race" and Gender; Some Feminist Interventions* (London: Taylor and Francis, 1994); Rey Chow, *Woman and Chinese Modernity* (Minnesota: University of Minnesota Press, 1991); and Chandra Talpade Mohanty, Ann Russo, and Lourdes Torres, eds., *Third World Women and the Politics of Feminism* (Bloomington: Indiana University Press, 1993).

12. Leila Ahmed, *Women and Gender in Islam*, p. 243. See also As 'ad AbuKhalil, "Toward the Study of Women and Politics in the Arab World: The Debate and the Reality," *Feminist Issues*, 13, no. 1 (Spring 1993), pp. 3–22.

13. Valentine M. Moghadam, *Modernizing Women: Gender and Social Change in the Middle East* (Boulder, CO: Lynne Rienner Publishers, 1993), p. 109.

14. *Ibid.*, pp. 6, 8.

15. *Ibid.*, p. 169.

16. Margot Badran, "Gender Activism: Feminists and Islamists in Egypt," in Valentine M. Moghadam, ed., *Identity Politics and Women: Cultural Reassertions and Feminisms in International Perspective* (Boulder, CO: Westview Press, 1994), pp. 203, 222. See also Margot Badran and Miriam Cooke, eds., *Opening the Gates: A Century of Arab Feminist Writing* (Bloomington: Indiana University Press, 1990); and Valentine M. Moghadam, ed., *Gender and National Identity: Women and Politics in Muslim Societies* (New York: Oxford University Press, 1994).

17. Darima Bennoune, "Algerian Women Confront Fundamentalism," *Monthly Review*, 46, no. 4 (September 1994), p. 35, and as quoted on p. 37.

18. Youssef M. Ibrahim, "Bomb at Algeria Police Housing Wounds 63," *New York Times*, March 11, 1995, p. A5.

19. John Darnton, "Discontent Seethes in Once-Stable Turkey," *New York Times*, March 2, 1995, p. A1.

20. See Nawal El Saadawi, *Memories from the Women's Prison* (Berkeley: University of California Press, 1983).

21. As quoted in Anne Weaver, "A Fugitive from Injustice," *The New Yorker*, LXX, no. 28 (September 12, 1994), p. 60.

22. Chris Hedges, "Key Panel at Cairo Talks Agrees on Population Plan," *New York Times*, September 13, 1994, p. A10. Also see further discussion of the issues in John Burns, "Bangladesh, Still Poor, Cuts Birth Rate Sharply," *New York Times*, September 13, 1994, p. A10; and Amartya Sen, "Population: Delusion and Reality," *New York Review of Books*, XLI, no. 15 (September 22, 1994), pp. 62–71.

23. Alan Cowell, "How Vatican Views Cairo," *New York Times*, September 18, 1994, p. A25; and Barbara Crossette, "Vatican Drops Fight Against U.N. Population Document," *New York Times*, September 10, 1994, p. A5. See also James Brooke, "With Church Preaching in Vain, Brazilians Embrace Birth

Control," *New York Times*, September 1, 1994. p. A1.

24. As stated in Barbara Crossette, "Women's Advocates Flocking to Cairo, Eager for Gains," *New York Times*, September 2, 1994, p. A3.

25. See the United Nations Report on the Fourth World Conference on women, Beijing, China, September 4–15, 1995, "Beijing Declaration and Platform for Action." Available from the United Nations, New York, NY 10017.

26. Alan Riding, "Women Seize Focus at Rights Forum," *New York Times*, June 16, 1993, p. A3.

27. Charlotte Bunch, "Women's Rights as Human Rights: Toward a Re-Vision of Human Rights," in Charlotte Bunch and Roxanna Carillo, *Gender Violence: A Development and Human Rights Issue* (Rutgers: Center for Women's Global Leadership, 1991), p. 8. Also see Bunch's statement "The Global Campaign for Women's Human Rights," available from the Center for Women's Global Leadership.

28. Asma El Dareet, *Woman, Why Do You Weep?* (London: Zed Press, 1982); Olaynka Koso-Thomas, *The Circumcision of Women: A Strategy for Eradication* (London: Zed Press, 1992); Awa Thiam, *Black Sisters Speak Out: Feminism and Oppression in Black Africa* (London: Pluto Press, 1986); Nahid Toubia, *Female Genital Mutilation: A Call for Global Action* (New York: Women, Ink., 1993); and Alice Walker, *Possessing the Secret of Joy* (New York: Harcourt Brace Jovanovich, 1992).

29. See the proceedings and annual reports of the International Reproductive Rights Research Action Group, Hunter College, 695 Park Ave, Rm. W1713, New York, N.Y. 10021. Also see Rosalind Petchesky and Jennifer Weiner, "Global Feminist Perspectives of Reproductive Rights and Reproductive Health," A Report on the Special Sessions Held at the Fourth International Interdisciplinary Congress on Women, Hunter College, New York City, June 3–7, 1990.

30. Deniz Kandiyoti, Introduction to Deniz Kandiyoti, ed., *Women, Islam and the State* (Philadelphia: Temple University Press, 1991), p. 5.

31. Kumari Jayawardena, *Feminism and Nationalism in the Third World* (London: Zed Books Ltd.), 1986.

32. Deniz Kandiyoti, Introduction to Kandiyoti, ed., *Women, Islam, and the State*, p. 4.

33. Margot Badran, *Feminists, Islam, and Nation*, p. 207.

34. Kumkum Sangari and Sudesh Vaid, "Recasting Women: An Introduction," in Kumkum Sangari and Sudesh Vaid, eds., *Recasting Women: Essays in Indian Colonial History* (New Brunswick, N.J.: Rutgers University Press, 1990), p. 17. See also Zoya Hasan, ed., *Forging Identities: Gender, Communities and the State in India* (Boulder, Colo.: Westview Press, 1994); and Vandana Shiva, *Staying Alive, Women, Ecology and Development* (London: Zed Books Ltd., 1989).

35. Hamid Mowlana, George Gerbner, and Herbert I. Schiller, *Triumph of the Image: The Media's War in the Persian Gulf—A Global Perspective* (Boulder, Colo.: Westview Press, 1992).

36. Cynthia Enloe, "The Gendered Gulf," in Jeffords and Rabinovitz, eds., *Seeing Through the Media*, p. 217. See also her *The Morning After* (Berkeley: University of California Press, 1993), especially chapter 6.

37. Cynthia Enloe, *The Morning After*, p. 216.

38. Carla Makhlouf Obermeyer, "Reproductive Choice in Islam," *Radical America*, vol. 25, no. 3 (July/September 1992, published January 1995), pp. 26, 32.

39. Deniz Kandiyoti, Introduction, in Kandiyoti, ed., *Women, Islam and the State*, pp. 2, 3.

40. *Ibid.*, p. 18.

41. Margot Badran, "Competing Agenda: Feminists, Islam and the State in Nineteenth- and Twentieth-Century Egypt," in Deniz Kandiyoti, ed., *Women, Islam and the State*, pp. 204–205.

42. Fatima El Mernissi, "Democracy as Moral Disintegration: The Contradiction between Religious Belief and Citizenship as a Manifestation of the Ahistoricity of the Arab Identity," in Nahid Toubia, ed., *Women of the Arab World* (London: Zed Books Ltd., 1988), pp. 37, 38.

43. Nawal El Saadawi, "The Political Challenges Facing Arab Women at the End of the 20th Century," in *ibid.*, p. 8.

44. See various discussions of this interpretation in Valentine Moghadam, ed., *Identity Politics and Women*.

45. Deniz Kandiyoti, Introduction, in Kandiyoti, ed., *Women, Islam and the State*, p. 18.

46. Afsaneh Najmabadi, "Hazards of Modernity and Morality: Women, State and Ideology in Contemporary Iran," in *ibid.*, p. 70.

47. Valentine Moghadam, *Modernizing Women*, pp. 88–89.

48. *Ibid.*, p. 89.

49. *Ibid.*, p. 149.

50. Margot Badran, *Feminists, Islam, and Nation*, p. 5.

51. Leila Ahmed, *Women and Gender in Islam*, p. 152.

52. Afseneh Najmabadi, "Veiled Discourse—Unveiled Bodies," *Feminist Studies,* vol. 19, no. 3 (Fall 1993), pp. 487, 511.

53. Marnia Lazreg, *The Eloquence of Silence*, p. 135.

54. Frantz Fanon, *A Dying Colonialism* (New York: Grove Press, 1965), pp. 44, 36.

55. *Ibid.*, p. 168.

56. As quoted by Valentine Moghadam in "Introduction: Women and Identity Politics in Theoretical and Comparative Perspective," in Valentine Moghadam, ed., *Identity Politics and Women*, p. 15.

57. Fouad Zakaria, "The Standpoint of Contemporary Muslim Fundamentalists," in Nahid Toubia, ed., *Women of the Arab World*, p. 32.

58. Leila Ahmed, *Women and Gender in Islam*, p. 26.

59. See Marilyn Rueschemeyer, ed., *Women in the Politics of Postcommunist Eastern Europe* (New York: M.E. Sharpe, 1994).

60. Kumari Jayawardena, *Feminism and Nationalism in the Third World*, p. ix.

61. McClintock, "No Longer in a Future Heaven," p. 122.

62. As quoted in Ulrike Helwerth and Gislinde Schwarz, "Germany: The Walls That Have Yet To Fall," *Ms. Magazine,* vol. 3, no. 6 (May/June 1993), p. 19.

63. Slavenka Drakulic, *How We Survived Communism and Even Laughed* (New York: W.W. Norton, 1991). See also Gordana P. Crnkovic, "Why Should You Write About Eastern Europe, Or Why Should You Write About 'The Other'," *Feminist Issues*, 12, no. 2 (Fall 1992), pp. 21–42.

64. Stephen Kinzer, "Feminist Gadfly Unappreciated in Her Own Land," *New York Times*, December 11, 1993, p. A11.

65. Mikhail Gorbachev, *Perestroika: New Thinking for Our Country and the World* (New York: Harper and Row, 1987), p. 103. See also Zillah Eisenstein, "Eastern European Male Democracies: A Problem of Unequal Equality," in Nanette Funk and Magda Mueller, eds., *Gender Politics and Post-Communism* (New York: Routledge, 1993), pp. 303–317.

66. Tatiana Bohm, "The Women's Question as a Democratic Question: In Search of Civil Society," in Magda Mueller and Nanette Funk, eds., *Gender*

Politics and Post-Communism, p. 151.

67. These activities were described by Sonia Licht at the public policy forum "Gender and Nationalism: The Impact of the Post-Communist Transition," sponsored by the Network of East-West Women, October 26–27, 1993, Washington, D.C.

68. Ros Coward, "Women of Peace Against Men of War," *The Guardian,* July 24, 1995, p. 11.

69. See "Special Issue: Between East and West, Gender in an Era of East European Transitions," *Social Politics,* vol. 2, no. 1 (Spring 1995).

70. These comments were made at the Network of East-West Women public policy forum, October 26–27, 1993, Washington, D.C. Also see her unpublished paper "Nationalism, Patriarchy and War," Zarana Papic, Faculty of Philosophy, Belgrade, Yugoslavia.

71. Marina Blagojevic, "War and Everyday Life: Deconstruction of Self/Sacrifice," *Sociology,* Belgrade, vol. XXXVI, no. 4 (October–December 1994), p. 473.

72. Dasa Duhacek, "Women's Time in the Former Yugoslavia," in Funk and Mueller, eds., *Gender Politics and Post-Communism,* p. 133.

73. Hilary Pilkington, "Russia and the former Soviet Republics, Behind the Mask of Soviet Unity: Realities of Women's Lives," in Chris Corrin, ed., *Superwomen and the Double Burden,* p. 209.

74. Stated in a letter announcing the journal, April 30, 1993. One Eye Open/Jednim Oken; c/o American Express, 110 00 Prague 1, Czech Republic.

75. Tatyana Mamonova, *Women's Glasnost vs. Naglost* (Westport, Ct.: Bergin and Garvey, 1994), pp. xiii, 21.

76. Ewa Hauser, Barbara Heyns, and Jane Manesbridge, "Feminism in the Interstices of Politics and Culture: Poland in Transition," in Mueller and Funk, eds., *Gender Politics and Post-Communism,* p. 269. See also John Darnton, "Tough Abortion Law Provokes Dismay in Poland," *New York Times,* March 11, 1993, p. A3; Stephen Engleberg, "Polish Limits on Abortion Create a New Clandestine Movement," *New York Times,* December 28, 1992, p. A10; and Ann Snitow, "The Church Wins, Women Lose," *The Nation,* 256, no. 16 (April 26, 1993), pp. 556–59.

77. Peggy Watson, "The Rise of Masculinism in Eastern Europe," *New Left Review,* 198 (March/April 1993), pp. 72, 78.

78. Jennifer Gould, "On Their Backs," *The Village Voice,* XXXIX, no. 2

(January 11, 1994), p. 18.

79. Hilary Pilkington, "Russia and the Former Soviet Republics, Behind the Mask of Soviet Unity: Realities of Women's Lives," in Chris Corrin, ed., *Superwomen and the Double Burden* (Toronto: Second Story Press, 1992), pp. 218-19.

80. Solomea Pavlychko, "Between Feminism and Nationalism: New Women's Groups in the Ukraine," in Mary Buckley, ed. *Perestroika and Soviet Women* (New York: Cambridge University Press, 1992), p. 80.

81. Mary Buckley, "Introduction: Women and Perestroika," in Mary Buckley, ed., *Perestroika and Soviet Women*, pp. 7, 11, 6. See also Steven Erlanger, "Bread Prices Rise; Russians Resigned," *New York Times*, October 17, 1993, p. A9; Judith Ingram, "On the Revolt's Front Line, Kiosks Feel the Fury," *New York Times*, October 19, 1993, p. A4; and Craig Whitney, "Western Europe's Dreams Turning to Nightmares," *New York Times*, August 8, 1993, p. A1.

82. Tatyana Mamonova, *Women's Glasnost vs. Naglost*, p. xv.

83. See: Mary Buckley, Introduction, in Mary Buckley, ed., *Perestroika and Soviet Women*, p. 11; and Julia Kristeva, *Nations Without Nationalism* (New York: Columbia University Press, 1993), p. 34. See also Igor Kon and James Riordan, eds., *Sex and Russian Society* (Bloomington: Indiana University Press, 1993).

84. Steven Erlanger, "Men, Mostly Nervous, Voted for Russian Right, Pool Says," *New York Times*, December 30, 1993, p. A10.

85. Vladimir Shlapentokh and Tatiana Marchenko, "Family Values on the Rise While Women Fall in Russia," *Feminist Issues* 12, no. 2 (Fall 1992), p. 45.

86. Sibylle Meyer and Eva Schulze, "After the Fall of the Wall: East German Families in Transition," unpublished paper, available from Technische Universitat Berlin, Institut fur Soziologie, Forschungsstelle, Hardenbergstr. 4–5, 1000 Berlin 12.

87. Judith Shapiro, "The Industrial Labour Force," in Mary Buckley, ed., *Perestroika and Soviet Women*, p. 24.

88. Myra Marx Ferree, "The Rise and Fall of 'Mommy Politics': Feminism and Unification in (East) Germany," *Feminist Studies*, 19, no. 1 (Spring 1993), p. 105.

89. Mariana Katzarova, "Opening the Door," *The Nation*, 257, no. 4 (July 26/August 2, 1993), p. 148.

90. Dorothy Rosenberg, "The Colonization of East Germany," in *Monthly*

Review, 43, no. 4 (September 1991), pp. 20, 32.

91. Anastasiia Ivanovna Posadskaia, "Men's and Women's Potential for Social Mobility and Changes in Working Conditions," *Sociological Research*, 31, no. 5 (September/October 1992), pp. 82, 84, 88. See also her "Self-Portrait of a Russian Feminist," *New Left Review*, 195 (September/October 1992), pp. 22–36.

92. Chris Corrin, "Hungary, Magyar Women's Lives: Complexities and Contradictions," in Corrin, ed., *Superwomen and the Double Burden*, pp. 46, 47. See also Janos Simon, "The Effects of Unemployment on Women's Situation in Hungary During Model Change"; and Julia Szalai, "Women and Democratization: Some Notes on Recent Trends in Hungary," unpublished papers delivered at the conference "Women and Political Transitions in South America and Eastern and Central Europe: The Prospects for Democracy," December 3–4, 1992, University of California, Berkeley.

93. Mita Castle-Kanerova, "Czech and Slovak Federative Republic: The Culture of Strong Women in the Making?" in Chris Corrin, ed., *Superwomen and the Double Burden*, p. 104.

94. Andrew Kopkind, "From Russia With Love and Squalor," *The Nation*, 265, no. 2 (January 18, 1993), pp. 50, 55.

95. Larissa Lissyutkina, "Soviet Women at the Crossroads of Perestroika," in Mueller and Funk, eds., *Gender Politics and Post-Communism*, pp. 281, 284. See also Mary Buckley, ed., *Perestroika and Soviet Women*; and Zillah Eisenstein, *The Color of Gender: Reimaging Democracy* (Berkeley: The University of California Press, 1994), especially chapter 1.

96. Zarana Papic, "The Possibility of Socialist Feminism in Eastern Europe?" unpublished paper presented at the International Association of Women Philosophers, Amsterdam, April 22–25, 1992.

97. Katrina Vanden Heuvel, "Right-to-Lifers Hit Russia," *The Nation*, 257, no. 14 (November 1, 1993), p. 490. See also her "From Proletarians to Pinups," *The Washington Post*, February 21, 1993, p. C4; and Andrew Kopkind, "From Russia with Love and Squalor," pp. 44–62.

98. As quoted in Allesandra Stanley, "Sexual Harrassment Thrives in the New Russian Climate," *New York Times*, April 17, 1994, p. A1.

99. Alessandra Stanley, "Russians and Americans Join in Anti-Abortion Fight," *New York Times*, May 19, 1994, p. A12. See also Vladimir Shlapentokh and Tatiana Marchenko, "Family Values on the Rise While Women Fall in

Russia," *Feminist Issues*, 12, no. 2 (Fall 1992), pp. 43–46.

100. Alena Heitlinger, "The Status of Women in Changing Economies: Czechoslovakia," unpublished paper presented at the annual meetings of the American Economic Association and the Association for Comparative Economic Studies, New Orleans, January 3–5, 1992, p. 23.

101. Slavenka Drakulic, "Women and the New Democracy in the Former Yugoslavia," in Funk and Mueller, eds. *Gender Politics and Post-Communism*, p. 124.

102. From personal correspondence, February 10, 1995.

103. Snitow, "The Church Wins, Women Lose," p. 557.

104. News from "Hidden Victims: Women in Post-Communist Poland," in *Helsinki Watch*, IV, Issue 5 (March 12, 1992), pp. 1–9.

105. Peggy Watson, "The Rise of Masculinism in Eastern Europe," *New Left Review*, 198 (March/April, 1993), p. 75.

106. Jane Perlez, "Why Poland Swung to the Left," *New York Times*, September 21, 1993, p. A6.

107. Jane Perlez, "Polish Senate Votes to Liberalize Law Restricting Abortions," *New York Times*, July 2, 1994, p. A3.

108. Jane Perlez, "A Painful Case Tests Poland's Abortion Ban," *New York Times*, April 2, 1995, p. A3.

109. See conference materials from the "European Conference on Abortion and Contraception," September 25–27, 1992, University II, Geneva, Switzerland (c/o NAC, Print House, 18 Ashwin St., London E8 3DR, England).

110. Stephen Kinzer, "German Court Restricts Abortion, Angering Feminists and the East," *New York Times*, May 29, 1993, p. A1.

111. Joyce Marie Mushaben, "Concession or Compromise? The Politics of Abortion in United Germany," unpublished paper presented at the 1993 American Political Science Association National Meeting, September 2–5, 1993, Washington, D.C., pp. 18, 21–22.

112. Stephen Engelberg, "Polish Limits on Abortion Create a New Clandestine Movement," *New York Times*, December 28, 1992, p. A10.

113. Anna Titkow, "Political Change in Poland: Cause, Modifier, or Barrier to Gender Equality?" in Funk and Mueller, eds., *Gender Politics and Post-Communism*, p. 255; and Ann Snitow, "The Church Wins, Women Lose," p. 558.

114. Introduction, in Funk and Mueller, eds., *Gender Politics and Post-*

Communism, p. 10.

115. For a sample of this discussion, see bell hooks, *Ain't I A Woman: Black Women and Feminism* (Boston: South End Press, 1981), and her *Feminist Theory: From Margin to Center* (Boston: South End Press, 1984); Gloria Joseph and Jill Lewis, *Common Differences* (Boston: South End Press, 1981; New York: Doubleday, 1986); and Barbara Smith, ed., *Home Girls: A Black Feminist Anthology* (New York: Kitchen Table Women of Color Press, 1983).

116. Charlotte Bunch and Roxanna Carrillo, "Gender Violence: A Development and Human Rights Issue" (Rutgers: Center for Women's Global Leadership, 1991).

117. Charlotte Bunch, "Women's Rights as Human Rights," in *Gender Violence*, p. 3.

118. Rey Chow, *Woman and Chinese Modernity*, p. 18.

119. Gayatri Chakravorty Spivak, "The Politics of Translation," in Michele Barrett and Ann Phillips, eds., *Destabilizing Theory: Contemporary Feminist Debates* (Stanford, Cal.: Stanford Univ. Press, 1992), p. 195.

120. From personal correspondence with Renata Salecl, July 22, 1995, Slovenia.

121. Chandra Mohanty, "Cartographies of Struggle" and "Under Western Eyes" in Chandra Mohanty, Ann Russo, and Lourdes Torres, eds., *Third World Women and the Politics of Feminism*.

122. Barbara Einhorn, *Cinderella Goes to Market: Citizenship, Gender and Women's Movements in East Central Europe* (London: Verso Press, 1993).

123. Linda Racioppi and Katherine O'Sullivan See, "Organizing Women Before and After the Fall: Women's Politics in the Soviet Union and Post-Soviet Russia," *Signs*, vol. 20, no. 4 (Summer 1995), p. 818.

124. See the conference papers from "Women and Political Transition in South America and East and Central Europe," University of California, Berkeley.

125. Larissa Lissyutkina, "Soviet Women at the Crossroads of Perestroika," in Funk and Mueller, eds., *Gender Politics and Post-Communism*, p. 276.

126. Barbara Einhorn, *Cinderella Goes to Market*, pp. 64, 65.

127. Mita Castle-Kanerova, "Czech and Slovak Federative Republic: The Culture of Strong Women in the Making?" in Corrin, ed., *Superwomen and the Double Burden*, p. 121.

128. See Vaclav Havel, *Living in Truth* (London: faber & faber, 1986), for a discussion of anti-political politics although he does not, himself, extend this concept to women's activities.

129. See Angela Davis, "Reflections on the Black Woman's Role in the Community of Slaves," *Black Scholar,* 3, no. 4 (December 1971), pp. 3–15; bell hooks, *Talking Back: Thinking Feminist, Thinking Black* (Boston: South End Press, 1989); and Barbara Smith, "Toward a Black Feminist Criticism," in Gloria T. Hull, Patricia Bell Scott, and Barbara Smith, eds., *All the Women Are White, All the Blacks Are Men, But Some of Us Are Brave* (New York: Feminist Press, 1982).

130. Cynthia Enloe, "The Globetrotting Sneaker," in *Ms. Magazine*, V, no. 5 (March/April 1995), pp. 10–15; and Annette Fuentes and Barbara Ehrenreich, *Women in the Global Factory* (Boston: South End Press pamphlet, 1984).

131. Bob Herbert, "Children of the Dark Ages," *New York Times*, July 21, 1995, p. A25.

132. Vaclav Havel, *Living in Truth*, p. 123.

133. As quoted in Barbara Einhorn, *Cinderella Goes to Market*, p. 188.

134. Hana Havelkova, "A Few Prefeminist Thoughts," in Funk and Mueller, eds. *Gender Politics and Post-Communism*, p. 65. See also Anna Hampele, "The Organized Women's Movement in the Collapse of the GDR: The Independent Women's Association (UFV)," in this same volume, pp. 180–93. For further discussion of women's informal actions see Mary Buckley, "Political Reform," pp. 54–71, and Ol'ga Lipovskaia, "New Women's Organizations," in Buckley, ed., *Perestroika and Soviet Women*.

135. Linda Racioppi and Katherine O'Sullivan See, "Organizing Women before and after the Fall," pp. 819, 830.

136. Tatyana Mamonova, *Women's Glasnost vs. Naglost*, pp. xiv, xix.

137. Laura Busheikin, "Is It Possible to Have Feminism Without Man-Hating?" *The Prague Post*, November 25–December 1, 1992, p. 9.

138. Josef Skvorecky, "Can There be Sex Without Rape?" *The Prague Post*, November 25–December 1, 1992, p. 9.

139. Katalin Fabian, "Overview of Women's Interest Articulation in Central and Eastern Europe," unpublished paper, Colleguim Budapest, Budapest Hungary, 1994.

140. See *What Can We Do For Ourselves?* East-European Conference,

Center for Women's Studies, Belgrade, June 1994.

141. Slavenka Drakulic, "Women Hide Behind A Wall of Silence," *The Nation*, 256, no. 8 (March 1, 1993), pp. 253–272; Jeri Laber, "Bosnia: Questions About Rape," *New York Review of Books*, XL, no. 6 (March 25, 1993), pp. 3–6; Paul Lewis, "Rape Was Weapon of Serbs, U.N. Says," *New York Times*, October 20, 1993, p. A1; Alan Riding, "European Inquiry Says Serbs' Forces Have Raped 20,000," *New York Times*, January 9, 1993, p. A1; and Laura Pitter and Alexandr Stiglmayer, "Will the World Remember? Can the Women Forget?" *Ms. Magazine*, 3, no. 5 (March/April 1993), pp. 19–22.

142. These statements were made in interviews in the film *War Crimes Against Women,* directed by Mandy Jacobson and produced by Bowery Productions, community television, telephone no. 212–219–1385.

143. Quoted in Karen Rosenberg, "A Day in Croatia," *The Women's Review of Books*, vol. XI, no 9 (June 1994), p. 15.

144. Cited in "letter for women in sarajevo," from "women in black," the "autonomous women's center." "belgrade women's lobby," April 20, 1995.

145. Transcribed from personal meetings and interviews, May 1995.

146. From personal correspondence, June 5 and 26, 1995.

147. From a statement "Who Are Women In Black?" written by Sasa Kovacevic, December 1994, belgrade, pp. 1, 2.

148. An interview with Antoinette Fouque, "Women in Movements: Yesterday, Today, Tomorrow," in Antoinette Fouque, Charlotte Bunch, Corinne Kumar D'Souza, Georgina Ashworth, Rosiska Darcy de Oliveira, *Terra Femina: Women and Human Rights* (Brazil: IDAC-Institute of Cultural Action, May/June 1993), p. 77.

149. Chela Sandoval, "U.S. Third World Feminism: The Theory and Method of Oppositional Consciousness in the Postmodern World," *Genders* 10 (Spring 1991), p. 15.

INDEX

A

Adelson, Leslie, 31–32
African American Women in Defense of Ourselves, 118
African National Congress (ANC), 56, 140
Agger, Inger, 60
Ahmad, Aijaz, 43, 90
Ahmed, Leila, 140, 141, 147
Aladdin, 137
albania, 152
algeria, 138, 142
Amber, Jeanine, 31
Anderson, Benedict, 52
Angelou, Maya, 121
Anthias, Flora, 64
Antin, Mary, 70
Anzaldua, Gloria, 70, 71, 94
Appadurai, Arjun, 102
Appiah, Kwame Anthony, 86
Arab Women's Solidarity Association, 143
Arendt, Hannah, 29, 48
Asia-Pacific Free Trade Agreement, 95

B

Babic, Mikica, 49
Badran, Margot, 111, 140, 142, 147
Baird, Zoe, 119
Bakhtin, Mikhail, 33
Balibar, Etienne, 35, 36
Banana Republic, 164
Barbie dolls, 54
Barnet, Richard, 88, 101
Bartky, Sandra Lee, 31, 41
Bellcore, 75
Bell Curve: Intelligence and Class Structure in America, The (Murray and Herrnstein), 79, 122
Benetton, 75
Bennoune, Darima, 142
Bernard, Elaine, 95
Bettelheim, Bruno, 28
Bhabha, Homi, 71–72, 74
Bhattachardee, Anannya, 52
Black Panthers, 49, 69
Blagojevic, Marina, 151
Bobbit, Lorena, 124
Bohm, Tatiana, 150

Borch-Jacobsen, Mikkel, 24–25
bosnia, war in
    Bill Clinton on, 45
    concentration camps in, 34
    cultural identity and, 49, 65
    ethnic cleansing in, 23, 24
    images of muslim women from,
    42
    rape in, 39–40, 59–60
    serb nationalism and, 26, 36, 51,
    56, 57, 58
    western image of, 37
    women in belgrade and sarajevo
    and, 167–69
    women's efforts to stop, 151
Brezinski, Zbigniew, 104
budapest, 104
buenos aires, 24
bulgaria, 152
Bunch, Charlotte, 144, 161
Bush, Barbara, 112
Bush, George, 69, 130
Busheikin, Laura, 165
Butler, Judith, 26, 53

C

Capital Cities/ABC Inc., 102
Castañeda, Jorge, 94
Castle-Kanerova, Mita, 163
Cavanagh, John, 88, 101
Centers for Raped Women, 151
Charles, Nick, 125
Charney, Craig, 56
Chattopadhyay, Bankimchandra, 38
chechnya, 24
chiapas, 95
Chinese Exclusion Act of 1882, 97
Chodorow, Nancy, 55

Chow, Rey, 56, 161
Citadel, 134–36
Clinton, Bill
    on affirmative action, 123
    on bosnia, 45
    global economics and, 86
    on haitian refugees, 43
    Hillary Rodham Clinton and,
    111, 113
    nominations and initial propos-
    als of, 118–21
    sexual scandals involving, 123,
    130, 133
Clinton, Hillary Rodham
    on attorney-general nomina-
    tions, 119
    mass marketing of, 115
    multiple images of, 111–12, 113
    nation building and, 128–33
    It Takes a Village, 130
CNN, 26, 96, 101, 141
Coca-Cola, 75
Contract with America, 79
Copelon, Rhonda, 59
Cosmopolitan, 137
Crisis Line, 151

D

Dairy Queen, 104
Davis, Angela, 51
Devan, Janadas, 53
Devji, Faisal Fatehali, 38, 50
Disclosure, 117
Disney World, 76
Dizdarevic, Zlatko, 57
Djokic, Maja, 24
Dole, Bob, 122
Drakulic, Slavenka, 150

Du Bois, W. E. B., 36, 37, 52
Dunkin Donuts, 104

E

Eagleton, Terry, 86
Eddie Bauer, 164
egypt, 140, 141
Einhorn, Barbara, 162, 163
Elders, Jocelyn, 120–21
El Saadawi, Nawal, 143, 146
el salvador, 74
Enloe, Cynthia, 145
Enzensberger, Hans Magnus, 126

F

Faludi, Susan, 134
Family Code, 142
Fanon, Frantz, 25, 26, 33, 60, 148
Farrakhan, Louis, 27
Fatherland Catholic Election
    Coalition, 158
Faulkner, Shannon, 134–36
Fest, Frau Anna, 39
Filipovic, Zlata, 26
Flowers, Gennifer, 123, 130
Foucault, Michel, 33
Fouque, Antoinette, 169
Frank, Anne, 28
Frank, Otto, 28
Freud, Sigmund, 31

G

Gates, Henry Louis, 72
Gates, William, 93
General Agreement on Tariffs and
    Trade, The (GATT), 95
General Electric, 100

Gevisser, Mark, 56
Gilman, Sander, 36, 38, 39
Gilroy, Paul, 25, 50
Gingrich, Kathleen, 129
Gingrich, Newt
    Contract with America and, 79
    Internet and, 111, 122
    nationalism of, 77
glasnost, 153, 155
Global Campaign for Women's
    Rights, 161
Godstein, Richard, 115
Goldberg, David Theo, 35
Goldstone, Richard, 59
Gorbachev, Mikhail, 150
Grant, Hugh, 114–15
Grosz, Elizabeth, 34
Guinier, Lani, 27, 119–20
gulf war
    germany and, 57
    images of muslim women from,
    42
    muslim women and, 148
    national identity from, 43
    new world order and, 96
    women in, 118, 128, 140, 145
    yellow-ribbon campaign of, 48
Gunew, Sneja, 68, 71, 75

H

Hackney, Sheldon, 78
haiti, 39, 43, 96
Haizlip, Shirlee Taylor, 35, 36
Harding, Tonya, 123
Havel, Vaclav, 150
Heitlinger, Alena, 161
Helms, Jesse, 122
Heng, Geraldine, 53

Hernton, Calvin, 38
Herrnstein, Richard
  *The Bell Curve: Intelligence and
  Class Structure in America,* 79,
  122
Hill, Anita, 114, 115, 118, 125
Hirsch, Marianne, 55
Hitchens, Christopher, 24
Hitler, Adolph, 26, 27, 29, 48
Hobsbawm, Eric, 104
Holocaust, 25, 34, 73
  denial of, 25, 28–29
Honda, 87
Hradilkova, Jana, 165
Huntington, Samuel, 78, 96–97
Hussein, Saddam, 96

I
Ibrahim, Youssef, 142
Ignatieff, Michael, 26
Independent Women's Forum, 122
International Reproductive Rights
  Research Action Group, 144
Interview with the Vampire, 124
iran, 138, 146
It Takes a Village (Clinton), 130

J
Jackson, Jesse, 121
Jacobs, Harriet, 13
japan, 78
Jesenka, Milena, 39
Jiaxiang, Wang, 143
John Paul II, 136, 143
Jones, Lisa, 33, 36, 72
Jones, Paula, 123
Jordan, Winthrop, 38

K
Kandiyoti, Deniz, 145, 146
Karadzic, Radovan, 57
Kennedy, Jacqueline, 115
Kennedy, John F., 98
Kentucky Fried Chicken, 104
Kerrigan, Nancy, 115, 123
Khomeini, Ayatollah, 147
King, Rodney, 43, 65, 125
Kinzer, Stephen, 51
Konstantinova, Valentina, 157
Kristeva, Julia, 30, 31, 33, 55, 74

L
Lacan, Jacques, 29
Lane, Charles, 79
Law on the Protection of Human
  Life, The, 158
Law on the Protection of the
  Family, The, 155
Lazreg, Marnia, 141
Lemsine, Aicha, 142
Lenin, Vladamir I., 86
Licht, Sonia, 150
Lipovskaia, Ol'ga, 154
Little Women, 124
Liu, Lydia H., 58
london, 24
los angeles, 37–38, 45
los angeles, 96
Lugones, Maria, 29

M
MacKinnon, Catharine, 59
Madonna, 115, 124
Maharidge, Dale, 78
Malcolm X, 75

Mamonova, Tatyana, 152, 155, 165
Mankind Quarterly, 79
Marshall, Stuart, 73
Martin, Emily, 91
Marx, Karl, 86
McClintock, Anne, 53, 139
McDonald's, 103, 104
Meir, Golda, 133
Melikyan, Gennady, 152
Menendez, Eric, 124
Menendez, Lyle, 124
Mernissi, Fatima, 148
Mexican Repatriation Campaign, 98
Meyers, G. J., 93
Milosevic, Slobodan, 36, 57
Mitsubishi Corporation, 92
Mladjenovic, Lepa, 168
Moghadam, Valentine, 142, 147
Mohanty, Chandra, 162
MTV, 101, 115
Muhammad, Khalid Abdul, 24
Murray, Charles
    *The Bell Curve: Intelligence and
    Class Structure in America*, 79,
    122
Myers, Dee Dee, 130

N
Nabisco, 75
Nasrin, Taslim, 143
Natarajan, Natalini, 54
National Origins Quota System, 98
National Rifle Association (NRA),
    126
new york city, 38, 45, 96
New York Times, 143
Nike, 105

Nixon, Richard, 48, 113
Noah, Yannick, 36
North American Free Trade
    Agreement (NAFTA), 95

O
Obermeyer, Carla Makhlouf, 145
O.J. Simpson trial, 114, 115, 125
oklahoma city bombing, 24, 25, 96
One Eye Open/Jednim Oken, 152
Outram, Dorinda, 33

P
Packwood, Bob, 118
Pahlavi, Mohammed Reza, 147
Papic, Zarana, 56, 151, 157
Parmar, Pratibha, 31
Pepsi-Cola, 89
perestroika, 16, 150, 153, 155
Petchesky, Rosalind, 144
Phillip Morris, 75
Piano, The, 124
Pocahontas, 75
poland, 100, 152
Political Party of Women and
    Mothers, 164
Posadskaya, Anastasia, 155, 162
Prague Post, 165
Price, Hugh P., 104
proposition 187, 77, 99

Q
Queer Nation, 49

R
Reagan, Nancy, 112

Reagan, Patti, 112
Reagan, Ronald, 69
Reebok, 105
Reed, Ishmael, 93
Reich, Robert, 90
Reich, Wilhelm, 25, 26
Rieff, David, 70
River Wild, The, 124
Rockefeller, David, 92
Rodney King trial, 45, 65
Rohatyn, Felix, 77
romania, 152
Rose, Jacqueline, 24, 25, 44
Rotoflow, 99
RU486, 119
Rushdie, Salman, 64
    The Satanic Verses, 44, 76
russia, 51, 100, 152
Rutherford, Jonathan, 25, 75
rwanda, war in, 25, 33, 60, 96

S

Said, Edward, 38, 54–55
Salecl, Renata, 50, 55, 158, 162
Salom, Nada, 27
Samokovlija, Isak, 65
Sandoval, Chela, 169
Sangari, Kumkum, 145
Sartre, Jean-Paul, 22
Satanic Verses, The (Rushdie), 44, 76
Saum, Elizabeth, 60
Scarry, Elaine, 34
Scheer, Robert, 92
Schlesinger, Arthur, 69, 70
Schwarz, Benjamin, 64
Self-Employed Women's
    Association, 132
Simic, Predrag, 57
Simpson, O. J., 114, 125
Sister Souljah, 121
Skvorecky, Josef, 165
Slim-Fast, 152
Smith, Susan, 125
Smith, William Kennedy, 124
somalia, 39, 87, 96
Sony, 87
Soros, George, 50
south africa, 39, 139
Spivak, Gayatri, 68, 161–62
Srivastava, Vinita, 73
Stalin, Joseph, 27
"State of Women in the World,
    The" *(Cosmopolitan),* 137
Szalia, Julia, 162

T

Tailhook scandal, 124
Takaki, Ronald, 25, 67
Taussig, Michael, 23
Thatcher, Margaret, 133
The Gap, 164
Theweleit, Klaus, 31
Thiam, Awa, 144
Thomas, Clarence, 115, 118, 125
Three Guineas, The (Woolf), 52
Thurmer-Rohr, Christina, 149
Thurmond, Strom, 122
Time Warner Communications, 101
Toll, Nelly, 13
Toubia, Nahid, 144
Tungsram, 100
Tyson, Mike, 124

U

U.N. Balkan War Crimes
Commission, 59
United Nations Commission for
Refugees, 94
United Nations Conference on
Population and Development
(1994), 143
United Nations Fourth World
Conference on Women, 143
United Technologies, 75

V

vagina dentata, 31
Vaid, Sudesh, 145
Vasconcelos, Jose, 72
Viacom, 101
vietnam, 89
Viva Zena, 151

W

Walesa, Lech, 158
Walker, Alice, 31, 144
Wallace, Michele, 49
Walt Disney Company, 75, 102
War Brides Act of 1945, 97
Weekly Reader, 75
Weeks, Jeffrey, 71
White House Travel Office, 132
Whitewater, 132
Winfrey, Oprah, 115
Wolf, Naomi, 127
Wood, Kimba, 119
Woolf, Virginia
The Three Guineas, 52
World Conference on Human
Rights (1993), 144

world war II, 25, 40, 73
See also Holocaust

Y

Yeltsin, Boris, 150
Yuval-Davis, Nira, 64

Z

zagreb, 104
Zapatista uprising, 95
Zhirinovsky, Vladimir, 155
Zizek, Slavoj, 27, 28